Ter Tria

TER TRIA:

OR THE

DOCTRINE

OF THE

Three Sacred Persons,

FATHER, SON, & SPIRIT.

Principall Graces,

FAITH, HOPE, & LOVE.

Main Duties,

PRAYER, } and { MEDITA-
HEARING, } and { TION.

Summarily Digested for the Pleasure and Profit of the Pious and Ingenious Reader.

By *Faithfull Teate* Preacher of the Word at *Sudbury* in *Suffolk*.

TRIA SUNT OMNIA.

LONDON,
Printed for *George Sawbridg* at the Sign of the Bible on *Ludgate* Hill. 1658.

TER TRIA

by Faithful Teate

with notes and a critical introduction by
Angelina Lynch

FOUR COURTS PRESS

Set in 10.5 on 13 point Bembo for
FOUR COURTS PRESS LTD
7 Malpas Street, Dublin 8, Ireland
e-mail: info@four-courts-press.ie
http://www.four-courts-press.ie
and in North America by
FOUR COURTS PRESS
c/o ISBS, 920 N.E. 58th Avenue, Suite 300, Portland, OR 97213.

A catalogue record for this title
is available from the British Library.

ISBN 978–1–84682–035–9

Printed England
by Antony Rowe Ltd, Chippenham, Wilts.

Contents

The Literature of Early Modern Ireland series

Forthcoming volumes in the series
Richard Nugent's *Cynthia* (1604) ed. Anne Fogarty
Henry Burnell's *Landgartha* (1640) ed. Deana Rankin
The anonymous 'Purgatorium Hibernicum' (1668/70) ed. Andrew Carpenter and Micheál Mac Craith
Henry Birkhead's *Cola's Fury* (1646) ed. Patricia Coughlan

Preface

This series of editions of English-language texts from seventeenth- and eighteenth-century Ireland has been undertaken in the belief that the study of Early Modern Ireland is entering a new and exciting phase. As thousands of web-based images of English-language texts from Early Modern Ireland have become available to scholars and students during the last few years (through 'Early English Books On-Line' and the 'Eighteenth-Century Collections On-Line', for instance), so the necessity for authoritative editions of the key texts has become ever more acute. Readers need to be able to set major works – all of them rare and several virtually unknown – into their cultural and political contexts. Interest in Ireland is constantly increasing and the publication of major projects such as the *Cambridge History of Irish Literature* (2006) helps quicken awareness of the significance of Early Modern Irish writing. What is needed now is a series of definitive editions of key literary and dramatic texts, edited to the highest standards and set into context by scholars and editors of international standing: such is this series.

The texts chosen for the first six volumes in the series – which is intended to be open-ended and, eventually, to make up an unrivalled resource for scholars and students of Early Modern Ireland – comprise poetic and dramatic texts which reflect the cultural energy of the age, and also Ireland's place within the British archipelago, in Europe and in the emerging British Empire. The editorial board is made up of leading scholars of the literature of Early Modern Ireland from the Republic of Ireland, from the USA and from the UK; all of us recognise the need for this series and we hope that the volumes will appear at the rate of two a year. Each text will be meticulously edited from the only printed edition or from the manuscript, and will be provided with an introduction by the leading authority on the work. This will set the work in context and explain its particular importance to the study of the writing of Early Modern Ireland. Each text will be provided with a full textual commentary. The list of the editorial board and the projected list of publications are listed opposite.

All members of the board, together with the editors of individual volumes, would like to thank Michael Adams and his staff at Four Courts Press for invaluable help. This project, like so many others, could not have come about without Michael's sense of vision and his enthusiastic support; all those working in the field of Early Modern Irish Studies are in his debt.

We would also like to express our gratitude to the Irish Research Council for the Humanities and Social Sciences which awarded a post-doctoral fellowship to Angelina Lynch in 2006, thus facilitating the launch and continuation of this scholarly project. Angelina Lynch herself has worked enthusiastically and tirelessly on these texts, and we are very grateful to her also.

Andrew Carpenter
General Editor
Dublin, April 2006

Acknowledgments

This book grew out of my doctoral thesis undertaken at University College Dublin from 2002 to 2005. I would like to express my gratitude to the Mícheál Ó Cléirigh Institute for the fellowship which funded my research at that time.

I would also like to thank my thesis supervisor, Andrew Carpenter, who introduced me to the work of Faithful Teate, and who has been a constant source of encouragement and support in bringing this edition to fruition. Thanks are also due to my thesis examiners Danielle Clarke and Tom Healy for their advice in shaping my doctoral research into a book. The staff at Four Courts Press were enormously helpful in pulling the book together.

I would also like to express my deep gratitude to Edwina Keown, Elaine Garvey, Eoin O'Shea, Jessie Magee, Grainne Elmore, Eibhlín Evans and Marie Glancy for their humour and support.

This book is dedicated with love and thanks to my mother Patsy, brother Daniel and to the memory of my father, Noel.

Introduction

One of the most exciting and appealing things about the long, devotional poem *Ter Tria, or the Doctrine of the Three Sacred Persons, Father, Son and Spirit; Principal Graces, Faith, Hope and Love; Main Duties, Prayer, Hearing and Meditation* by the Irish puritan preacher Faithful Teate is the energy and freshness of its language. Published in 1658, on the cusp of the Restoration, the poem incorporates many of the philosophical, theological and political discourses of the time. It is full of the emotive language of puritan fervour and private revelation, yet it also stresses the ordered and hierarchical nature of God's universe in a manner that anticipates the literature and philosophy of the Augustan age. It delights in the 'wit' of extended metaphor and wordplay that we have come to associate with the Metaphysical poetry of George Herbert, yet its intermittent grandiloquence is also reminiscent of the occasional poems of Edmund Waller – Teate quotes both poets with admiration in the preface to one of his sermons.[1] *Ter Tria* also anticipates, especially in the three central poems, 'Faith', 'Hope' and 'Love', the earthy and colloquial figures of Bunyan's allegories in a manner which may have accounted for its ensuing popularity with non-conformist readers after the Restoration.

What is also exceptional about *Ter Tria* is the way in which it walks a rhetorical tightrope between deference and bravura, righteousness and playfulness, in its rendering of the biblical source material. Indeed, the impression so commonly communicated by the language of seventeenth-century, religious verse – human humility and sense of mystery in the face of God – fails to materialize. To some degree, this confidence can be explained by the poem's historical moment. *Ter Tria* is a poem that was fashioned to appeal to the ruling authority of the time – God's righteous representative on earth, Oliver Cromwell, as well as his son Henry, the then lord deputy of Ireland, to whom it is dedicated.

In some ways *Ter Tria* is an interesting counterpoint to *Paradise Lost.* If Milton's epic constitutes a lament for the high ideals of a republican commonwealth lost to the lord protector and then to the restored monarchy,

1 Faithful Teate, *A discourse grounded on Prov. 12. 5: the thoughts of the righteous are right* (Dublin, 1666), sig. A3.

Teate's nine-part poem – which incorporates long, dramatic renderings of the Fall and Christ's Passion – echoes with the triumphal tones of one who believes that the divine will has at last found its true, earthly expression in Cromwell's godly rule. Unlike *Paradise Lost*, which Milton wrote from a position of disillusionment and obscurity, *Ter Tria* was the fruit of a period of material and political security for Teate – security which he had not experienced since, as a 14-year-old boy, he had been driven from his native Cavan amidst the chaos and violence of the Ulster rising of 1641. Indeed, as we shall see, it is likely that the enthusiasm for Cromwell's protectorate that underpins the politics of *Ter Tria* was born out of the civil disruption and sectarian violence that had marked his childhood in Ireland.

II

Teate was born in Ballyhaise, County Cavan, in about 1626,[2] the eldest son of a puritan doctor of divinity also named Faithful (hereafter referred to as Dr Teate), a landowner of planter stock who had been educated at Trinity College Dublin under James Ussher. The Teate family was forced to flee from their home at the time of the 1641 rising during which Protestant settlers were killed by Irish natives embittered by years of discrimination. The 1641 rising was a catastrophic event which plunged the country into nearly twenty years of war. It was also a defining moment in Irish Protestant history and was referred to for generations after as undeniable proof of the barbarity and godlessness of the native Irish. At the time, many Protestants also believed that the insurgents had the secret support of the king. Charles I had long been suspected of being a crypto-Catholic – his queen, Henrietta Maria, was Catholic and Charles himself and given his full support to the high-church Anglicanism of Archbishop Laud. Laud's preference for a ceremonial style of worship and his questioning of the doctrine of predestination had not endeared him to Irish Protestants; nor had his insistence, in 1634, that the more rigidly Calvinist articles of the Church of Ireland be replaced by the Thirty-Nine Articles of the Church of England. Hence, in the eyes of some Protestants, the 1641 rising was God's punishment for the crown's toleration of Catholicism in Ireland and, as a consequence, those who escaped were believed to have been rescued by divine providence as reward for their unyielding stance against popery.

It is possible to see this mythologizing process at work in the various accounts of Dr Teate's escape from Cavan to Dublin. According to Dr

2 *Alumni Dublinenses*, ed. G.D Burtchaell and T.U. Sadleir (London, 1924). According to the Trinity College register, Teate entered the college in November 1641, aged 14.

Teate's own deposition of March 1642, on the morning of 23 October 1641, 'fearing of a rebellion and seeing them begin to arise', he filled his pockets with gold and silver and set out for the refuge of Dublin with his eldest son and namesake, the future author of *Ter Tria*.[3] It appears that he was forced to leave his wife and other children behind in Ballyhaise, and, although they eventually joined him in Dublin, they suffered 'ill usage' at the hands of the insurgents, as well as terrible weather *en route*.[4] A pamphlet, published anonymously in London to alert English readers to the situation in Ireland, elaborates the story to suggest that God had shown 'extraordinary providence' to Dr Teate. The author claims that on the road to Dublin, exhausted, bleeding and near death, Dr Teate 'came to a house where accidentally an Irish Chirurgion [surgeon] was, who formerly never had reported thither ...' The surgeon attended to Dr Teate's injuries, allowing him to continue his journey. Similarly, according to the same report, Dr Teate's wife, travelling separately with her infant son (probably Faithful's brother, Joseph) and both being close to starvation 'found a little Irish Mader [drinking vessel] full of Butter-milke ... whereby the baby was preserved alive.'[5] Over fifty years later, William Turner used the story to demonstrate the 'existence of good angels' in *A Compleat History of Remarkable Providences*.[6]

Once in Dublin, Dr Teate was appointed temporary provost of Trinity College, where he enrolled the young Faithful. Dr Teate had most likely been offered the position because his hardline puritanism agreed with the politics of those who had appointed him, the then Lord Justices Borlase and Parsons, who were known supporters of Parliament in the dispute with the king that was to lead to civil war in England the following year. By May 1642, Dr Teate was sufficiently accepted by the city authorities to be allowed to preach the funeral sermon of the controversial governor of Dublin, Sir Charles Coote, a soldier whose military success in repelling the insurgents was tainted with accusations of brutality; he was reported to have killed many innocent Catholic civilians in Wicklow. In the sermon, which he delivered in Christchurch cathedral, Dr Teate called for violent revenge against the 'Antichristian and bloody adversaries in Ireland'.[7]

3 Raymond Gillespie, 'The murder of Arthur Campion and the 1641 rising in Fermanagh' in the *Clogher Record* (1993), pp. 52–66, p. 61.

4 St. John D. Seymour, 'Faithful Teate', in the *Journal of the Royal Society of Antiquaries of Ireland* (1920), pp. 39–45, 39.

5 G.S., *A briefe declaration of the barbarous and inhumane dealings of the northerne Irish rebels* (London, 1641), pp. 10–11.

6 William Turner, *A compleat history of the most remarkable providences* (London, 1697), p. 12.

7 Faithfull Teate D.D., *The souldiers commission, charge & reward* (London, 1658), p. 14. See also Raymond Gillespie, 'The crisis of reform, 1625–60' in *Christ Church cathedral, Dublin:*

Dr Teate's political views were eventually to cost him his position at Trinity College when the outbreak of the English civil war forced all Irish men to declare for Parliament or the king. Dublin was still in the hands of the Royalists under the lord deputy, Ormonde, and in August 1642, Teate's patron Parsons was arrested and imprisoned in Dublin Castle, along with three other parliamentary supporters.[8] In April 1643 Dr Teate was ordered to quit the college because he had shown himself as 'ill-affected' towards 'the present established government under His Majesty's subjection'.[9] Probably angered at Ormonde's decision to negotiate with the 'bloody' Catholics, Dr Teate left Ireland for England some time before 1648 in which year he appears as minister at Salisbury cathedral. What is certain is that his son Faithful matriculated from Pembroke College, Cambridge in 1646, most likely by incorporation of the studies he had previously undertaken at Trinity College Dublin.[10] The whole family may have left Dublin in that year or, alternatively, Dr Teate, realizing his position in Dublin and at Trinity College was precarious, may have sent his son to England ahead of him. Whatever the case, it is likely that Faithful Teate remained at Pembroke College for some two years and he is recorded as taking his MA in 1650, at the age of 23. By 1644, Cromwell had established his authority in the university, and in that year several of the Royalist masters, including Benjamin Laney of Pembroke College, were ejected from their positions. By the time Teate arrived at Pembroke, therefore, it would have been under the control of Parliament and the Presbyterians, allowing the young puritan to take orders.

As well as beginning his theological education, it is probable that Teate first began experimenting with verse at Cambridge. The years before Teate's arrival had seen the publication of volumes of poetry by Cambridge graduates that would have been widely circulated and read by young scholars with an interest in devotional verse. These included Herbert's *The Temple* of 1633 and Milton's 1645 edition of his poems. Religious emblem books by poets such as Francis Quarles, George Wither and Christopher Harvey also commanded a wide readership and inform the imagery in *Ter Tria*. Teate was also at Cambridge at the same time as the Cambridge Platonists, a diverse group of philosophers, whose treatises were often concerned with reconciling Cartesian empiricism with the existence of God – a theme which emerges several times in *Ter Tria*.

a history, ed. Kenneth Milne (Dublin, 2000), pp. 195–217, p. 204.

8 Brendan Fitzpatrick, *Seventeenth-century Ireland: the war of religions* (London, 1987), p. 182.

9 Seymour, 'Faithful Teate', p. 40.

10 S.C. Roberts, 'The quest for Faithful Teate', *Times Literary Supplement*, 19 April 1941, p. 196.

Following his ordination, Teate seems to have received his first living in 1649 as rector of Castle Camps, Cambridge, the second of three 'Intruders', that is, ministers appointed by Parliament. The first of these 'Intruders' had been Nahum Kenetie whose daughter, Katherine, Teate married. According to the parish records of Castle Camps, Teate remained there until 1656. However, he was also minister at Sudbury, Suffolk from 1651 when he was granted license to preach at St Peter's and St Gregory's. In 1655, *A Scripture-map of the wildernesse of sin, and way to Canaan* – Teate's extended meditation on the Song of Solomon, described as 'Being the summe of LXIV lecture sermons preached at Sudbury in Suffolk' – appeared in print. The *Scripture-map* also contains Teate's first published verse, his 'Epithalamium, or a Love-Song of the Leaning-Soul' which comes with a separate title page at the end of the volume. The poem is a first-person account of overcoming temptation in a phantasmagoric landscape modelled on the desert of the Song of Solomon. Teate intended the 'Epithalamium' to perform the same role as a sermon, to elucidate the meaning of Scripture for the benefit of his reader, and he seems to have seen verse as the most fitting form for commenting on the Song of Solomon, perhaps the most famous of the poetical books of the Bible. As he says in the preface, addressed to the 'Christian, Pious and Prudent Reader':

> the matter … is experience, though the form be Verse. My Text being one of the highest and sweetest straines, Of the Song of Songs, best SONG that ever was Penned; my Discourse being but an Explanation of that Text, and my Verse but a Contraction of that Discourse.[11]

In 1656, two more of Teate's sermons, *The Character of Cruelty in the Workers of Iniquity* and *The Cure of Contention among the People of God* were printed together in one volume. According to the title page, they had been preached on the 'Day of Publick Humiliation upon occasion of the late sad Persecution in Piedmont', in commemoration of the Protestant Waldenses who had been massacred in the valleys of Piedmont in 1655. The sermons are dedicated to 'His Highnesse Oliver Lord Protector of The Commonwealth of England, Scotland and Ireland' and show Teate to be an unequivocal Cromwellian apologist. The first of the sermons, *The Character of Cruelty in the Workers of Iniquity*, is addressed to the 'Sons of Violence' and begins with typical Old Testament righteousness:

11 Faithful Teate, 'Epithalamium, or a love-song of the leaning-soul', *A scripture-map of the wildernesse of sin* (London, 1655).

> *Yee Men of Belial; The God of Peace hath sent mee this day to proclaim war against you, for waging war with his People; who will* shortly bruise you (*with Satan, your leader*) under his feet, *except you speedily* humble your selves under his Mighty hand.[12]

Teate is referring ostensibly to the French Roman Catholics responsible for the massacre, although rumours propagated by Charles Fleetwood, the lord deputy of Ireland, that Irish Catholics had been involved in the bloodshed may have been in the forefront of Teate's mind. The second of the sermons, *The Cure of Contention among the People of God*, is a pragmatic rebuke to those responsible for infighting within the Commonwealth. Teate's sermon was published just after Cromwell had dissolved the Barebones Parliament, or the 'Assembly of Saints', as it had been dubbed, and assumed almost monarchical status. Seen in this light, Teate's assertion that 'there is too great a proneness in Gods own People to eat each other' and his distrust of too 'fiery zeal' could be seen as a politic appeal to left-wing Parliamentary and religious agitators for reconciliation and an end to dissent. As he warns towards the end of the sermon:

> If Saints that *complain most* of one another, and *strive most* when they are asunder, would but *complain together* to the *Lord* of themselves, and *strive together* in Prayer; these *latter* and *better Complainings* and *strivings* would be of farre more force to *put out* the other, then the *Sunne* is of, to *put out the fire*. But alas! Instead of taking this course, have wee not rather been *watching for one anothers haltings*, while God has been *waiting for all our healings*?[13]

The possible political expediency of these sermons provides an interesting context to the first edition of *Ter Tria*. The poem was published while Teate was still resident in Sudbury, in July 1658. As already mentioned, it is prefaced with a Latin dedication to Henry Cromwell, Oliver's youngest son who, the previous year, had been appointed the new lord deputy of Ireland, responsible for the country's ecclesiastical reform. Ireland was suffering from a dearth of able 'Ministers of the Gospel' and it is likely that, with his dedication to Henry Cromwell, Teate was angling for a position in his home country. Indeed Teate's father, Dr Teate, had been personally directed by the lord deputy to preach at Drogheda and had returned to Ireland in 1658. A year later, in 1659, Teate himself was awarded a posi-

12 Faithful Teate, *The character of cruelty in the workers of iniquity* and *the cure of contention among the people of God* (London, 1656), sig. A1.
13 Teate, ibid., p. 151.

tion in Limerick due to start on 25 March, and followed his father to Ireland. By the time Teate left Sudbury for Limerick, he was the father of seven children – sons Faithful (the third), Nahum, Joseph and Theophilus, and daughters, Mary, Fidelia and Ann.[14]

Whether Teate ever arrived in Limerick or not is uncertain, but in May 1660, he was directed to preach at St Werburgh's in Dublin. Dramatic political and ecclesiastical change, however, ensured that Teate's career would come full circle. Just as his father had been censured in Ireland in the 1640s because of his puritanism and his support for Parliament, and forced to leave the country, now the son was made to suffer the same fate. After Oliver Cromwell's death in September 1658, attempts had been made in England to continue with the Commonwealth under his son Richard, but they ended in failure. In May 1659 Richard was overthrown by military coup, and the following month Henry relinquished his position in Ireland, having refused overtures from the army to assist in the restoration of Charles II. In May 1660, the same month that Teate was appointed to St Werburgh's, Charles II was declared king in Dublin. Puritan ministers in Ireland were anxious to retain the reforms enacted under Henry Cromwell, but the reinstallation of episcopacy and the Book of Common Prayer in 1661 made this seem unlikely. In May 1661 a declaration ordering all ministers to conform to government by episcopacy was drawn up and ordered to be read at Sunday services all over Dublin. One month later, Teate was ordered to appear before the Irish parliament to answer charges of preaching contrary to the declaration, and was suspended forthwith.[15] It seems as though Teate may have seen his removal coming as, in 1660, he had published in Dublin one of his sermons, *The Uncharitable Informer charitably informed that Sycophancy is a Sin*, addressed 'To the Principal Officers of the English Army within these Three Nations' in which he railed, with Swiftian acerbity, against an Ireland 'replete with angry humors, and distempered with tongue-dysenteries'. It appears that Teate remained in Dublin until 1664. In July of that year he made a will in which he stated he was 'of Dublin, clearke' and intended 'speedily a journey into England'. The following September he made a second will in which he said he is 'late of Dublin, now of Holyhead, and intending a voyage into Ireland'.[16]

It seems that Teate did return to Dublin, as another of his sermons, *The Thoughts of the Righteous are Right*, was printed in Dublin in 1666. In the Preface he quotes Edmund Waller: ''Tis not that which first we Love / But what Dying we approve' as well as his beloved, 'Holy Herbert': 'My

14 Seymour, 'Faithful Teate', p. 44.

15 St. John D. Seymour, *The Puritans in Ireland, 1647–1661* (Oxford, 1921), p. 201.

16 Seymour, 'Faithful Teate', p. 44.

Soul's a Shepheard too, A Flock it feeds, / Of THOUGHTS, and Words, and Deeds'. The Herbert quotation points to the theme of the entire sermon – that those who are righteous in their hearts will triumph, even if they are forbidden to be righteous in word and deed – a theme which must have been intended to console Low Church men like himself, who had been forced to tolerate episcopacy after the Restoration.

Teate died in 1666 at the age of 40 and three thousand mourners were said to have attended his funeral.[17] His reputation as a preacher and a poet must have been sufficient to warrant both a London reprint of *The Thoughts of the Righteous are Right* and a second edition of *Ter Tria* in 1669. The second edition of the poem differs from the first principally in the inclusion of a dedicatory poem by John Chishull, 'Minister of the Gospel' at Tiverton in Devon. Both the metrical freshness of Chishull's couplets and his delight in playful imagery and puns, evident in lines such as: 'Let all wise-hearted savo'ring things Divine / Come suck this TEAT that yields both Milk and Wine' chime with some sections of *Ter Tria*. Chishull also has the confidence to call on 'Baxter or Boyle', that is, Richard Baxter and Michael Boyle, two famous clerical writers and wits, to read and learn from Teate's poem.

Although Teate's sermons and poems are his only works to survive in print today, the *Catalogue of Early Dublin Printed Books* lists a volume of *Meditations* by Teate as having been printed in Dublin in 1672; no copy of this work can be traced.[18] However, a third edition of *Ter Tria* was published in Leipzig with a German translation by Gottfried Wagner in 1699, forty years after it first appeared, which testifies to the lasting and far-reaching popularity of the poem with seventeenth-century readers.[19]

Teate's love of poetry, if not his politics, was inherited by his son Nahum Tate (1652–1715), who graduated from Trinity College Dublin in 1672 and, shortly afterwards, moved to London where he began his literary career. During the 1680s Tate wrote a great deal of verse in support of Charles II in decorous rhyming couplets that seem a far cry from the colloquial freshness of some parts of *Ter Tria*. Indeed, Nahum's decision to change his last name from Teate to Tate may have reflected a desire to distance himself politically and artistically from his father. In 1696, Tate compiled an anthology of religious verse, *Miscellanea sacra, or Poems on Divine and Moral Subjects*, but neglected, strangely, to include any lines from his father's poem. Nahum Tate became poet laureate in 1692, and in 1700, with Nicholas Brady, completed *A New Version of the Psalms of David, fitted to the Tunes used in Churches*.

17 Phil Kilroy, *Protestant dissent and controversy in Ireland, 1660–1714* (Cork, 1994), p. 42.

18 *Catalogue of early Dublin printed books, 1601 to 1700* (Dublin, 1898), p. 146.

19 *A catalogue of English books printed before 1801 held by the University Library at Göttingen*, ed. Bernhard Fabian (Hildesheim, 1987) p. 634.

Despite initially being criticized for an inappropriate modishness of language, the new Psalms eventually became popular throughout the Anglican communion, and some are sung in churches to this day.

III

One can learn much about Faithful Teate's reasons for writing *Ter Tria* by examining the prefatory material. The title page addresses the poem to the 'Pious and Ingenious Reader' and promises such a reader both 'Pleasure and Profit.' In the prefatory poem 'The Author to the Reader' Teate goes on to make a clear distinction between 'Luxuriant Vicious Wit' whose 'leud Poetrie' constitutes a 'wanton Rape on a fair Muse' and religious poetry which 'Chastly' serves the 'grave Body of Divinity'. For a puritan like Teate, it was essential to stress the spiritually instructive nature of his verse and to distinguish *Ter Tria* from secular poetry and its worldly concerns. In doing so, he was attempting to assuage the suspicion with which poetry was regarded in some circles of radical Protestantism. In the popular consciousness, puritanism has long been associated with a dislike and suspicion of aesthetic production but in actuality, attitudes towards art and poetry within seventeenth-century puritanism were multitudinous, ranging from open hostility to enthusiastic praise. At the heart of these varying attitudes lay a tension between the uses of art and religion, between the writings of the classical world and the Bible, that had existed since the birth of Christianity, but which re-emerged during the reformation. Some puritan theologians felt that the rhetorical artifice of poetry, with its direct appeal to earthly senses, drew the believer's attention away from spiritual concerns, and, furthermore, associated it with the ostentatious rituals of Catholicism and also, from the 1630s onwards, with Laudian worship. Why did man need poetry when all that was beautiful and true was to be found in the word of God, in 'A book whose ev'ry leafe, whose ev'ry line / Outshines the milky way' (Spirit, 265–6)? More commonly, puritan ministers and scholars, the majority of whom had been educated in classical literature at university, tried to accommodate their love of poetry with their love of God. They argued that the use of classical rhetoric in both sermons and poetry was acceptable if divinely inspired and employed to serve the higher purpose of glorifying God and spreading His Word.[20] After all,

20 See, for example, John Smith, *The mysterie of rhetorique unvail'd, wherein … the tropes and figures are severally derived from the Greek into English, together with lively definitions and variety of Latin, English* [and] *scriptural examples … conducing very much to the right understanding of Scripture* (London, 1656).

poetry had a biblical precedent in the Psalms and the Song of Solomon and the majority of puritan theologians and preachers felt that while secular poetry was sinful, religious poetry could be beneficial if used for suitably didactic purposes. In 'The Author to the Reader' Teate himself draws a parallel between his role as a poet and preacher and that of the prophet David, believed to be the author of the Psalms.

It seems inevitable that lyric poetry – with its emphasis on expressing the private feelings of the subject – would becomes a vehicle for Protestant worship. After all, one of the defining principles of radical Protestantism is that God is to be found not in a mediating ritual such as the mass but in both the subjective experience of the believer and in the Bible – a divine manifestation of all human experience. Underlying this relation between the Bible and human experience was the hermeneutics of typology. Typology was the practice of interpreting certain events in the Old Testament (types) as foreshadowing Christ's ministry in the New Testament (antitypes). Protestant exegesis broadened this pattern by 'emphasizing instead the contemporary Christian as antitype, recapitulating in himself the experiences recorded in the Old and New Testament.'[21] Thus the Bible and the life of the good Protestant were parallel texts, to be read and deciphered together, and throughout the seventeenth century Protestant devotional culture became a self-consciously literary one based around the documenting of experience, and then the relation of that experience – in a multitude of ways – to the Bible. The literary nature of Protestantism was consolidated by the rapid growth of the printing press which not only enabled access to English translations of the Bible but to all the devotional literature that the holy book inspired, so that by the time Faithful Teate was writing *Ter Tria* there existed an array of printed texts designed to assist the laity in relating their own lives to Scripture. As Raymond Gillespie comments, 'Protestantism in all its forms used print as a way of giving shape to the religious impulse.'[22] These printed texts included sermons, treatises, autobiographical writing, dream journals and, of course, poetry.

An appetite for devotional verse in the mid-seventeenth century is exemplified by the long-lasting popularity of the meditative poetry of George Herbert. Herbert was influential for all devotional poets, including Teate, and commanded a wide readership across the spectrum of Protestantism. *The Temple*, published in 1633, became an alternative Psalter

21 Barbara K. Lewalski, 'Typology and poetry: a consideration of Herbert, Vaughan and Marvell' in *Illustrious evidence: approaches to English literature of the early seventeenth century* (Berkeley, 1979), 41–69, p. 43.

22 Raymond Gillespie, *Reading Ireland: print, reading and social change in early modern Ireland* (Manchester, 2005) p. 146.

for the Protestant laity, running to eleven editions before the end of the seventeenth century. Although Herbert had not been a supporter of religious dissent, his lyrics which give voice to an intensely personal, private dialogue between man and his God – a dialogue mediated through the phrases of Scripture – seemed perfectly attuned to puritan sensibilities, and his poems were quoted by dissenters during the Civil War.[23]

The reception and appropriation of the poems that make up *The Temple* provides a good example of how private, spiritual experience became public, confessional discourse in the seventeenth-century religious sphere. Herbert, who did not write his 'private ejaculations' with publication in mind, ended up being quoted from pulpits. *Ter Tria*, however, seems tailor-made for a large audience and its author alert to this very transference of religious 'experience' from the private to the public realm. In *Ter Tria*, Teate takes the defining characteristic of seventeenth-century Protestant lyric poetry – the presumption of a dialogue between the individual conscience and God, articulated through His Word – and stretches it into an interior drama of Homeric proportions.

All of the nine poems which comprise *Ter Tria* contain echoes of the Biblical and typological imagery found in *The Temple,* imagery that would have constituted a second language to a readership steeped in the practice of Biblical exegesis. Yet Herbert and Teate are radically different poets. While the Biblical discourse that comprises *The Temple* seems to exist in a hermetic, self-referential sphere referring to nothing but the private dialogue between the poet and his God, the language of *Ter Tria* lets in the sights and sounds of the corporeal world, as if Teate has transformed Herbert's cloistered conversation into a public debate. Teate's language also tends towards the colloquial, sometimes to the extent of bawdiness. One can see the influence of Herbert in the following stanza from Teate's poem 'Love':

> Then if thou smile, thy favour, Lord, shall be
> Like rain upon mown grass to me.
> Or like warm Sun-beams that succeed some shower
> Till joyes poor Bud's a full-blown flower. (Love, 631–4)

However, in the following lines, also taken from 'Love', Teate writes with a sense of the grotesque more akin to Swift:

> Hell hath deflour'd the earth, and now I see
> 'T would put its leavings off to me,
> Dawbing false paint on th' face oth' wrinkled Creature,
> Hav'ng worn and spoil'd its native feature. (Love, 227–30)

23 See Elizabeth Clarke, *Theory and theology in George Herbert's poetry* (Oxford, 1997) p. 129.

The differences between the two poets also extends to form. Although, *Ter Tria* often draws on the dialogic structure and Calvinist imagery of the lyrics of Herbert, it is not a lyric poem but rather an epic lyric. Each of the nine sections has a distinct stanza form ranging from the elaborate twelve line constructions of 'Son' to the four-line rhyming couplets of 'Meditation', from which Teate never deviates (in the case of 'Son', for over two and a half thousand lines). This constant repetition of a stanza form which never deviates significantly in metre or rhyme over such a length, projects Augustan confidence rather than Metaphysical doubt – creating a sense of balance and order which counteracts any tendency towards abasement or uncertainty.

For example, the private, questioning nature of Herbert's lyrics is also built into the construction of his poetic line. In the poem 'Praise (I)' Herbert addresses the powerlessness of the poet in the face of God:

> To write a verse or two, is all the praise,
> That I can raise:
> Mend my estate in any ways,
> Thou shalt have more.
>
> I go to church; help me to wings, and I
> Will thither fly;
> Or, if I mount unto the sky,
> I will do more.

Teate addresses the same subject in the opening poem 'Father' but in a manner which communicates confidence rather than humility:

> My Pen is but a feather'd vanitie,
> Like me that write;
> Yet shall this feather,
> If thou'lt indite,
> Help me flie thither
> Where Angels wings make Pens beyond the skie.
>
> (Father, 7–12)

This stanza typifies the striding rhetorical pattern of 'Father'. Teate builds clause upon clause as if building a staircase, in a manner which makes conditionals sound like affirmations, and questions like imperatives. The request for God's assistance and sanction to write the poem, 'If thoul't indite', reads like a barely necessary aside to an approving patron.

In many ways, surety of patronage is key to understanding *Ter Tria*. The poem weaves Biblical and civic imagery together to paint the

Cromwellian Protectorate as a godly millenarian state which must be defended from its enemies. In this respect, Teate has more in common with the occasional poets of the late seventeenth-century – Waller, Marvell and Dryden – than the poets of meditation, Donne, Herbert and Vaughan. That Teate intended *Ter Tria* to be read as a validation of the Protectorate is made clear by the prefatory poem 'To the Pious and Ingenious Author of this Tripartite Poem' written by William Jenkyn, a prominent puritan commentator who had been imprisoned in 1651 for his involvement in a plot to overthrow Cromwell and re-establish the monarchy under Charles II. He was later released only on the condition that he publicly endorsed the authority of Parliament and it seems that his poem in honour of *Ter Tria* was to serve as an extension of that endorsement of the Protectorate. In the poem he echoes *Ter Tria's* 'Tripartite' structure by denouncing 'Austria, Spain [and] the Pope'.

Opposition to Cromwell's regime came not only from Catholic states and exiled Royalists but also from Protestant factions such as the Levellers, the Fifth Monarchists, the Ranters and the Quakers who believed that the new puritan state was not radical enough. The nature of Teate's dedication to Henry Cromwell may have had a specific political resonance in this regard. In the dedication, Teate refers to 'D^no^ *Henrico Cromwell,* DIGNISSIMO HIBERNIÆ PRÆFECTO SACROSANCIÆ INDIVISÆQ, TRINITATIS CULTORI INDIVISO TRIPLICI DIVINAR^m^' which translates as 'the most illustrious Lord, Lord Henry Cromwell, Most dignified protector of Ireland, and of the worship of the most holy, undivided and indivisible Trinity'. One of Henry Cromwell's objectives as lord deputy in Ireland had been to neutralize the influence of radical Protestant sects such as the Baptists and the Quakers whom he described, in a letter to John Thurloe in 1656 as 'our most considerable enemy'.[24] The Quakers were strictly opposed to the idea of an ecclesiastical hierarchy and challenged many of the cornerstones of puritan theology and practices as espoused by the new state, including the doctrine of the Trinity. Thus, the Trinitarian structure of Teate's poem could be seen as a declaration of the sound conservatism of his theological and political principles geared towards securing an appointment in Ireland.

Indeed, it is clear from *Ter Tria* as well as from the sermons that Teate privileged order, unity and stability over individual freedoms and, that unlike Milton, he was not in the least perturbed by Cromwell's decision to curb the powers of Parliament through the Instrument of Government in 1653. In *The Character of Cruelty in the Workers of Iniquity,* published in 1656, Teate urges

24 T.C. Barnard, *Cromwellian Ireland: English government and reform in Ireland, 1649–1660* (Oxford, 1975), p. 109.

Protestant factions of all persuasions to present a united front against the common enemy of Catholicism and to stop offering each other as 'Morsells for the Teeth of the ungodly', going on to comment that '*Unitie* is as essential, to all that is truly *Evangelicall*, as is *Veritie*'.[25] As we shall see, the opening poem 'Father' dramatises this creed – affirming the 'Veritie' of Cromwell's dictatorial state by aligning it with the 'Unitie' of Creation before the Fall.

IV

The fourth poem in *Ter Tria*, 'Faith', opens with a dramatic journey:

Faith, I'll begin
With thee; for thou wast th' first,
When bloody sin
Had made me all accurst,
That shew'd th' avenger posting after me,
And had me to some refuge-City flee. (Faith, 7–12)

The primary allusion is to the gospel story of the infant Christ fleeing into Egypt in order to escape Herod's butchers. However, it is probable that Teate saw Christ's journey as a type of the enforced exile of his own family to Dublin and then to England in the aftermath of the 1641 rising in Ulster. As we have seen, Protestants were encouraged to relate their own individual and collective experiences to the Bible and the association of Protestantism with the Israelites of the Old Testament and the ministry of Christ in the New Testament was common practice in Reformation exegesis. The Geneva Bible, for example, contained marginal notes which encouraged readers to interpret the Biblical battles between God's chosen people and their enemies as types of the battle between godly Protestants and the Catholic Anti-Christ. Teate draws on this interpretive tradition in 'Father' by suggesting a typological connection between the Biblical stories of the Fall and Christ's redemptive ministry, and the king's corruption and Cromwell's restoration of the 'true' Church. Although Teate's refashioning of the Biblical story of the Fall in 'Father' can not be read as a sustained political allegory, it is undeniable that his readership would have associated the poem's rhetoric of kingship, sovereignty and millenarianism with the contemporary political landscape. Much recent scholarship has demonstrated how certain Biblical and Classical tropes took on different political significances and were appropriated for different causes – the king or Parliament, Republic or Protectorate – in texts published throughout the 1640s and

25 Teate, *The character of cruelty*, p. 86.

1650s.[26] As already mentioned, Teate was writing *Ter Tria* during the most conservative phase of Cromwell's rule which could explain why he needed to find a poetic language which honoured Cromwell's revolutionary assault against the 'corruption' of Charles I during the civil war period, and yet also validated Cromwell's growing conservatism – demonstrated by his decision to subordinate the powers of Parliament to his own rule in 1653.

In 'Father', Teate accomplishes this primarily by forging a link between the benevolent power of God and the orderliness of His Creation on the one hand, and Cromwell and his Godly Protectorate on the other. The prelapsarian world of Genesis is described not as a royal court but in the language of civic, commercial and domestic routine. The earth is both a 'Minting-house' where mist is 'coyn'd' into clouds, and a 'Treasurie' stocked with 'golden Lightnings' and 'silver Rain'. It is a 'distillatorie' of rain, and a 'Confectionary' of snow. Teate makes the analogy clearer by the use of military imagery in his description of the oceans:

Under the covert of these surging Seas
Those Armed Bands
(Each jointed scale
Like Armour stands,
Or Coats of Male)
March here and there securely as they please.
(Father, 325–30)

England's island status meant that its ability to defend itself and its colonies rested squarely with the power of the navy, a reality not lost on Cromwell who oversaw massive naval expansion from 1649 onwards. The strength of the navy during the Commonwealth period was undoubtedly the reason for England's victory in the war with Spain, but its primary role was 'to defend the regime at home and keep the Stuarts at bay'.[27] In this context, Teate's personification of the fish as soldiers marching under the sea echoes Edmund Waller's glorification of the English navy in 'A Panegyrick to My Lord Protector':

The sea's our own, and all nations great,
With bending souls, each vessel of our fleet,
Your power extends as far as winds can blow
Or swelling sails upon the globe may go …

26 See, for example, David Norbrook, *Writing the English republic: poetry, rhetoric and politics, 1627–1660* (Cambridge, 1999).

27 Bernard Capp, *Cromwell's navy: the fleet and the English revolution, 1648–1660* (Oxford, 1989), p. 1.

In the midst of delineating the different aspects of Creation, Teate addresses God directly: 'Earths Fabrick Fair / Thou didst erect / And hang i'th' Ayr / To shew its makers Independency' (Father, 345–8). Through a punning allusion to Cromwell's political affiliation to the Independents, uncorrupted Earth, in all its 'Fabrick Fair', becomes a symbol of the Protectorate. Finally, Teate ends his description with a direct allusion to Parliament:

This spacious House thus built, and furnisht so;
Come let's convey
Our Image just,
Did th' Father say,
To breathing dust;
Leaving our likeness to keep House below.

Then was clay stamp'd, by Act of Parliament,
With God's bright face:
A Creature Crown'd
With Life and Grace:
Heav'n-born, Heav'n-bound,
Of upright aspect, of Divine descent.

(Father, 397–408)

Paradise is called a 'spacious House', an image that recalls Marvell's description of the new Protectoral government as a 'house' with Cromwell as the 'protecting' roof in 'The First Anniversary of the Government under His Highness the Lord Protector', published in 1655. Teate's Adam, the first 'king', is given authority to rule 'by Act of Parliament', an image which simultaneously alludes to King Charles I and his attempt to ride roughshod over Parliament in the years leading up to the civil war, and to Cromwell's attempt (however transparent) to retain the appearance of libertarianism by refusing the Crown in 1657. Teate is careful to stress the qualities that made Adam a fit leader before his corruption:

His Diadem was bright Intelligence
Wisdom in full,
Whose ev'ry spark
Makes Diamonds dull,
And Gems look dark;
His Ermine Robe was purest Innocence.

(Father, 469–74)

In what must be interpreted as an attack on the corrupt flamboyance associated with the court of King Charles and the ceremonial style of worship inaugurated by Archbishop Laud, Teate renders the superficial regalia associated with kingship redundant – Adam's 'Diadem' and 'Ermine Robe' *are* his 'bright Intelligence', 'wisdom in full' and 'purest innocence' which make 'Diamonds dull'. Similarly, Teate's description of Adam's fall can be read in the context of the politics of the 1630s and 1640s. The poem stresses the role of Eve, the 'Royall consort' in spreading the 'gangrene' of corruption, perhaps an allusion to Charles' wife Henrietta Maria who had been instrumental in attempting to harness the support of the Catholic Irish to her husband's cause during the 1640s. 'Father' ends with the promise of the redemptive ministry of Christ:

> *Adam* comes forth but in a new Edition:
> Gods bright Portraiture
> Is new imprest,
> The Divine Nature,
> On mans brest;
> Clear from all treason, and from all Misprision.
> (Father, 703–8)

Again, Teate's use of a pun is revealing, the word 'misprision' meaning both a clerical mistake – as in a misprint – and the crime of deliberately concealing knowledge of treason. During the Commonwealth period, various plots to overthrow the lord protector were uncovered, and printed accounts of 'treason' and 'misprision' were disseminated widely.[28] It is as if, in using the language of the law, Teate is drawing a parallel between Christ (the 'new Edition'), and a loyal, Cromwellian subject, if not Cromwell himself. Teate's use of 'book' imagery – comparing Christ to a 'new Edition' – affirms yet again the theological centrality of the Word to puritan worship. What is therefore remarkable about the second and longest poem of *Ter Tria*, 'Son' a verse paraphrase of the Gospels, is the liberty that Teate takes with his divine source material – the extent to which he feels licensed to appropriate 'God's mind sent us in black and white.'

V

Putting words into the mouth of God is a bold act of creativity for any poet. It implies strong, undoubting religious and rhetorical conviction, and is relatively rare in seventeenth-century verse. The poets who did attempt

28 See, for example, *The true case of the state of Sir John Gell, prisoner in the tower: accused of high treason, and misprision of treason* (London, 1650).

it made the Messiah a relatively anodyne, dispassionate figure who spoke either in the lofty, elevated language of officialdom, or else did not deviate significantly from the words designated to Christ in scripture. Thus Milton's Christ in *Paradise Lost* and *Paradise Regained* is an idealized philosopher and rhetorician, Herbert's Christ in 'Sacrifice' is circumscribed by the language and the structure of the liturgy, and in *Salve Deus Rex Judæorum*, Aemelia Lanyer's Christ is virtually silent, His quiet suffering paraphrased by the poet.[29] In Teate's 'Son', a verse paraphrase of the Gospels and a tour-de-force of hyperbolic narrative, Christ is unequivocally colloquial and partisan, and revels in invective. The following stanza is taken from a description of the 'Agony in the Garden' and depicts Christ's response to Judas' betrayal:

Thou send'st me to my cross: But I'll be even.
Thou shal't hang first,
Thief that thou art!
Thou'st broke thy faith, and thou shalt burst
Asunder, false perfidious heart!
'Tis fit such pay be to such traitours given.
Into the second Adam's garden creep
Dost thou, Serpent?
That way
Betray
The innocent?
Methinks thou smil'st as Crocodiles do weep. (889–900)

The poem's use of heterometric lines, combined with the heightening effects of alliteration and repetition, serve to replicate the exaggerated slowing and quickening of pace associated with the hyperbole of the pulpit preacher. This dramatic stanza form complements the content – an Old Testament view of retribution voiced by Christ in a manner that is rare in religious verse of the period. The unequivocal rejection of the central gospel message of forgiveness that the speech implies is shocking, but although it may have been rare in poetry, it was common practice in the anti-Catholic literature of the time – Cromwell, for example, appropriated the story of the Israelite's destruction of the 'ungodly' Canaanites in the book of Joshua to justify the violence meted out to the Irish Catholics in his invasion of Ireland in 1649. Indeed it is possible to hear echoes of Cromwell the iconoclastic soldier in Teate's portrayal of Christ in 'Son', with Christ's con-

29 See Danielle Clarke (ed.), *Isabella Whitney, Mary Sidney and Aemilia Lanyer: Renaissance women poets* (London, 2000), p. xxxi.

demnation of Judas becoming a condemnation of those 'traitours' who had killed Protestant settlers in the 1641 rising in Ireland from which Teate and his family had barely escaped with their lives. The poet's father, Dr Teate, had dubbed the Irish insurgents as 'bloody Cannibals' and 'incarnate devils', and in one of his own sermons Teate himself renounced the doctrine of 'turn the other cheek' with explicit reference to 1641:

> I remember once in *Ireland*, one went about to disswade the souldiers from opposing the Rebels; for said he, *If one smite thee on the one cheek, turn to him the other*, and this he called a Scripture – self Resignation mistaking that Scripture, and opposing it against the Law of *Self-preservation* written indelebly in all our hearts ... natural conscience did abominate it.[30]

Christ's mercy, it seems, did not apply to the Catholic 'Judas', and it is tempting to see all the gospel 'traitors' in 'Son' as enemies of the Protectorate who must be overcome by an, at times, decidedly militaristic Messiah. This view is demonstrated by the following description of Christ's temptation in the wilderness:

The fierie Serpent of the Wilderness
Finding Christ there,
Doth spit and bite;
But th' Brazen Serpents hard and clear,
Scorning the tempters craft and spight,
The Bullet's batt'red, but not the fortress.
Our Lord now learns to fast that we might feast,
And to be tempted,
That wee
Might bee
Thereby exempted:
Or succour'd so as still to have the best. (Son, 133–44)

Christ is presented as a model soldier who is both 'hard and clear', adjectives that suggest physical strength and an untainted conscience, and allude to the iconographic image of Cromwell fighting for God with both sword and Bible. Satan is a 'batt'red' bullet who is unable to dent the fortress, Christ.

What is also apparent in 'Son' is Teate's fondness for proverb and colloquialism. The free movement of material between the oral and the writ-

30 Teate, *A scripture-map of the wildernesse of sin*, pp. 223–4.

ten was widespread in the seventeenth century, and proverbs were used widely in sermons to explain a theological point in condensed, pithy terms that the average layperson could comprehend. Similarly, 'Son' is littered with colloquialisms which often function as didactic interpolations within the gospel narrative. After describing the high priest Caiaphas' condemnation of Christ, Teate breaks off to declare: 'Thus men teach Parrots speak, but when they know not;' (529), he rebukes 'doubting' Thomas with the wonderful: 'His faith must go on stilts, or not at all' (2329); earlier, he reacts to Christ's blindfolding with:

Oh! how these Bats project to blind the Sun!
Moles plot and think
(How wise they are?)
With a poor clout thus to hood-wink
Jacobs true bright and morning star. (Son, 1021–5)

Through his use of idiomatic language Teate contemporizes the gospel narrative, equating the high priests with a con artist who has underestimated the intelligence of his would-be victim. However, it is not only the poet's interpretive voice that is coloured by the idiomatic. Teate makes no attempt to distinguish his own narrative voice from those of the other 'speakers' in 'Son' – namely Pilate, Peter, Thomas and most significantly, Christ. Thus when Christ compares Judas to a weeping crocodile, and when he raises the communion wine at the last supper and addresses his disciples with a drinking oath, 'here's an health likewise / To you, not mee' (601–2), he is using the language of the commoner, rather than that of a celestial king.

The degree of license that Teate takes with his source text is demonstrated in the verse description of the passion. There is a precedent for poetic meditation on the life and particularly the death of Christ which derives from the teaching laid out by the Jesuit St Ignatius of Loyola in his *Spiritual Exercises*. The *Exercises* stressed the importance of contemplating the Passion as a means of drawing the soul closer to God, and placed particular importance on the 'composition of place', that is, on an imaginative visualization of Christ's suffering. This meditative technique had a profound influence on Protestant poets of the seventeenth century, including Donne and Herbert, and was also adapted by puritan divines such as Richard Baxter who, in the *Saints Everlasting Rest* (1653), called fervently for good Protestants to 'Look well upon him [...] his Hands were pierced, his Head was pierced, his Sides were pierced, his Heart was pierced with the sting of thy sins'. Baxter's meditative approach is much in evidence in Teate's poem 'Son'. At the moment of Christ's death on the cross, the poet breaks away from the central narrative to contemplate how he may strive to emulate such serenity:

Then Christ, in sweet submission, *bowes his head*
To all Gods pleasure:
I think on't still:
Lord make the bowing heart my treasure
An heart to bow to all thy will;
That dying I may say, *all's finished.* (Son, 1813–18)

However, for the central act of the poem (lines 559–1812), Teate takes the 'composition of place' technique a step further by having Christ narrate his own suffering, in effect rewriting the passion from the perspective of its central protagonist. The poet also weaves his sermonizing ministrations on the passion into Christ's first-person account in a manner which makes it difficult to tell where one voice ends and the other begins. Take, for example, the following stanza which shows Christ reacting to his disciples' indifference during his 'agony' in the garden of Gethsemane:

What, can I not one hours short watch obtain?
One houres? I say.
Oh you'l be tempted;
Watch, for your own sakes then, and pray:
Oh! pray that you may be exempted.
There are no vapours left in my parcht brain:
I'm past all sleeping now, but th' sleep of death.
But, Oh! let pass
This cup!
Drink't up.
Thy sword, Alas!
In thine own fellow-shepheard dost thou sheath.
(Son, 853–65)

The constant movement from the first to the third person is typical of 'Son', and has the overall effect of fusing the voice of Christ with that of the poet, so eradicating any sense of reverential separateness implicit in a marked division between the divine subject and the human interpolator. In the last two lines of the stanza, is Jesus referring to himself in the third person, or is it a rebuke from Teate directed at the disciples, and therefore at all sinners? Is the italicized line '*Drink't up*' Christ urging himself on, or the encouraging voice of Teate? This poetic ventriloquism is even more marked in the section of 'Son' that narrates Christ's trial at the hands of the chief priests, Herod and finally Pontius Pilate:

Now th'Judge of all stands bound at Pilats bar.
Great God is tried
For's life, by man:
Yet by this stranger justified,
Say mine own people what they can.
Hurried to *Herod* next, and's men of war.
Herod forsooth would see a miracle
And doth, whilst I
Sustain
Disdain
So patiently,
Who could scoule these proud scorners quick to Hell.
(Son, 1201–12)

The first three lines are spoken in the third person and have the omniscient tone of the poet setting the scene for Pilate's condemnation of Christ. Yet the fifth line introduces the first person possessive pronoun, 'Say mine own people what they can', which indicates that it is actually Christ who is speaking, in effect, narrating his own judgment in the third person.

The license taken with the gospel text in 'Son' – the invention of speeches for Christ and the interweaving of His divine testimony with the poet's own – can be seen as a logical extension of the Protestant belief that Scripture is about the Christian's own life experience. However, this conflation of the human and the divine works to varying ends. On a general level, Teate's use of the colloquial and proverbial democratizes the Biblical text by infusing it with the common language of the people, but with the attendant, perhaps unintentional result that the divine Word seems contemporized to the point of demystification. 'Son' seems not so much an esoteric meditation *on* the Bible but a self-assured, wholesale occupation of it.

VI

The third poem in *Ter Tria*, 'Spirit' marks a definitive change in emphasis. If 'Father' and 'Son' are structured around historical narratives, and are occupied with establishing parallels between Biblical events and the contemporary political stage, then 'Spirit', and all of the poems that follow, are more concerned with staging the inner drama of the soul. In fact, the remaining seven poems in *Ter Tria* amount to a kind of puritan 'Song of Myself', and draw on a wide range of imagery to demonstrate some of the central tenants of reformed spirituality. One such idea is that the third person of the Trinity is constantly present in the believer, communicating messages from God designed to keep sinful impulses at bay, and that these interventions were felt as physical, often turbulent sensations:

> Calms are not alwayes profitable for me,
> Therefore the winds are sometimes high;
> This Spirit blusters and is stormy,
> That I might groundfast in humility. (Spirit, 217–20)

Behind this image of the blustery storm raging in the soul of the believer is the idea of the Spirit as an agent of mortification, His 'sharp rod' hammering the heart into obedient submission to God. Images of battered, melted and penetrated hearts litter 'Spirit':

> Melt, stony heart! till all becomes one river:
> Doves do delight near ponds to dwell:
> Groans are best musick to a griever:
> Such is Gods dove, whose groanes thy duty tell.
> (Spirit, 353–6)

Teate's reference to 'groanes' as the 'best musick' is rooted in the idea, derived from Augustine, that 'ejaculatory' prayer consisting of unmediated, spontaneous physical responses such as groaning and weeping, was the truest way to demonstrate the Spirit's power over the heart. There is nothing spontaneous, however, about the manner in which Teate draws out the central conceit – the dove happily dwelling by the 'pond' of the poet's melted heart. This kind of emblematic thinking – in which a quasi-logical link is established between a sentiment and an image – underpins much of the 'wit' in *Ter Tria*. The most pertinent examples turn on the metaphor, deeply embedded in puritan discourse, of the Holy Spirit as a writer – God's authorial persona. Just as the 'light' of the Spirit inspired the authors of the Bible, so it now inspires the author of *Ter Tria*:

> My callow muse hath pinions but no wings,
> Pinions indeed of ignorance;
> Yet th' Dove that hatcheth other things
> Can fledge mine infant muse with utterance.
>
> But th'ther day I saw a Lamb take wing
> And flie to Heaven from an hill:
> I watcht to see if any thing
> Would fall from him in flight, and found a quill,

Of which I made a pen, and fell to write
The story; writing, found a Verse;
Whilst on mine hand a Dove did light,
And bad me with the Lamb the Dove rehearse.

(Spirit, 5–16)

The poet's 'pinions', a word meaning both bird feathers and a quill, are steeped in 'ignorance' and it is only when he finds a 'quill' which falls from the 'Lamb … in flight', that is, the ascending Christ, that he is able to find his 'Verse'. Thus Teate is tacitly presenting himself as an apostolic poet whose 'pen' is a channel through which the Holy Spirit works, and *Ter Tria*, by extension, as a parallel gospel.

In the latter half of *Ter Tria*, the pedagogical practices of 'writing' and 'reading', so central to Bible-centred, Puritan worship, are put to metaphorical use to demonstrate the correct way for the Godly to receive the Holy Spirit. The poet uses the lexicon of book production, for example, to admonish seventeenth-century materialist philosophers such as Thomas Hobbes whose controversial treatise, *Leviathan*, had been published in 1651. Although Hobbes never espoused atheism, his belief that nature could be understood by rational deduction alone and his assertion that religious belief came about because of an ignorance of the laws of nature were interpreted by many as an assault on the literal truth of the Bible, a claim that would certainly have offended a puritan preacher such as Teate.[31] Teate may have had *Leviathan* in mind when writing the following stanzas:

Yet some by reason, some by newfound light
Not only leave to question take
But mend this Book and set it right
By Tables of Errata's they would make.

So much is good, and 'tis Canonicall,
As to mans reason is commensur'd:
Gods light, by mans, must stand or fall:
And so the Sun by th' Sextons Clock is censur'd.

Methinks I love the Author for the Book:
The Book for the' Author much more love;

31 Teate felt the need to qualify Descartes' famous assertion 'Cogito ergo sum' with reference to scripture: 'And as naked *Thinking* is the surest argument of *meer being*, so is *well-thinking* (if our Text be true) an Evidence of *well-being*': *A discourse grounded on Prov.* 12. 5, p. 2.

When op'ning into it I look
My God, I can't forget thy sweet-spread Dove.
(Spirit, 276–88)

In accordance with the philosophical ideas of his contemporaries, the Cambridge Platonists, Teate seems to advocate a compatibility between 'reason' and divine revelation. Reason is not merely a faculty for processing sense impressions, but a gift from the Holy Spirit which enables those with faith to comprehend God's 'Book'. On the whole, however, Teate eschews the mystical language of Henry More and Nathaniel Culverwell in favour of more homely imagery:

For since th' incarnate word his tender love
In blood to write us condescends,
What wonder that his own dear Dove
In ink and paper praies us to be friends?

The image of the Spirit as a dogged clerk, rendering the 'tender love' of Christ the 'incarnate word' intelligible on earthly 'ink and paper' – has a concrete utility that suggests that the Bible was seen as much as a day-to-day, practical self-help book as a mystical text. Indeed, the extent to which the Bible had become socialized by the mid-seventeenth century is evident by the way in which Teate consistently depicts the 'Book' and its 'author', the Holy Spirit, in language taken from the material worlds of education, commerce and the home. When Teate states that:

This Book doth sanctifie the shelf,
The heart, I mean where it's sincerely laid
(Spirit, 275–6)

he neatly compacts both the literal and symbolic location of the Bible in the godly household.

The great majority of seventeenth-century devotional verse in English is steeped in this kind of metaphorical 'wit', but what marks Teate apart is the way he ostentatiously underlines his own ingenuity and playfulness. Indeed, the conceits of the latter poems of *Ter Tria* are shot through with a bravura that seems almost incongruous with their divine subject matter. For example, in the fourth poem 'Faith', that 'principal grace' is personified as an apothecary administering to the poet's sick soul:

But lest I should
In bleeding faint, Faith took
Some Cordialls roll'd

In Bible leaves, a Book
Whose ev'ry leafe, said Faith, rich drugs conteins
As I compound them, sov'raign for heart-pains.
(Faith, 265–70)

Here, Teate takes the literal image – the 'Book' – and transforms it into the metaphor that represents it – the 'rich drugs'. We are shown the 'leaves' or pages being torn from the Bible and used to roll up 'Cordialls' to ease the 'heart-pains' of the poet. Teate does not just deliver the pun, he deconstructs the pun by dramatizing the process of linguistic association that makes it work. This flamboyant playfulness, combined with an almost comic blending of the domestic and the divine, gives an injection of freshness into the most common of Biblical and cosmic tropes. This is demonstrated admirably in the eighth poem, 'Hearing', which is structured around puns which invoke the multiple Biblical senses of the word 'ear':

The Humble Hearer may invite
God Guest-wise to a Disht Delight
A fervent *whole broke-heart* serv'd up in *Tears*
The *Bread* bee'ng made o' th' *Contrite hearers Ears*.

Nay God invites Himself to *sup*
Where such delights are so serv'd up
By a *clean hand*, where th' *ear* and the *heart's* kept hot
God is Mans *Guest*, and Heav'n will pay the *shot*.
(Hearing, 117–24)

The image of God as a genial dinner guest, happily digesting His children's repentance 'serv'd up' in the metaphorical dish of 'Bread ... made o' th' Contrite hearers Ears' and then charging the 'shot' or bill to 'Heav'n' is a wonderfully colloquial rendering of the Last Supper.

All of these examples demonstrate the transparency of Teate's use of metaphorical language, a language which lends itself to explanation rather than ellipsis, to extrapolation rather then contraction. This transparency is, in part, a product of the poem's didacticism, as if the poet, like the good minister he is, wishes to take the readers by the hand and guide them safely through the maze of symbolic connections towards salvation.

VII

Ter Tria is without doubt a text that will hold great interest for scholars of the literary culture of Ireland and England during the Civil War and

Commonwealth period. Teate led a somewhat hyphenated existence – travelling from war-torn Ireland to the relatively cloistered worlds of Cambridge and Suffolk, and then back to Ireland again. Indeed his short life was marked by journeys back and forth over the Irish Sea – and perhaps in consequence, *Ter Tria* seems caught between two worlds, striving to incorporate the private intensity of the lyric into what is essentially a public, occasional poem.

Ter Tria is also a major addition to the corpus of seventeenth-century devotional verse as a whole. Not only does it traverse the boundaries which separate different literary genres and labels – poem and sermon, Metaphysical and Augustan verse, lyric and epic – but it also demonstrates a colloquial freshness and bold playfulness in its refashioning of the biblical text which is always engaging and, at times, a real delight.

A note on the text

In most respects, including punctuation and spelling, this edition reproduces the 1658 (first) edition. Words where the old spelling may cloud the meaning for readers have been footnoted. The only exception to this relates to 'than' and 'then' which were often used interchangeably in Teate's time, and have been amended to their modern forms. Any obvious misprints have been silently corrected. Biblical quotations are taken from *The Authorized King James version with Apocrypha*, ed. Robert Carroll and Stephen Pricket (Oxford, 1992).

Punctuation was relatively arbitrary in the seventeenth century, partly due to its perfunctory application at the printing press. In places were the punctuation interferes with intelligibility, it has been silently amended or removed. Apostrophes for possession were not used in the seventeenth century and, as their absence does not interfere with understanding, they have not been added.

TER TRIA

ILLUSTRISSIMO DOMINO[1]

D[no] *Henrico Cromwell,*

DIGNISSIMO HIBERNIÆ

PRÆFECTO SACROSANCIÆ

INDIVISÆQ, TRINITATIS

CULTORI INDIVISO

TRIPLICI DIVINAR[m] GRATIAR[m]

Coronâ ORNATISS[mo]

TRIBUS Que Apprime Christianis

OFFICIIS INTEGERRIME DEDITO,

TRIPLECEM HANC TRIADEM

SACROR[m] POEMAT[m]

CHRISTIANÆ DOCTRINÆ

SUMMAM IN SUMMÆ OBSERVANTIÆ TESTIMONIUM Humill[m].

F.T.

L. M. D. D. D.

1 The dedication reads: 'To the most illustrious Lord, Lord Henry Cromwell, Most dignified protector of Ireland, and of the worship of the most holy, undivided and indivisible Trinity of the three Divine Graces of the most ornate crown, here presented in a compendium dedicated to the triadem of Christian doctrine in sacred verses for the edification of the worthy faithful. Your most humble servant, F[aithful] T[eate].' The letters L.M.D.D.D. stand for the Latin phrase 'Licentiatus Magistris Doctus Doctrina Divina' which may be translated 'Learned and Licensed Master in Holy doctrine'. (My thanks to Dr Declan Downey of the Department of History, UCD for invaluable help with this translation.)

The Author to the Reader

Oft have I seen Luxuriant Vicious Wit
A wanton Rape on a fair Muse commit:

At once distaining,[1] by leud Poetrie,
The Writers Paper-sheets, and Readers Eye.

And may I not oblige the thrice three Muses[2]
Chastly to serve so Sacred thrice three Uses?[3]

Is the grave Body of Divinity
Less Currant for the feet of Poetry?

Are Truths, for being short and sweet, less sound?
Or streames, for running smoothly, less profound?

David a Prophet, yet in Verse excels:[4]
'Twas ECCLESIASTES made the Canticles.[5]

1 i.e. staining, corrupting.
2 According to classical literature, Zeus and Mnemosyne had nine daughters known as the Muses who were invoked to provide inspiration for artists.
3 i.e. the nine sections of *Ter Tria.*
4 The book of Psalms was attributed to the Old Testament king and prophet David.
5 Ecclesiastes is another of the 'Poetry Books' of the Old Testament traditionally attributed to Solomon who was said to have composed the Song of Solomon otherwise known as the Canticles. Ecclesiastes takes its name from the Hebrew word for 'preacher'. Here, Teate is suggesting that preachers can also be poets.

To the Pious and Ingenious Author of this Tripartite Poem[1]

Before your *triple Poems* I admit,
These *Votes*[2] made up of *Threes*, may well be writ.

May *Understanding*, *Will*, and *Memory*
Know, *Love*, and *hold* thy Sacred Poetry.

May *Heav'n* be th' *fuller*, Earth the *better*, *Hell*
The *thinner*, by the Truths, you write so well.

May *pride of life*, the *lusts* of *flesh* and *eye*,
Be poyson'd by these leaves of thine, and die.

If any other three, I'de wish were down,
'Tis *Austria*, *Spain*, the *Pope* with's triple Crown.[3]

This *latter Vote* if th' *King* of *Kings*[4] would make
An *Act*, I'de willingly the *Earth forsake*.

1 This verse preface was written by William Jenkyn (1613–83), a prominent puritan commentator who had been imprisoned in 1651 for his involvement in a plot to overthrow Cromwell and re-establish the monarchy under Charles II. He was later released after publicly withdrawing his opposition to the government.

2 Vote = a petition or a request, but also a prayer or intercession.

3 Triple crown = the papal tiara. At the time this poem was published, England was at war with Spain. In January 1658, Cromwell had made a speech to parliament accusing Catholic Spain and Austria of being in league with the pope in order to bring down the 'true religion'. See *The writings and speeches of Oliver Cromwell*, ed. Wilbur Cortez Abbott (Oxford, 1937), p. 752.

4 i.e. Christ.

Father

Thou that *begin'st* All things, begin my verse
My words are winde;
Thy words are works:
Thou'lt lightness find
Where darkness lurks:
My Pen and Ink may me not Thee reherse.[1]

My Pen is but a feather'd vanitie,[2]
Like mee that write;
Yet shall this feather,
If thoul't indite,[3]
Help me flie thither[4]
Where Angels wings make Pens beyond the skie.

Father, mine Inks dark hue, presents[5] mine heart.[6]
Ink's not more dark,
Ink's not more black;
One beam, one spark
Supply this lack.
Father of Lights,[7] now shew thy perfect Art.[8]

1 The poet does not wish his poem to 'reherse' (i.e. merely to practise with imperfect results) but successfully to dramatize the glory of God.

2 The word 'vanity' is used in the Bible to mean total spiritual emptiness and worthlessness as opposed to mere conceitedness. For the puritans, the word became associated with the search for knowledge and achievement solely for its own sake and not for the glory of God.

3 i.e. enable me to set this poem down in words.

4 Cf. Herbert, 'Praise (1)', line 6, in *The complete English poems*, ed. John Tobin (London, 1991).

5 i.e. brings my heart into your presence.

6 Cf. Herbert, 'Good Friday', lines 21–4.

7 'Every good gift and very perfect gift is from above, and cometh down from the Father of lights, with whom is no variableness, neither shadow of turning'. James 1:17.

8 i.e. creation. Calvin refers to God as the 'Artificer' whose works show 'exquisite workmanship'. John Calvin, *Institutes of the Christian religion*, ed. John T. McNeill (Philadelphia, 1961), p. 56.

Lord teach me speak, and I'll not hold my peace,
Which if I should,
The stones would come;[9]
Though deaf, yet would
They not be dumb;
Break into praises, stonie heart, for these.

No man hath seen thee, Father, but He who
Did sometime come
(Thy Son it was)
Thy bosom from,
Thy Looking-glass,[10]
Hee's the wise Child that doth his Father know.

Who else[11] sings Thee, sings what he hath not seen:
My Verse hath feet,[12]
And fain would run,
Thy praise to meet;
But, lest the Sun
Should hurt weak sight, the clouds do interveen.

Then may I in thy Son thy self discover;
Sure Hee's the Mirrour
That shews thy face:
Prevent mine errour;[13]
Christs flesh like glass
A brighter Glory, but unseen doth cover.[14]

Since then I must be silent, or begin
To sing th' unseen;

9 i.e. come alive and speak. In St Luke's Gospel, the Pharisees command Jesus to rebuke his disciples for proclaiming him the 'King'. Jesus replies, 'I tell you that, if these should hold their peace, the stones would immediately cry out.' Luke 19:40.

10 Calvin describes Christ as '... the mirror wherein we must, and without self-deception may, contemplate our own election.' *Institutes* III. 24. 5, p. 970.

11 i.e. anyone other than Christ.

12 with a pun on iambic feet.

13 '... man never achieves a clear knowledge of himself unless he has first looked upon God's face.' Calvin, *Institutes*, I.1.2, p. 37.

14 'They who break a Crystall, may see their face in every peece and parcell; so in every-thing of Christ there is an image of God.' John Saltmarsh, *The smoke in the temple* (London, 1646) p. 65.

Father of Mercies,
That set'st the screen,[15]
Forgive my Verses:
O thou that vail'st[16] their subject, vail their sin.

Father's a word my child learns first to mutter,
And thy child too,
Thy new born Babe
First thing't can do
Is to cry Ab;[17]
But both come last to know what first they utter.[18]

Thou art the Father of that Son that made
That womb on earth
That, without Father,
Did give him birth;
And might the rather,
He bee'ng begot where He no Mother had.[19]

Then shall I call thee Father? Lord, thy Son
Was call'd no less
Before his birth;
Prophets confess
He had on earth
His children, seed and generation.[20]

Th' Eternall Father call we Thee? or rather
Thy Child, thy Son
Born to restore us,
Thine Holy One
Giv'n to us, for us?
I'll call Thee th' Everlasting Fathers Father.

15 screen = a piece of material which is held in front of the face to protect it from a fire. Christ incarnate is a kind of screen that allows man to see God without being blinded by His glory.

16 vail = veil or cover.

17 = Abba, the name Jesus used when addressing God: 'And he said, Abba, Father, all things are possible unto thee.' Mark 14. 36.

18 Teate quotes 'Mr Edmund Waller' in the preface to his sermon *Right thoughts* (Dublin, 1666): ''Tis not that which first we love / But what Dying we approve.', sig. A2.

19 A reference to the belief held by some Protestants that Christ was 'begot' in Heaven.

20 i.e. the children of God who existed on Earth before the birth of Christ and who prophesised his coming.

All that's in God is God ; and needs must bee.
Thou mad'st mine eye,
Could'st thou forbear
Thy self to spie?
Or so to rear
The blessed Image of thy self in Thee?

Surely thou could'st no more thy self not view;
Then, Lord, not love
Thy self when seen;
From whence thy Dove,
As hatcht between
Thy face and Looking-glass, sprung forth and flew.[21]

Then shall I not beleev Thou'rt One, yet Three?
Father, and Son,
And sacred Spirit,
That equall run,
One bliss inherit?
Lord, I'll believ Thee surely such to bee.

Yet thou'rt the FATHER still: Those sparkling things,[22]
Are Sons of God:
Those winged flames
That flie abroad,
(Thou know'st their names)
Made without Bodies, made all face and wings.

Faces they have, and eyes and tongues, with these
To see and sing:
But O their Grace!
A sixfold wing
To ev'ry face!
Wise, happy, humble, obedientiall.

Lend's wings, dear Dove; we lag and lose our traffick.[23]
Poore short-leg'd Rhymes,

21 The 'Dove' or holy spirit is a product of both God 'Thy face', and Christ, God's 'Looking-glass' i.e. his human incarnation.

22 i.e. angels.

23 communication.

Verses on foot
Reach Seraphims,
They cannot do't,[24]
Lord, now if ever make my Muse seraphique.

Or if I mayn't have wings, and so keep sight
Of these bright flames,
Shades of thy glory,
Yet tell's[25] their names
And tell's their story;
And lend's a quill, dear Dove, and I'll go write.

Write Angels. Lord, 'tis done:[26] but who are they?
Servants, or sons?
Subjects or Kings?
Footstools, or Thrones?
Inferiour things,
Or Principalities? What shall I say?

Sometimes I hear thee call them Elohim;[27]
Yet they were made:
These plumed[28] things
Are but the shade
Of thy bright wings,
Before whose Sun-shine, all these Stars are dim.

Sometimes't should seem that they but servants are;
Or Ministers
To wait upon
Salvations heirs,
And guard thy Throne.
Yet these stand cover'd where thy sons stand bare.[29]

24 i.e. verses on foot (double meaning with metrical 'feet') cannot reach seraphim (the highest order of the angels). seraphick (line 84) = seraphic, having the attributes of the seraphim.

25 i.e. tell us.

26 i.e. a short dialogue: 'Write the word Angels.' 'Lord, 'tis done.'

27 One of the Hebrew names of God, or 'the gods'.

28 i.e. with wings.

29 i.e. yet these stand with their wings covering their heads while your sons stand bare-headed.

Servants they are, and yet Dominions:[30]
Each holds his Crown
By casting it
Most humbly down
Before thy feet.
Father, thy Throne's erected on the Thrones.

Thousands of thousands of the finite Gods
On ev'ry side
I mean the Cherubs,
When thou dost ride,
Some serv for stirrups,
And some thou holdest in thy hands for rods.

Arch-Angels, Angels that sixwinged Nation[31]
Stand trembling, Lord,
Prest to obey
Their Makers word;
And glad they may
By all their running but maintain their station.

These can't forget that early Funerall;[32]
These can't forget
Those morning Stars
That rose and set,
Whose inbred wars
Blew up themselves. But ——— oh their fall!

Yet thou'rt the FATHER still: these Absoloms[33]
Their beeings had
And beauties, Lord,
But not their trade
Nor Traitours sword
From Thee, from whom All good, and only comes.[34]

30 'Because he exercises and administers his authority in the world through them, they the angels are sometimes called principalities, sometimes powers, sometimes dominions.' Calvin, *Institutes*, I. 14. 5, p. 165.

31 Angels were sometimes portrayed as having six wings.

32 A reference to the fall of Satan and the angels; see 2 Peter 2:4; Jude 6; Revelation 20:1–2 and Isaiah 14:12–15.

33 Absalom rebelled against his father, King David. II Samuel 14–18.

34 i.e. and only good comes.

How came these then to fall? 't should seem that under
Their Angels wings
Each laid some evil
(Oh wretched things!)
And hatch't a Devil.
And so by sinning sing'd their wings. What wonder?

Thy fine white linnen, Lord, sin burnt to tinder.[35]
Satan's thy creature,
But now doth want
First form and feature,
Oh miscreant!
Thou mad'st him bright, but sin turn'd all to cinder.

Yet thou'rt the FATHER still: those Stars in view,
Lanterns hung out
In all mens sights
Thy Court about,[36]
Those various lights
FATHER of Lights there dwelling clearly shew.

That golden Globe comes trundling from thine hand:
Father, thou saist,
Thou Sun of mine
Run East and West,
Cease not to shine
Rounding my Bowling-green of Sea and Land.[37]

That burnisht silver Ball's hurl'd forth by Thee:
That Moon of thine
That always ranges,
Doth sit and shine,
In constant changes,[38]
Says plainly, He that changeth not made mee.

35 Tinder to catch a spark, and so make fire, was formerly made of partially charred linen.

36 This refers to a Ptolemaic conception of the universe according to which stars rotated around the earth on the outermost sphere. The poet is comparing the stars to 'lanterns' which are hung outside God's 'court' i.e. the Earth to signal his residence there.

37 Again, a reference to the Ptolemaic view that the sun orbited the earth.

38 According to the Ptolemy the moon was part of the corporeal, changeable universe, unlike the upper Heavens (the sun, planets and stars) which were celestial and thus immutable.

The Pleiades,[39] cluster of six, call'd seaven:
The signes twice six;
The Errant Train:
The Stars that fix:
The Northern Wain
And all the Constellations of the Heaven:

The Great Orion with those Bands of his:
Stars Great and Least:
The Milkie way,
With All the Rest,
Doth plainly say
That He whose Breasts drop Lights their Father is.[40]

The Archt Expanse, whose Props who can descry?[41]
That surging Roof,
And Saphyre-cieling
Yeelds ample proof,
To all mens feeling,
It had its rise from Thee, O thou most High!

Those stately Offices all on a row,[42]
Standing about
Thy spangled Court,
And yet without
For greater Port;
Thee Father of Heav'ns Family do show.

There stands thy Minting-house, thy Bulloign[43] brought
From 'ts place of birth;
Vapours, I mean,

39 The Pleidades is a group of small stars in the constellation Taurus, commonly spoken of as containing seven stars though only six are visible to the naked eye. Other references in this stanza and the following one are to stars, constellations and the signs of the zodiac. 'The Northern Wain' (line 196) refers to the seven bright stars in the constellation known as the Great Bear, often called 'Charles's Wain'.

40 'Lights', i.e. the stars of the Milky Way, drop from God's 'breasts' as milk does from mothers'.

41 descry = catch sight of.

42 This seems to be a reference to the planets, which stand about God's spangled court but stay outside it, so that they make a more impressive 'port' or train of attendants.

43 bullion. The stanza refers to the mist and fog.

From drossie earth
Are there made clean;
And, as thou pleasest, cast and coyn'd and wrought.

There stands thy Treasurie, that doth contain
Gems in great store
Of orient hue:
Who can count o're
Thy Pearls of dew?
Thy golden Lightnings? or thy silver Rain?

There stands thy Wardrope.[44] Lord, the purple shrouds
Which thou dost use,
And dapled skie,
Like Ermins, shews
Thy Majestie.
And when thou wilt thou wear'st the gold-fring'd clouds.

There stands thy stable-room. Sometimes thy mind's
To ride abroad;
That men below,
There is a God
Above may know
Hearing the neighings of thy prancing winds.

There's thy distillatorie. Thence thou dost
Heav'ns drops distill
In such great store
Earth drinks its fill
Till 't needs no more.
Then the cold ashes are cast forth in Frost.

There stands thy great Confectionary. There
Those heaps of Snow
Double-refin'd
Do clearly show,
And bring to mind
That they belong to th' Great Confectioner.

44 Creation is 'like a spacious and splendid house, provided and filled with the most exquisite furnishings'. Calvin, *Institutes*, I. 14. 20, p. 180. Cf. Herbert, 'Providence'.

'Tis He that makes those Frost-works. He that makes
Moist Drops, when cast
In's Comfit-mold,[45]
Hail stones at last,
When they grow cold,
'Tis He that candies all the Icie flakes.

There stands thy Magazine.[46] Thou dost erect
Thy flaming forges,
And there prepare
Thy shafts and scourges,
Weapons of War
Which, when thou wilt, thy Rebell foes correct.[47]

Storms, tempests, thunders, thunder-bolts, with these,
Great and small shot,
Brimstone and fire,
Father, what not?
If thou require,
Dart thence to chastise those that thee displease.

Whole *Egypt* from thy storm of Hailshot runs.
His Heathen-Head
That Royal slave
Slunk under-bed;
When th' Heavens gave
But one round volley from thy greater guns.[48]

Thou'rt the Rains Father. Frost thou'st gendred?[49]
What Prose or Verses
Can better shew
Thy tender Mercies
Than melting Dew?
This shews thine Heart, and hoary frost thine Head.

45 A mould for shaping sweets or sweetmeats.

46 A place for storing ammunition and artillery.

47 i.e. they correct those who rebel against you.

48 One of the plagues which Moses caused to smite the land of Egypt was a terrible hailstorm (Exodus 9:23–5); Pharaoh sent for Moses and Aaron and entreated them to tell the Lord to send no more hail.

49 engendered, created.

Th' Ancient of Days begat me, says the Snow.
The Lord of Hoasts
's my Fathers Name,
The Thunder boasts,
And Lightnings flame.
I carry Fathers Colours, says the Bow.

So thou'rt the FATHER still: Lord, 'tis alledg'd
By th' Feather'd Hosts,
That here and there
Th' Aeriall Coasts
And Quarters bear,[50]
Under thy Wings they were both hatch'd and fledg'd.

That Bird of Paradise, Lord, thou must owe it.[51]
With chattring cryes,
Swallows and Cranes
Plead th' Only wise
Did hatch our Braines
And He that made our season, made us know it.

'Twas God All-seeing made my piercing Eye
Doth the Eagle say.
To th' God of Love
Our broods we lay,
Saith Stork and Dove:
If these be ours, sure we're thy Progenie.

With early visits and salutes from Earth
Up the Lark climbes,
As if it meant,
With Seraphims
Of high descent
By vieing notes and wings, prove equall birth.

The plumed Ostriches forget their young;
But thou their Father
With careful hand

50 i.e. that sustain themselves [i.e. fly] here and there about the borders and other parts of the air.

51 i.e. you must acknowledge that you made the bird of paradise.

Their Eggs dost gather
Laid in the sand,
Hatching to life, and hiding them from wrong.

The goodly Peacock with his Argus-train,[52]
His Angel plumes,
His well-set border,
Strongly presumes[53]
To th' God of Order,
Unto whose pomp this splendour doth retain.[54]

The tumbling Deeps where all the waters gather[55]
Roundly declare
That Name of His
Whose Counsells are
The Great Abyss:
Seas swell too big to own a meaner FATHER.

Surely the Ocean's thine. Lord is it not?
Thou bid'st it boyle,[56]
But not boyle o're:
And't does recoile
Within the shore,
Thou dost both furnish, Lord, and salt the Pot.

Thou, Great-House-keeper, must the Fish-pond owe,
Whose banks and shores
Are Rocks and sands,
Whose fullness stores
All Coasts and Lands,
For thou the greatest Family canst show.

These Water-works are thine invention, Lord.
Is th' Oceans force,
When most serene,

52 The patterns on a peacock's tail or train resemble eyes and were sometimes likened to the eyes of Argus, a jealous husband who, in classical mythology, is said to have had one hundred eyes with which to watch his wife.

53 presupposes.

54 belong.

55 For the following five stanzas, cf. Edmund Waller, 'A Panegyrick to my Lord Protector', lines 41–56.

56 'He maketh the deep to boil like a pot.' Job 41:31.

Charg'd by thine Horse,
Thy Winds, I mean?
What mighty banks and trenches, Lord, appear?[57]

Under the covert of these surging Seas
Those Armed Bands[58]
(Each jointed scale
Like Armour stands,
Or Coats of Male)
March here and there securely as they please.

Leviathan,[59] that moving Mount or Fort,
Who can deride
Stormes battering,
Of Sons of pride
Thou call'st Him King;
There tumbles he to make his Maker sport.

So thou'rt the FATHER still. Ev'n Earth can cry
From Cliffs and Mountains,
Hills high and steep;
Springs, Mines, and Fountains
That run so deep,
How deep's thy wisdom, Lord? thy pow'r how high?

Thou gav'st the Rocks their Rise. Springs sprang from thee.
Great Architect!
Earths Fabrick fair
Thou didst erect,
And hang i'th' Ayr
To shew its Makers Independency.

Thy very foot-stoole,[60] Lord, thou dost inlay
With Mines of gold,
And silver Ore;

57 Cf. *Ovid's Metamorphoses* (Arthur Golding, 1565), I. 37–40: 'And here and there he cast in seas, to whom he gave a law: To swell with every blast of wind and every stormy flaw / And with their waves continually to beat upon the shore / Of all the earth within their bounds enclosed by the afore.' ed. Madeleine Forey (London, 2002), p. 32.

58 i.e. of fish.

59 A mythological sea monster whom God was said to have defeated. See Psalms 74. 13–14.

60 'Thus saith the Lord, the Heaven is my throne, and the Earth is my footstoole …' Isaiah 66:1.

Who can unfold,
Or prize the store,
Wherewith thou dost enrich poor dust and clay?

This inlay'd foot-stoole thou hast round beset
With Vegetants.[61]
Who can declare[62]
Those various Plants,
Their Vertues rare,
That spring from dust of heav'nly Fathers feet?

Those short-lived Beauties that the Florists gather
Look up a while,
With a fair Eye;
Give God a smile:
And though they die
Yet leave such seed as plainly shews their Father.

Thou'rt fruitfull Parent of All Trees fruit-bearing.
Who doth not see
Earth doth but nurse
These Plants for thee?
Thine Heav'ns disburse
Continuall payments for these Plants up-rearing.

Some Trees there are, though suckled with earths sap,
Yet run upright;
As if they meant,
By their vast height,
Prove their descent,
And lay their Leavie[63] Locks in Fathers lap.

Others there are too weak to rise alone,[64]
Yet seem to know
Where Father dwells;
Why should they go
To Neighbours else
To borrow clutches,[65] to run up upon?

61 i.e. vegetation. 62 i.e. set out the details of … 63 i.e. leafy.
64 a reference to creeping plants such as ivy.
65 clutches = tight grips for shoes.

The Herds, the Folds, the Beasts innumerable:
The multifarious
Creeping Creatures,
Whose food is various
As their features,
Cry still to God, our FATHER, spread our Table.

Father, to Live, thy gift alone can bee;
Earth's cold and dead,
And cannot give
To what it bred
To breathe or live,
Surely the fountain of all Life's with thee.

This spacious House[66] thus built, and furnisht so;
Come let's convey
Our Image just,
Did th' Father say,
To breathing dust;
Leaving our likeness to keep House below.[67]

Then was clay stamp'd, by Act of Parliament,[68]
With God's bright face:
A Creature Crown'd
With Life and Grace:
Heav'n-born, Heav'n-bound,
Of upright aspect, of Divine descent.

Father, thy foot-steps we may find and gather
All other-where,
But in this creature,
Thy face shines clear,
Witness his feature;
Who reads mans face may quickly spell[69] his Father.

66 i.e. the world. Cf. Marvell, 'The First Anniversary', lines 75–98, *The poems of Andrew Marvell*, ed. Nigel Smith (Harlow, 2003).

67 i.e. leaving man (who is made in the image of God) to look after the world.

68 i.e. by God, the supreme authority – since parliament was the supreme authority in England and Ireland when Teate wrote this poem. 'stamped' because the ruler's face was normally stamped on a coin.

69 i.e. recognize.

Said I, one may? my God, I should have said
One might have done:
But things fall cross:[70]
Flesh turns to stone,
Pure Gold to dross,
Silver degenerates to dirt and lead.

Said I, there is? I should have said there was:
My God! there was
Thy countenance
So in his face,
That ev'ry glance
The shining Sun in brightness did surpass.

Father, this walking, talking Plant was Hee
Whom thou didst love,
Whom thou didst prize
All Plants above.
Thy Paradise
Thou soon didst quit when thou hadst lost this Tree.[71]

From th' side whereof a female plant did spring
A splendid pair,[72]
Now as th' Earth begins
T'outshine the Ayr,
Where Heavens bright twins
(The Sun and Moon) their Light, as tribute, bring.

Woman to man's a gift of Gods own giving,
(That man alone
No more might be;
Yet as much one,
And one with thee.)
A gift endors'd with Donors Name, the living.

This Royall consort to compleat mans joy
Thou God of Union
Didst well provide

70 fall away from perfection.
71 this Tree = Adam. God himself left Paradise after Adam had sinned.
72 Eve was formed from Adam's rib. See Genesis 2:21–2.

For chast Communion
As his dear Bride
Whom thou has crown'd on Earth as thy Viceroy.

So th' little world, with greatest work and skill,
Was fram'd at last,
And being the best
Its grace was past[73]
To rule the rest.
Nothing's forbidden but its knowing ill.

Upon thy foot-stool[74] thou hadst built a Throne
For man to sit,[75]
My God, at thine;
And at his feet
Thou didst consigne
All other things in due subjection.

Thou gav'st him Life, 'twas fit should'st give him Law
His fear did fall
By thy command,
On Creatures All
In Sea and Land;
He standing only in his Fathers Awe.

His Diadem was bright Intelligence
Wisdom in full,
Whose ev'ry spark
Makes Diamonds dull,
And Gems look dark;
His Ermine Robe was purest Innocence.

A Rationall Plant-Animal was he;[76]
Could vegetate,[77]
Could Move and walk,
Could contemplate,

73 i.e. it was given dispensation … 74 i.e. Earth.

75 i.e. Adam whom God made sovereign over Paradise. See Genesis 2:15.

76 According to alchemical lore, Adam was the first natural philosopher and had a unique, God-given insight into all the laws governing the natural world.

77 i.e. grow.

Discourse and talk:
Fair Issue of the Blessed Trinity!

Parents own Picture! wise, just, holy Son!
Thou mad'st that star,
His Heart, to be
Triangular,[78]
Yet one with thee,
Who art the Ever-blessed Three in One.

That Instruments Three Strings thou God *Trin-Une*,[79]
(Th' Intellect, Will
And Memory)
Didst Wisdom's skill,
And Sanctity,
And Righteousness give charge to keep in Tune.

And, Oh! What rare and ravishing content
My God did take?
Till, on a day,
A fall did crack
(spoiling his play)
That strings together with the Instrument.[80]

But, oh, what tongue? what pen? what prose? what verse?
What tears? what cryes?
What melting moans?
What sobs? what sighs?
What piercing groanes
Can mans so suddain, so sad fall reherse?

Of late a most compleat and upright Piece
My God did frame,
Of crooked bone:

78 In the Old Testament the heart was used as a metaphor for what is purest and best about mankind. It was regarded not only as the seat of emotions but also wisdom. See 1 Kings 3:12. Because of its triangular shape, it also became an emblem for the Holy Trinity.

79 This refers to the Christian doctrine of the Trinitarian God i.e. the Father, Son and Holy Spirit.

80 A reference to the Fall – Adam has ruined himself, i.e. become a cracked instrument, through his own disobedience and hence spoiled God's 'play' or plan.

But th' Serpent came,
When God was gone
And wound his work to greater crookedness.

Wound out of Heaven, but into Paradise,
In a Friends guise,
That cankerd Devil,
By fallacies,
Drew *Eve* to evil:
And thus the Mother of all living dies.

Man being thus on th' one side mortified,
How quickly doth
The Gangrene spread?
Infecting both
The heart and head.
Thus *Adam* liv'd and reign'd, rebell'd and died.

Down comes the Son by leaping Fathers hedge:
An Apple there,
As some do gather,
But a choak-Pear[81]
As I think rather,
Did tempt him, Oh my teeth are yet on edge!

Oh fruit, Death was thy fruit! thy gall,[82] thy soot
Mee thinks I tast
With all my bread;
Which makes me hast
Unto the dead;
Thou bredst that worm that kill'd me in my root.[83]

Which bee'ng once wither'd, root and branch did fall
With such a weight
Made the earth to groan
From such an height

81 An unpalatable piece of fruit but also figuratively something which is hard to believe or accept i.e. 'difficult to swallow'.
82 The contents of the gall bladder, i.e. bile, proverbial for its bitterness.
83 This line refers to the doctrine of original sin which states that mankind's sinful nature is inherited from Adam's transgression.

Man fell upon
The inferiour creatures, and so crusht them all.

These subjects, thus opprest, soon take up Arms
'Gainst Rebell-Man,
Heav'ns deputie,
(Who first begun
to mutinie
Against his Sov'raign) to revenge their Harms.

For sin that made man Naked, Arm'd the Earth:
So poor man scrambles,
In sweat and blood,
'Midst thorns and Brambles
For sorry food,
Till's Dust turns thither whence it had its Birth.[84]

Now the Earth, that sometimes own'd him for its King
Makes him Distrain[85]
With plow or spade
For every grain,
Or't can't be had,
That wont, of'ts own Accord, its Tribute bring.

Man having broke Gods Peace, all turns to strife:
'Gainst his Creatour
Ev'n Dogs proclaime
Fal'n man a Traitour.
A two edg'd Flame[86]
Cries Come not, Rebell, near this Tree of Life.

Besides these wares without, that worm doth gnaw
Mans inmost soul;
A worm late breeding
O th' fruit he stole,

84 See Genesis 3:17–19.

85 Distrain = to perform an obligation in order to make satisfaction for some wrong done to another (*OED* 7 a). Here the sense seems to be that man must toil to claim back the Earth that was his before the Fall.

86 God placed in Eden 'a flaming sword which turned every way' to guard the tree of life. Genesis 3:24.

Whereof man feeding
Became as broken as his Makers Law.

Yet thou'rt the FATHER: these mourning Verses
Do prove thee so;[87]
Mans miseries,
The Creatures wo,
And all their cries
Plainly Proclaim thee FATHER of all mercies.

The Providence and Patience towards man
Do seem to strive,
O blessed strife
Who shall reprieve
The Traitours life,
By lengthening out his poor contracted span.

Though man made so much haste to stir thine ire;
Yet thou art slow,
My God, thou art;
I find it so;
Thou melt'st mine heart
With burning Coles, but of another fire.

Thine En'my hungers, and thou giv'st him food:
Thine En'my thirsts,
Thou giv'st him drink:
Oh! mine heart bursts.
Oh! Who would think
Man were so bad, that sees his God so good?

Father, Thou mak'st thy Sun still shine on those
That low'r on thee;
And when Heav'n lowers
'Tis love we see;
For fruitfull showrs
Thou makest them to fall on thankless foes.

Man, what art made of? Dost not feel that Sun,
Dissolve the Ice?

87 The poem both mourns the fall of man and testifies to the power of God's mercy.

But thou art Clay,
Th' harder for this:
Yet showrs, we say,
Soften the hardned Clay; But thou art stone.

Father, When man had ceas'd thy sonne to be,
And turn'd thy foe,
Yet didst thou not
Desert him so;
Nor hast forgot
To set thy child, though batter'd, on thy knee.

When man first stript himself, and shew'd his shame,
Cloaths from the Backs
Of Beasts less wild,
Mans FATHER takes
To dress his Child:
Man lost his Robe, and Beasts must bear the blame.

Could I, to cloath a Foe, and thus strip a Friend?
My God! My God!
What have these done?
And yet thy Rod
Due to thy Son
Falls on these servants backs that never sind.[88]

Thus Man's both fed and clad at thine expense,
Kept at thy charge,
Yet keeps it not;
But lives at large,
As having got
His force to fight thee from thy Providence.

Heaps upon Heaps! One load upon another!
God gives Man store,
Like a Dear Friend,
Man sins the more,
Till in the end,
Or Mercies sins, or sins do Mercies smother.[89]

88 i.e. sinned.

89 i.e. until either God's mercy defeats man's sin or man's sin defeats God's mercy.

Yet thou'rt the FATHER still: of mercies, Father:
When through sins curse,
Such Rebels dye;
Thou dost yet nurse
Their Progenie:
As th' Hen her Chickens, so thou dost them gather.

Thus are all things conserved since the fall;
Both man and Beast:
The Raven's fed:
The Lillie's drest;[90]
Then put to Bed.
All's kept in'ts kind, or Individuall.

How beauteous in its season is each thing?
Summer supplies
What Winter spends:
When Autumn dies,
Such stock descends
As may set up the next succeeding Spring.

Thy Providence makes Clouds feed th' Earth with Rain:
Th' Earth feed the Plant;
Plant, th' Animal:
So there's no want,
Nor wast at All.
Then th' Earth with Vapours feeds the Clouds again.

By these, the Marshes make the Mountains drink,
And liquid Seas,
At thy Commands,
Water, by these,
The parched Lands.
Who, but thy self should such a thing forethink.

Thou dost for ev'ry mouth provide a Meat:
For ev'ry meat,
A mouth provide:
Thy Board's full set

90 See Matthew 6:26–28.

On ev'ry side:
If ought do fall to th' ground, that th' earth doth eat.

Father, for All things thou dost well provide.
Thou didst Erect
This fair Creation,
And dost project
Its perservation:
And being the House-Keeper, art the great House-Guide.

Thou serv'st Thy self of All. Ev'n Satans Brain
Ripens thy Plot;
And his design,
When he thinks not,
Promoteth thine:
Thou mak'st that Black-smith forge his own dark chains.

Thou mak'st mans wrath praise thee: And all his evil
Thou turn'st to good:
In all mans Story,
Ev'n in mans blood,
Thou sav'st thy glory:
Goodness rules all in spight of man and Devil.

Yea, such is Fathers care, and Fathers skill,
When foolish man,
Led by that elf,[91]
Doth all he can,
T'undo himself,
T' extract mans greatest good from such an ill.

So thou'rt the FATHER still: Thy new Creation
Most sweetly shews
Thy Father-hood;
My God renews
Faln man to good:
By a new word through th' Spirits Incubation.

Adam comes forth but in a new Edition:[92]
Gods bright Portraiture

91 i.e. Satan.

92 i.e. Christ. Use of the imagery of text production in conceits designed to elucidate theological beliefs occurs time and time again in *Ter Tria*.

Is new impress,
The Divine Nature,
On mans brest;
Clear from all treason, and from all Misprision.[93]

Father, thou soak'st this Adamant[94] in blood
Of thy first-born.
Mine heart, I felt,
Did this impress[95] scorn,
And would not melt
Till that red Sea resolv'd it to a flood.[96]

Father, I heard thee beg the Rebels peace,
Rising betimes
To ope thy doores:
For all my crimes,
My God implores
Me to take pardon for my wickedness.

Then said I, turn me O my Lord my God!
And I will turn
To bear thy yoak;
Mine heart doth burn
That I it broke.
O my dear child! Ile run and burn my rod.

Thus spake my father. Pains oth' second birth
Did pinch and grieve,[97]
But Gods dear strength
Did soon relieve:
And at the length,
His child bee'ng washt and drest, my God makes mirth.

93 misprision = a clerical error but also a crime similar to treason (*OED* n1. 1 b).

94 Adamant = a rock of legendary impermeability associated with the diamond: 'Yea, they made their hearts like adamant stone, lest they should hear the law, and the words which the Lord of hosts hath sent in his spirit by the former prophets.' Zechariah 7:12.

95 impress = a mark made by a seal or stamp. The poet seems to be saying that his hard heart scorned or rejected the impression that God's mercy sought to make on him and required the blood of Christ's sacrifice to soften it.

96 A reference to the blood of Christ's sacrifice.

Nor doth mans elder brother grudge or grieve,[98]
But sing and smile,
Angels do shout
Heav'n rings the while
Th' whole court throughout,
To see poor spend-thrift man return and live.

Man thus adopted and regenerate
Searcheth his Fathers
Last Testament,[99]
And thence man gathers
Heav'ns full intent
For his inheritance and future state.

Thou prov'st thyself my FATHER all these waies.
Now let thy Dove
Teach me to fear,
To serve and love
Thee, Father Dear,
Proving my self thy Child, ev'n all my dayes.

If you call on the FATHER, *passe the time of your sojourning here in fear,*
I Pet.1.17[100]

97 A reference to the birth of Christ.

98 i.e. the angels, who were created before man.

99 Here, the poet is referring to the belief that the life of Christ told in the Gospels was prefigured in the Old Testament.

100 The full quotation is: 'And if ye call on the Father, who without respect of persons judgeth according to man's work, pass the time of your sojourning *here* in fear.'

Son

O Let that Dove, that sometimes did thee[1] Crown
With yellow Gold,
And Silver Plumes,
Unto thy Poet Thee unfold,
That humbly by thy leave presumes,
To spread thy fame, and scatter thy Renown.[2]
Let thine Heroick Spirit guide my Verse
If thou the thing
Indite,
I'le write
Touching the King.[3]
What my weak willing heart would fain reherse.

'Twas when *Augustus Caesar* laid a Tax[4]
On all the Earth,
Grace call'd for Thee.
'Twas then thy Mother gave thee Birth,
That thou might'st set all nations free,
Heavens fair Impression's stampt on Virgin Wax.
To us a Child is born, grace gives a Son,
Heav'ns were too bold,
To say
That they
That King can hold,
Who now into a Manger crouds His Throne.[5]

1 i.e. Christ.
2 'Son' begins by invoking the muses, a rhetorical device common in verse of the period. However in this case, the muse invoked is not a classical God but the Holy Spirit.
3 i.e. Christ.
4 Augustus Caesar was ruler of the Roman Empire which controlled Palestine at the time of Christ. Every inhabitant had to pay a poll tax. See Matthew 22:17.
5 For the story of the birth of Christ, see Luke 2.

For since sin made man bruitish like the Rest,[6]
My God did lay,
The Bread of Life,
Come down from Heav'n 'mongst Oats and Hay,
That man might find his food as rife,
Yea find his Saviour whilst he seeks his Beast.
'Tis not the Cloth but Crown that shews the King.
A Cave's a Court,
If there
Appear
The Prince's Port.[7]
Wise men, what means your Star, your sparkling thing?

Sure you can read by that Orientall light
What is this stranger,
That makes his Bed,
In this poore Cottage, Crib, and Manger;
Hav'ng no where else to lay his Head?
'Tis Christ, Earths Joy, Hels torment, Heav'ns Delight.
Satan, 'tis Christ my Crown, but Christ thy terror,
Bite if thou dare;
His heel,
I feel,
Is somewhat bare;
But thy bruis'd head shall ever rue thine error.[8]

All wise men do, but foolish sinners do not
Lye prostrated,
Before this Babe,
Being lodg'd in such a poore straw-bed;
Nor, to this new-born child, cry, Ab;
They're so unwise their Masters crib they know not.
My Lord at eight daies old began to bleed[9]
For my disease:

6 Cf. Thomas Hobbes, *Leviathan*, ed. C.B. MacPherson (1651), 'And the life of man, solitary, poore, nasty, brutish and short.' (London, 1968), p. 186.

7 Port = a prince's attendants; in this case, the three wise men.

8 This line refers to God's rebuke for the serpent's corruption of Eve: 'And I will put enmity between thee and the woman, and between thy seed and her seed; it shall bruise thy head, and thou shalt bruise his heel.' Genesis 3:15.

9 This refers to the Hebrew rite of circumcision which takes place eight days after birth.

To free
Poore mee,
Not for's own ease:
Surely this martyrs blood's the Churches feed.[10]

Then went he to his Temple with his Mother.
One Dove,[11] me thought,
That blessed maid,
Might then have spar'd, that Lamb be'ng brought
Before the Lord, whose fleece it laid
But rightly on, the worlds whole sin might smother.
From thence, my Lord, posts into Egypts Land.[12]
Have at thy head,[13]
Black Prince,
For since
Egypts dark bed
Hath lodg'd this light, what dungeon can with-stand?

When *Bethl'hem* first gave Judahs Lion[14] breath
He boldly wades
Through th' seav'nfold stream:[15]
The Dragons country[16] he invades,
On their own ground thus daring them.
Thence safe returning dwells at Nazareth.
Can any good come thence? fair Nazerene!
Thou dwellest there:
But, Lo!
The Snow
Is not so cleare
As thou canst make the Black-Moore[17] sinner clean.

10 i.e. food.
11 Mary brought the infant Jesus to Jerusalem to 'offer a sacrifice according to that which is said in the law of the Lord, A pair of turtledoves …' Luke 2:22–24.
12 For the story of Jesus' flight from Herod to Egypt, see Matthew 2.
13 'Have at thy head' is a phrase of defiance, here addressed to Herod. The sense seems to be: What dungeon of yours can incarcerate Jesus since 'Egypt's dark bed' has given lodging to his light?
14 A Messianic title for Christ found in Revelation 5:5.
15 A reference to the Red Sea: 'And the Lord shall utterly destroy the tongue of the Egyptian Sea; and with his mighty wind shall he shake his hand over the river, and shall smite it in the seven streams …' Isaiah 11:15.
16 i.e. Egypt (the crocodiles of the Nile were often referred to as 'dragons').
17 Black-Moore = blackamoor, a dark-skinned person.

At twelve years old, my Lord went thence to sit
I' th' Temple, which
Ne'r shines so bright
As when my Saviour doth enrich
Its darkened windows with his light,
There sits the child to teach the Doctours wit.[18]
The seav'ntieth week be'ng come, the time foreset,
In *Daniels* book,[19]
Foretold
Of old:
My Saviour took
Baptism to him a type of's bloody sweat:[20]

Then was the water washt that scoures my dress,[21]
My God, my Christ:
Thou could'st not need
For thine own sake a *John Baptist*:
But that thou mightest cleanse thy seed,
Thou'rt pleas'd thus to fulfill all righteousness.
Jordan's the cleaner, Lord, for washing thee;
Hath *John* indeed,
To be
By thee
Baptiz'd, such need?
O my baptiz'd Redeemer! Sprinkle me.

Christ, thence ascending, meets his own dear dove
Descending,[22] while
The bridegroomes[23] friend,
The *Baptist*, doth both see and smile,
Whose ears that heavenly voice attend

18 According to Luke 2, Jesus debated in the Temple at the age of 12.
19 These lines refer to a prophesy in Daniel 9:24: 'Seventy weeks are determined upon thy people and upon thy holy city, to finish the transgression, and to make an end of sins …' Christians interpreted this as a reference to the timing for the second coming of Christ.
20 The water used for Christ's baptism is a 'type' or anticipation of the blood he will shed at his death. For the story of Christ's baptism by John in the river Jordan, see Mark 1:4–11.
21 i.e. that cleanses my soul.
22 'And he saith unto him, Verily, verily, I say unto you, Hereafter ye shall see heaven open, and the angels of God ascending and descending upon the Son of man.' John 1:51.
23 Christ is referred to as the 'bridegroom' in Mark 2:19.

O Son of all my pleasure, all my love:[24]
From Egypt call'd, th' baptismal sea be'ng crost,
My Lord, sets foot
In hast[25]
On th' wast:
Heav'n drives him to't;
To learn in'th' desart, how to seek the lost.

Now with the Lion doth the Lamb converse[26]
God sends his Child,
His hand to lay;
Upon these Beasts that are most wild
Till he hath taught them to obey:
Tygers, Wolves, Leopards, Beasts most fell and fierce.
My Lord's sent thither sure to learn to tame
Mans bruitish heart;
(More wild,
Less mild,)
By dear bought art;
To turn the Savage sinner to a Lamb.[27]

The fierie Serpent of the Wilderness
Finding Christ there,
Doth spit and bite;
But th' Brazen Serpents[28] hard and clear,
Scorning the tempters craft and spight,
The Bullet's batt'red, but not the fortress.
Our Lord now learns to fast that we might feast,
And to be tempted,
That wee
Might bee
Thereby exempted:

24 'And there came a voice from heaven, saying, Thou art me beloved Son, in whom I am well pleased.' Mark 1:11.

25 i.e. haste

26 See Isaiah 11:6–9.

27 The passage which follows refers to Satan's temptation of Christ in the desert. See Matthew 4:1–11.

28 The 'brazen serpent' was made by Moses at the command of God to heal the pain caused by snake bite: 'Make thee a fiery serpent, and set it upon a pole: and it shall come to pass, that every one that is bitten, when he looketh upon it shall live.' Numbers 21:8. Because of its life-giving powers the brazen serpent became an Old Testament type for Christ.

Or succour'd so as still to have the best.
If thou be th' Christ, this Stone to Bread convert,[29]
Why foole, the Stone,
Which thou wouldst move,
Is Bread already, or there's none,
My Lord was hungry for my love;
Yet hee's the strength'ning Bread of poor mans heart.
Taking this Rock thence to a Mountain high,
Saith Satan, see;
If thou
Wilt bow
And worship me:
Those Kingdoms all i'le give thee instantly.

Why, foole! Must th' Son buy freedome of a slave?
Hark how thy Chain
Doth clatter at
Thine heel . My Lord was born to raign;
An Universall Monarchs state,
To him long since Heav'ns Letters Pattents gave.[30]
To th' Temples Pinacle, the Churches Head,[31]
Is hurried next:
Bee'ng there,
I heare,
Hell took a Text;
The Wolf by preaching would the Lamb preach dead.[32]

Jump down; 'Tis written th' Angels shall thee catch,
Sayth' Tempters lips;
And that he might
Perswade my Lord to leap, he skips
Those words should set his Doctrine right;

29 See Matthew 4:3–4.

30 Letters patent was an open document conferred by a monarch granting a patent or a right. Christ has received his authority to reign over Earth from Heaven.

31 According to 1 Corinthians 3:16, the Church would become the new Temple and open the way for the revelation of God to all nations.

32 Wolves are identified with persecutors throughout the Old and New Testaments: 'I send you forth as lambs among wolves.' Luke 10:3. In the following stanza, the wolf, i.e. Satan, tries to persuade Jesus to jump from the Temple by quoting Scripture. However he misquotes, and is called to task by Christ. See Matthew 4:6–7.

Angels our wayes ('tis not our Trespass) watch.
Thy neck-verse[33] found, in reading, dost thou Falter,
Yet seem to preach?
For thee
Can be
No Clergy, Wretch!
Thus *Haman* sometime handsel'd[34] his own halter.[35]

The tempter bee'ng at last turn'd off the Ladder,[36]
My Lord sits still
Bee'ng firmer stone,
Then th' wrestling-place, the Pinacle
From whence he threw bold Satan down:
Then th' Angels bring a Chariot from his Father.[37]
This chosen vessel these temptations season.
Now he'll begin
To preach
In each
Place he comes in.
BELEEV'S his doctrine; MIRACLES, his reason.

Yet who makes Use? for ev'ry tribe but one[38]
This great High Preist,
'Mongst all, doth get
Whom very near his sacred breast
As precious Jewels he may set;
And of this twelve, one's but a *Bristow* stone.[39]

33 A 'neck-verse' refers to a Latin verse which was set before one claiming benefit of clergy. In Teate's day, being able to read was taken as a sign that you were a member of the clergy, and thus immune from prosecution in secular courts. Thus by reading the verse you could 'save your neck' from hanging. Satan is trying to avoid defeat by quoting scripture, i.e. his 'neck-verse'.

34 handsel = to be the first to use something.

35 This line draws a parallel between Satan and Haman, a Persian politician who was executed on the gallows he had ordered erected for the Jewish hero Mordecai. See Esther 7. 10.

36 i.e. to be hanged.

37 Cf. Milton, *Paradise Lost*, VI. 749–53, in *The poems of John Milton*, ed. John Carey and Alistair Fowler (London, 1968).

38 Each of the twelve apostles was to judge one of the twelve tribes of Israel on the day of reckoning. See Matthew 19:28. Teate here makes an exception for Judas whose eventual treachery discounts him.

39 i.e. Bristol Stone. The Bristol Stone is a transparent rock-crystal, resembling the diamond in brilliancy. Judas is a fake among the other 'precious jewels' i.e. the disciples.

For his first proof Christ water turns to wine,
At th' marriage-feast.[40]
O pure!
Sirs, sure
It may be guest
You to your wedding did invite the Vine.[41]

If this free vine doth yield so rich a store;
Who can expres
What plenty shall
Flow from thy cross, my God, thy press
When they have bruis'd thy clusters all?[42]
May this Vines blood be my wine evermore!
Well done for th' first: canst do't again? Lord, do it;
Convert my Verse,
To thine
Own wine,
My water-terse:[43]
Renew thy miracle upon thy Poet.

Soon after to his temple goes my God,
His house of Pray'r
Where th' sheep and dove
Are sold as if there were a fair.[44]
But where is innocence and love?
'Tis time, Lord, in thine house to use thy rod.
Doth av'rice with thy temple make thus bold?
The next step hence
That we
Shall see
This sinne commence,
The temple of thy body must be sold.

To seek the sun-shine, comes a man by night,[45]
Hav'ng seen the things

40 See John 2:6–10.

41 The 'vine' is a name given to Christ in John 15:1.

42 The poem is anticipating the crucifixion when the vine's clusters, i.e. Christ's body, shall be bruised and made to bleed. See Revelation 14:19–20.

43 terse = polished, refined or perfected (*OED* 2). The poet is requesting God to transform and perfect his 'Verse' just as Christ turned water into wine.

44 This stanza refers to Christ's cleansing of the Temple. See Mark 11:15–19.

45 This line refers to the Pharisee Nicodemus who was sympathetic to Jesus but was too frightened to support him openly. See John 3:1.

My Lord had wrought.
Heav'ns mysteries my Lord forth brings,
But finds the teacher how untaught?
Night's most within, but Christ turns all to light.
After, this Fountain, thirsting, seeks a well:
But finds a ditch
Within
With sinne
All foul, the which
He searcheth first; doth all her doings tell:

Then, by revealing her, himself reveal
To be the Christ:
Samaria finds[46]
What blind Jerus'lem sought and mist.[47]
Thou'rt Christ to all kindreds and kinds,
That by beleiving set to thee their seal.
Then say's Disciples, Master, eat we pray
But he had got
A meat
To eat
Which they knew not
For he'd gone eating, *working,* all the day.[48]

Bee'ng thence return'd again to *Galile*,
A Noble man,
For's dying son
Begs a Reprieve of's Soveraign,[49]
The man beleev'd it should be done,
And what he first beleev'd did quickly see.
Happy that Son, whom Gods Son quickeneth!
More noble sure,
He is
For this

46 Samaria was the capital city of the district north of Judea. The two kingdoms shared a historical antipathy which led to Samaritans being regarded as unclean by the Jews. This stanza refers to the story of the Samaritan woman at the fountain who gives Jesus a drink of water and recognizes him as the Messiah. See John 4:4.

47 i.e. missed.

48 'Jesus saith unto them, My meat is to do the will of him that sent me, and to finish his work.' John 4:34.

49 See John 4:47.

Ev'n for his cure,
Bee'ng thus by th' Prince of life repreiv'd from death.

Then to Bethesda's Pool, Salvations Well[50]
Carries a cure
And gives't away;
The Jews this carriage can't endure,
But think Christ hurts the Sabath Day,[51]
Whilst he, poore man, for whom 'twas made doth heale.
Is there no cure, my God, for unbelief?
'Mongst all thine art,
Doth there
Appear
None to impart,
To this disease a fruitable[52] releif.

My Lord invites five thousand to a feast:[53]
No store of dishes
Bee'ng drest or cook'd;
That, by five loaves and two small fishes,
Their unbelief might all be chok'd,
Whilst in their mouths their meat's so much increast.
Yet the next day, as if they'd ne're been fed,
These very men
Do fret,
And whet,
Their teeth agen,
Not to feed on, but to back-bite[54] Heav'ns Bread.[55]

After, The man born blind to sight's restor'd
By paste of clay,[56]
Surely I should

50 A pool in Jerusalem where Jesus is said to have healed a paralyzed man during the sabbath. See John 5:9.

51 It was considered a sin to carry out any task, including performing miracles, on the sabbath.

52 The word 'fruitable' is a coinage by Teate, and here has the same sense as 'fruitful'.

53 For the story of the miracle of the multiplication of the loaves and fish, see John 6:1–15.

54 i.e. spit out …

55 The day after witnessing the miracle of the multiplication of the loaves and the fishes, the crowd question Jesus' claim to be 'Heav'ns Bread', i.e. the son of God. See John 6:16–71.

56 See John 9:1–41.

Have blinded seeing eyes that way,
Bee'ng so far, Lord, from doing good.
Yet Jews in these new eyes, can't see the Lord.
Thou tak'st a living mon'ment from a grave.[57]
Thy foes may see
The dead
Raised;
Yet they'd kill thee;
Oh, my deare Lord, what sign would sinners have?

Devils are all cast out,[58] but unbelief;
Dead Palsies too,
Receive their cure;
But Oh, Dead hearts, what aileth you,
That you do more and more obdure.
Not miracles, but blood must cure this grief.
Ah! My dear Lord, the wither'd hand is heal'd:[59]
And yet the hand
Of faith
Who hath?
Jews still withstand:
And after all, to whom's thine arm reveal'd?[60]

Feavers are quench'd; yet fury burns amain:
Issues of blood
Are stanched quite:
All evils but their spleen find good;
And th' bloody issues of their spite.[61]
Oh! how Jews hate the good Samaritan![62]
Do Pharisees wash oft? Ah! they have need:[63]
Leperds do clear,[64]

57 A reference to the raising of Lazarus from the dead. See John 11:1–44.

58 See Mark 1:25.   59 See Matthew 12:13.   60 See Luke 1:51.

61 A reference to Jesus' healing of a woman with a haemorrhage in Matthew 9:20–22. The poet is suggesting that Jesus can staunch all 'issues of blood', except those caused by the Pharisees' 'spleen' or spite, lines which hark forward to their role in Christ's crucifixion.

62 For the parable of the Good Samaritan, see Luke 10:33.

63 The poet is referring to the Jewish tradition of ceremonial washing before eating. The Pharisees rebuked Jesus and his disciples for not adhering to this custom, but were labelled hypocrites for caring more about superficial rituals than true love of God. See Mark 7:1–6.

64 In the second edition of *Ter Tria*, 'leperds' has been corrected to 'leopards'. However, the first edition spelling better serves to highlight a possible play on words: lepers in the

But then
These men
The liv'ry wear.
Gehazi's curse is on them and their seed.[65]

Who cures their Phrensies, can't their rage allay,
They contradict
The tongue that taught
The dumb to speak: yea when convict[66]
By the strang cures my Saviour wrought
In Falling-sicknesses, yet fall away.
Creeples[67] get legs; yet mens opinions halt
Who thou shouldst be:
One while
They smile,
Then lowre on thee;
But thou art still the same: Lord! where's the fault?

For thy good works their hardned hearts do stone thee.
Sure it displeases
That they have health,
And that thou carri'st their diseases;
Scatt'ring amongst thy poor the wealth.
My God ev'n of thine own how few do own thee!
Oh! how they daily carpe at righteousness!
Life may not live,
If they
But may
The sentence give.
They plot to bring salvation to distress.

To drag the resurrection to the grave:
Earths health to anguish:
How fain would they
See their dear-cheap Physitian[68] languish

Bible were afflicted with spots all over their skin, and Teate may be suggesting that Jesus can cure 'lepers' of their impurities (e.g. Luke 5:12–13), but Pharisees, like leopards, cannot change their 'spots'. See Jeremiah 13:22.

65 See 2 Kings 4:12. Gehazi was a servant of Elisha who falsely claimed a reward for curing a man of leprosy and was afflicted with leprosy as punishment.

66 i.e. convinced.

67 i.e. cripples.

68 i.e. Jesus who cures the people of their afflictions without charge. See Matthew 9:12.

Who freely cures them all the day.
Him to destroy they plot, he them to save.
My Lord, thy patience is a miracle
'Mongst all the rest
(As wee
May see)
None of the least.
My Lord! If I may judge, it doth excell.

Oh! how they grudge my Lord his drink and food!
The Bread, the Vine,
Sent down to us,
As bee'ng a bibber of much wine[69]
They tax, and call him gluttonous,
Who's only greedy for to do them good.
These dunghils to asperse[70] the sun begin.
He casts out evil,
Yet they
Do say
He hath a Devil;[71]
Sinner, they call the fountain ope for sin.[72]

Hee is the Son o'th' Carpenter, say some;[73]
The Son of God,
You might have said,
Who rais'd Heav'ns roof you see so broad,
Such Carpentry's no such mean trade,
Helping to ground-fill all this lower room.
Others object, that they his country know,
The place from whence
He came
Can name,
And how long since.
Why, Sirs, pray when did you to Heaven go?

69 'The Son of man is come eating and drinking; and ye say, Behold a gluttonous man, and a winebibber, a friend of publicans and sinners!' Luke 7:34. Bibber = drinker.

70 asperse = to defame.

71 See John 8:48–9.

72 All spiritual graces communicated by the holy spirit are compared to a fountain in Zechariah 13:1. The poem is rebuking the unbelievers who think the 'fountain', i.e. Jesus, to be an agent of sin.

73 See Matthew 13:55.

Then they perswade us that the King speaks treason
Because he makes
Himself to be
God as he is: Because he takes
His own, they cry out robbery.
Lord, all men have not Faith, all have not reason.
Sometimes he is not *Cesars* friend, they say,[74]
Who's *Cesars* King.
Yet hee,
We see,
Makes fish to bring
Tribute to him, that he may *Cesar's* pay.[75]

Then they crie out, that he's the sinners friend.[76]
But, Oh! that they
That thus exclaime,
Had rightly known what now they say,
The counsel that to sinners came,
From his deare friendly lips they'd more attend.
To make Christ clash with Moses they project.[77]
The great Law-giver
Doth teach
Its breach;
This they deliver
Who would the coppy by the Proof correct.[78]

How sharp their sight to find faults where are none?
But Oh! how dim
For to descrie
That radiant deity in him?
And most of all, how blind to spie
Those great prodigious evils of their own?
The Temple he'd destroy, and then rebuild[79]
This, Jews object;
But what
Of that?

74 See Matthew 17:24.

75 See Matthew 17:27.

76 See Matthew 9:11, Mark 2:6, Luke 5:30.

77 See John 9:29.

78 The Pharisees try to make Moses' Old Testament teachings (the copy) clash with those of Jesus (the proof). See Matthew 19:3–9.

79 See Matthew 26:61.

Themselves project
How th' Temple of Christs Body might be kill'd.

How malice mixt with blindness all misconstr'es!
My Lord so spake
As n're did Man:
Yet's words and works too they'll mistake,
Say he or do he what he can.
To match his miracles they bring forth monsters,
Have Rulers or have Pharisees beleev'd?
The Law we know;
Say those
His foes.
Ah! if t'were so
The Law-Maker would sure have been receiv'd.

Yet this good Shepherd finds some stragling sheep:[80]
The Gospel-net
Some Fishers takes:[81]
Some at receipt of custome set
Christs customers his market makes.[82]
And what he finds hee'll spend his life but keep.
Some wise and noble too, although not many
King Jesus Court
Can show:
And so
To keep his Fort
There's one Centurion,[83] Lord, 'tis well there's any.

Mary th' unclean from whom as many Devils,
As muddie *Nile*
Hath streams, are cast:[84]

80 Jesus is referred to as the 'good shepherd' in John 10:1–19. The following passage describes the appointing of the apostles.

81 Peter, Andrew, James and John were fishermen. See Matthew 4:18–22.

82 A reference to Matthew who was a tax collector before being called to follow Christ. See Matthew 9:9.

83 This is most likely a reference to the story of the healing of the Centurion's slave in Luke 7:1. The Centurion believes that he is not worthy to have Christ in his house but that if he only said the word his slave should be healed. The incident is related as an example of Gentile faith.

84 A reference to the prostitute Mary Magdalen who was cured of 'seven devils' by Christ

Each flood had its own Crocodile:
Yet she becomes one stream at last
Of Gospel-penitence for all her evils.
Christs feet washt with all her tears her haire makes dry;
And Christ agen
With blood
Makes good
Her waies unclean:
And with forgiveness wipes the weepers eye.

A *Canaanite* to th' King of *Hebrews* comes,[85]
Begs and implores
At *Israels* feast
Some succour from those sacred stores[86]
That Jesus for the Jews had drest.
Whil'st Children slight their bread, she leaps at crumbs.[87]
A little man, but sinner not the least[88]
Climbes up on high
That he
The tree
Of life might spie;
And in the fruitless *Sycamore* a feast.

Mary, the Lords *Messiah*, doth annoint;[89]
Disciples grudge,
And think't too good
For him who thinketh not too much
To spend on them his precious blood.
See how one *Judas* puts all out of joynt?
Bee'ng thus annointed Christ as King appears,
And forth doth go,
As King

after she washed his feet and dried them with her hair. See Luke 7:37–50 and Luke 8:2. The Nile was said to have seven streams.

85 A reference to an incident related in Matthew 15:22 where Christ heals the daughter of a Canaanite women. This is another example of Gentiles being rewarded for their faith.

86 stores = food. (Christ nourishes believers.)

87 'But he answered and said, It is not meet to take the children's bread, and to cast it to dogs. And she said, Truth, Lord: yet the dogs eat of the crumbs which fall from their masters' table.' Matthew 15:26–7.

88 A reference to Zacchaeus, the tax collector who climbed a sycamore tree to see Jesus. See Luke 19:1.

89 See Luke 7:37–46.

Riding
To *Sion* so
Who brings salvation, him an *Ass-Colt* bears:[90]

Thus foolish things, and things that men despise
The Lord doth chuse;
That this dumb Ass
Might preach performance to the Jews
Of what of old forespoken was;[91]
And Christ by weakness might confound the wise.
Judah! thy scepter's gone, but *Shiloh's* come.[92]
Jerusalem!
Look out,
And shout,
For *Davids* stem
Now springs a fresh in thy Law-givers room.[93]

Children, by their Hosannahs loudly cry'd,
Do testifie
My Saviours praise,
That he might still his foes thereby,
His Name these Babes and sucklings raise,
Whilst th' Elders and the Fathers him deride.
Thus whilst the Fathers fall ith' Wilderness,
Children inherit;
Why, lo
Ev'n so
It pleas'd the Spirit,
What men deny, to teach poor Babes confess.

What Jews reject poor Greeks make friends to see.[94]
Sion, take heed

90 According to Matthew 21:2. Jesus rode into Jerusalem, also known as 'Sion' or Zion, on an ass.

91 i.e. what was prophesised in the Old Testament.

92 'The sceptre shall not depart from Judah, nor a lawgiver from between his feet, until Shiloh come; and unto him shall the gathering of the people be.' Genesis 49:10. Shiloh was taken to be a messianic title for Christ.

93 This refers to the belief in Jewish theology that the Messiah would be a descendant of King David.

94 The term 'Greek' was often used in contrast to 'Jew' to denote Gentiles in general. See John 12:20.

Thou be n't the hive
That others do with hony feed,
Not tasting what it self doth give;
Whilest Gentiles steal away thy Christ from thee.
What needs more proof? my Lord puts on the rack
Devils themselves
(Though Jews
Refuse,
As worser elves)[95]
Till they to him a full confession make.[96]

Would you beleive, if your high Priest should tell
Or who's the Christ,
Should testifie?
Sure your own *Caiaphas*[97] little mist
Saying 'twas meet this man should die
For th' people, that they perish not: GO-SPELL:[98]
How sweetly sings this Swan before them all![99]
Though envy fumes
His skin
Within
His whited plumes,
Their High Priest sings Heav'ns High Priests Funeral.

Thus men teach Parrots speak, but when they know not;
The High Priest cries
(And surely hee
Should know) this mans your Sacrifice.
Yet Christ their Saviour must not be;
My Lord, men do confess thee though they do not.
This Sacrifice the Priest plots how to kill,
And yet there was
More Priest
In Christ

95 i.e. devils.

96 Jesus refers to Jews as devils in John 8:44. The poem seems to be saying that Christ will not be able to redeem the Jews until they recognise him as the Messiah.

97 Caiaphas was the high priest in Jerusalem who, according to John 18:13, was partly responsible for trying Jesus after his arrest.

98 A play on words: GO-SPELL = Go! Acknowledge! i.e. praise the Messiah, which is the function of the Gospels.

99 The swan is said to sing only once in her life, just before she dies.

Then Caiaphas.
Thus types the truth, shadows would substance spil.[100]

Innocent Lamb! although thou knew'st this plot,
Yet, Oh how fain
Would'st thou get up
To be in read'ness to be slain
'Gainst th' Passover; that all might sup?
My Lord thou seest thy death but shun'st it not.
This is the Paschall Lamb[101], sure I may call it
Immaculate;
O God,
Thy blood
Sprinkles my gate;
Yet is thy bitter grief my bitter sallet.[102]

I' th' upper room my Lord bespeaks the feast[103]
For his dear Friends;
That they might know
That from above their chear descends;
Who'l Feast with Christ must upwards go.
But, Oh! how dear for all pays this dear guest?
Desiring I've desir'd this feast to eat
With you, before
I go
Unto
The other shore.
Oh! how my Lord hungers to be my meat?

Yet Friends, there's something I must sadly say:[104]
You're not all clean,

100 This is most likely a reference to the division between Judaism and Christianity. In Hebrews 10:1, Paul compares Jewish law to a mere shadow of the reality or 'substance' that is to come in Christ.

101 Paschall = Passover; the Jewish feast celebrating the exodus of the Israelites from Egypt. The day was celebrated by the ritual slaughter and consumption of lamb. In early Christian theology the 'Paschal Lamb' came to represent Christ's suffering and sacrifice.

102 sallet = a measure or vessel for wine (*OED* 1 b).

103 The following passage is an account of the Last Supper. See Matthew 26:20–30, Mark 14:17–26, Luke 22:14–39, John 13–17. Bespeak = call to order.

104 The poem switches to a first person narration as Jesus denounces Judas Iscariot for his betrayal. See, for example, Mark 14:18.

'Mongst you doth sit
(The man that dips with me, I mean)
A Devill, yet an Hypocrite,
That shall this night the God of truth betray.
'Tis my Purse bearers plot his Lord to sell,
Who had him bought:
The wretch
To Preach
I sometime taught,
But not to sell me, or himself to Hell.

Judas! canst thou find death in such a Pot?
Plot such a matter
Against thy Master?
Whilst thy sop softens in my platter,
Who of each dish made thee a taster,
Hardens thy heart the whilst, *Iscariot*?
Will nothing serve but sops in blood next meal?
My Purse,[105] my dish
Were free
To thee
What more could'st wish?
Wretch! what thou dost do quickly:[106] Run, and sell.

Pensive Disciples when they hear, and know it,
Each fears for one:
But he that bears
The bag,[107] is lag; perdition's Son,
He is the last that doubts or fears:
Slow to confess, but Oh! how swift to do it.
Come children take this bread, 'tis broke for you:
Much good may't do you;
'Tis drest,
And blest,

105 'And he said to them, When I sent you without purse, and scrip, and shoes, lacked ye anything?' Luke 22:35. Here, 'purse' is most likely used synonymously with 'scrip', a small pouch for carrying food.

106 See John 14:27.

107 Judas was carrying a bag when ordered from the room, leading the disciples to think that Christ was merely sending him out for supplies. John 14. 29. Hence in Teate's time 'To bear the bag' was an idiom meaning to be dismissed.

Take it unto you,
And therewithall my broken body too.
Come my Disciples, here's an health likewise
To you, not mee:
Let it go round,
Salvations cup's the cup you see:
Your health is in my bloody wound,
Think of my blood as oft as ye drink this.[108]
Your Makers broken Law your bloody sin,
And bleeding heart
Bring mee
To see
And feel this smart.
Who would Hell conquer must with death begin.

My Testament I leave you seal'd in blood:
You I bequeath
When ere I die
Full conquest over sin and death
With life and peace; which by and by
I the Testatour[109] by my death make good.
Pledge mee, dear friends, this blood was broach'd;
I'll drink no more
Of wine
Oth' vine,
Till bee'ng got ore,[110]
I may in Fathers kingdome drink it new.

Come let's now sing, saith Christ, see'ng all my sorrow
Is but your Crown:
Thorns at the breast
Make musick, when the Spirit's down,
Yea sometimes musick of the best;
Let's sing to night, for I must dye to morrow.
My Lord then riseth up from whence he sate
Whom winds obey,

108 A reference to the Protestant rejection of transubstantiation. The wine is not Christ's actual blood as is suggested in the Gospels, but a symbol designed to aid remembrance of his sacrifice.

109 Testatour = one who makes a will. Christ is giving his last testament to his disciples.

110 i.e. until I have ascended into Heaven.

And seas
With these,
Disciples may
Now see him, that he may be gracious, WAITE.

Sure whilst my Saviour SERVES,[111] who ever came
See'ng him so drest,
Waiting on all
Girt with a Napkin, scarce had guest[112]
This were the feast of's Funerall,
But Marriage-Supper rather of the Lamb.
After the wine my Lord doth water take;
Heav'n stoops to meet,
And bow
As low
As sinners feet.
Oh what clean work Christs Blood and Spirit makes.

Peter, thou think'st that I stoop down too low,[113]
And sai'st I shall
Ne're wash thy feet;
Then canst thou have no part at all
In *Davids* Son, nor be made meet
I th' new Jerusalems clean streets to go,
Streets that are pure as gold and clear as glass:
This Basin is
Thy way
I say
To this fair bliss:
Israel to *Canaan* must through *Jordan* pass.[114]

Sirs, see you what I h've done, and do you know it?
You call me well
Say'ng I'm your Lord:
If I then stoop, Oh! never swell.

111 Jesus washes the feet of the disciples. See John 13:4.

112 i.e. guessed.

113 See John 13:6.

114 Canaan was the 'Promised Land' to which the Israelites fled after their escape from Egypt. To do so, they had to cross the river Jordan. See Joshua 4:10. Here, Jesus seems to be suggesting that the washing of the disciples' feet is a symbolic re-enactment of baptism. See John 13:6.

If I have wash't your feet, afoard
You to do likewise: Happy if you do it.
Servants, my Livery you must wear is Love.[115]
This bowl's my Spirit,
Which I
Now die
That you may 'nherit:
The Lamb goes hence that he may send the Dove.

Oh may this towell bind your hearts in one!
My bending down,
Teach them to bow!
May pride and sinful passions drown
In this full Basin. Men shall know
By this that your[116] mine when I am gone.
Gone? I'll go too, saith *Peter*, Lord I will
What ere comes on't.
Oh no!
Not so;
'Tis a sore brunt.
Best metall melts when men their Maker kill.

Nay Lord, though all men run, I'll stand by thee:
Run friends or foes,
Foes to pursue,
Or friends to scape the hands of those.
Poor man I'll tell thee what's more true,
Ere th' Cock crow twice I thrice denied must be.[117]
Sure *Peters* courage strangly is come on.
My Passion, lo!
He did
Forbid,
Now he'll dye too.
Yet when the Shepheard dies, the sheep will run.

Let not your hearts be troubled, but believe
In God and Mee;
I ride before

115 See John 13:34. 116 i.e. you're.
117 For Jesus' prediction of Peter's denial see John 13:36.

To see things may in red'ness[118] be,
Behold I'll meet you at the door:
My Fathers house can me and you receive.
Whither I go ye know, and th' way ye know.
Saith *Thomas,*[119] Nay
Lord, we
Can't see
Which is the way:
For, we alas! know n't whither thou dost go.

Thomas, I am the true and living way.
My flesh I gave,
(Knowest thou me)
A path-way unto Heav'n to pave,
Cemented with blood to be,
So that who walks in me can't go astray.
Shew us the Father, Lord, that's all our bliss;
Doth *Philip* say.
How long
Among
You must I stay,
Ere you know me, saith Christ, why here he is.

Judas replyed, but not th' *Iscariot*, Lord,
How is't that thou
Thy self to us,
But not unto the world dost shew
Thy blessed self revealing thus:
Why, I will do't to all to keep my word,
Peace I leave with you, my peace I you give,
Not as the world,
When here
And there
You're tost and hurl'd,
The sweetest calme shall then your hearts relieve.

Friends, if you love me let me go, don't grieve me.
Oh! how your sobs

118 i.e. readiness.

119 There follows a dialogue between Jesus and the disciples Thomas, Philip and Judas. See John 14:5.

Do antedate
My Passion! O my pulse vies throbs.[120]
Oh let my grief in yours abate;
My fathers arms are ready to receive me.
Sirs, I can't stay to talk: yonder's the Prince
The world that swaies.
O see
How hee
Doth's legions raise;
Yet of one single fault can't me convince.[121]

I am the vine, ye branches bring forth fruit:
My blood's your sap:
My blood's your seed:
'Tis well for you that others tap
The vessel, that the vine may bleed:
The hand that empties me doth you recruit.[122]
O if you love your selves let me go send
That guide to you
That shall
Ev'n all,
Ev'n all things shew.
I h've much to speak which you can't yet attend.[123]

A little while I disappear, Anon
I'm seen agen;
For to the Father
I go; say they, what may this mean,
This little while? we cannot gather.
Why, Friends, when Winter's over, Spring comes on.
Truth, Lord! we now believe. Ah do you so?
Just now comes on
An houre
Whose showre
Will make you run,
Whilst solitary to my grave I go.

Yet am I not alone: Oh blessed Father!
Thou'rt with me still:

120 vie = to increase in number. My pulse increases my 'throbs' or pain.
121 i.e. convict.
122 i.e. fill you up.
123 i.e. listen to.

Now glorifie
Thy Son, thy Son: when *Butchers* kill
Thy Lamb, Oh take me up on high
And thine and mine Lord with me, to me gather:
These are thy stock I kept, and did improve them.
For these I pray,
And all
That shall
Their word obey:
Lord, here's thine own again; O keep them, love them!

Then his Disciples forth my Lord doth lead.
Cedron[124] ith' way
Makes me bethink
What th' Psalmist of th' High Priest do say,
He of the brook ith' way shall drink
Therefore he shortly shall lift up the head.[125]
Thence they together to the garden pass,
Where grew that store
That can
Fall'n man
Make as before:[126]
Sure my Redeemers Rue's[127] that herb of grace.

'Twas in a garden *Adam* did undo us;
There grew that fruit
Whose bitterness,
That man for ever might not ru't,
My Lord did tast and squeeze and press:
Then from a Garden brings our cure unto us.
O mount of Olives! O *Gethsemane*!
To all else yet
A soile
Of Oyle![128]

124 Cedron = Kidron; a valley which Jesus and the disciples crossed after the Last Supper. See John 18:1.

125 'He shall drink of the brook in the way: therefore shall he lift up his head.' Psalm 110:7.

126 Here the poet is drawing an analogy between the Garden of Eden, the location the Fall and the Garden of Gethsemane where Jesus' sacrifice of his own life will redeem sinful mankind.

127 Rue = compassion (*OED* n1 2) but also a medicinal herb.

128 The name 'Gethsemane' means 'oil press'.

Of bloody sweat
Only to me —— sinner! here's Oyl for thee.

Sirs, sit you here, *Peter*, and *James* and *John*,[129]
Oh! I begin
To feel such smart
Amazeth me that n'ere knew sin:
Yet how it cuts my very heart!
Sirs, sit you down. I must pray or I'm gone.
This cup, this cup, O Father! may it pass![130]
This cup, this cup
May't pass!
Alas!
Must I drink't up?
Why, all thy vials dregs are in this glass.

Ah! friends your heav'ness doth augment mine too.
How can your eyes
Continue shut
So near such strong and bitter cries?
Dulness, I now perceive, can cut:
Will you not watch with him that's sick for you?
You three of all I chose for sentinels:
I bade you lie
Perdieu,[131]
But you
Sleep, though I die.
Yet in weak flesh a willing spirit dwels.

But though my foot-guard sleeps, mine horse men watch
Though men do grieve me
Yet at the length
Mine Heav'nly Angell doth relieve me,
Heav'ns succours reinforce my strength.
Sin, do thy worst now, thou'lt meet with thy match,
Yet, Oh this cup! this cup! Lord let it pass

129 The poem again moves into the first person as Jesus denounces the disciples for falling asleep. For an account of 'The Agony in the Garden' see Matthew 26:36–45, Mark 14:32–41, Luke 22:39–47.

130 See Matthew 26:39, Mark 14:36, Luke 22:42.

131 Perdieu = on guard.

If't be thy will;
Yet thine
Not mine
Perform thou still.
Thy scalding wrath, Lord, cracks my brittle glass.

Sin ent'red man at first but by one hole:[132]
But ev'ry pore
Throughout my skin,
My God! my God! becomes a door
Whence blood goes out whilst wrath comes in.
Such anger, through thine anger, melts my soul.
Can you get sleep, whilst in this scalding bath
I melt away,
Blood-wet
In sweat?
Sirs, think I pray,
'Tis for your feavers sake of sinne and wrath.

What, can I not one hours short watch obtain?[133]
One houres? I say.
Oh you'l be tempted;
Watch, for your own sakes then, and pray:
Oh! pray that you may be exempted.
There are no vapours left in my parcht brain:
I'm past all sleeping now, but th' sleep of death.
But, Oh! let pass
This cup!
Drink't up.[134]
Thy sword, Alas!
In thine own fellow-shepheard dost thou sheath.

Oh! how thy wrath my flow'r to hay converts!
My bones do start,
My flesh consumes,

132 A reference to the misogynist belief that women, through Eve's transgression, were responsible for the advent of sin on earth.

133 Cf. Herbert, 'Sacrifice', lines 29–30.

134 The italics may signify that this is intended to be the voice of God commanding his son although this is impossible to ascertain conclusively.

My skin is parcht, as bottles[135] are
I'th' smoak, Lord, through thine angry fumes.
Disciples, now sleep on, and rest your hearts.
This restless night of mine procures for you
A day of peace;
My show'rs,
Your flow'rs,
Your joyes increase.
Never did night yield such a blessed dew:

Honey to mine, though Gall and Blood to me:
I mean those drops
Which from my brow
Bedew the ground.[136] Sinners, what crops
May your dear Lord expect from you?
But now let's rise; yon Traitour comes, I see.
Your saviour's given into sinners hands.
Judas! Art come?[137]
Thou'lt soon
Be gone
Hence to thine home.
Whilst thou twists mine, I faster knit thy bands.

Thou send'st me to my cross: But I'll be even.
Thou shal't hang first,
Thief that thou art!
Thou'st broke thy faith, and thou shalt burst
Asunder, false perfidious heart!
'Tis fit such pay be to such traitours given.
Into the second Adam's garden creep
Dost thou, Serpent?
That way
Betray
The innocent?
Methinks thou smil'st as Crocodiles do weep.[138]

135 bottle = a bundle of hay or straw.

136 'And being in an agony he prayed more earnestly: and his sweat was as it were great drops of blood falling down to the ground.' Luke 22:44.

137 A reference to Judas Iscariot's betrayal of Jesus in the Garden of Gethsemane. For an account see Matthew 26:47. There is no source in the Gospels for the majority of the hyperbolic denunciation that follows.

138 Cf. Francis Quarles, 'Fraus Mundi', lines 12–16, *The Penguin book of Renaissance verse*, ed. David Norbrook (London, 1992).

Canst kiss, and court me still? Hail! Master, Hail!
'Twas sometimes said,
O kiss the Son
Lest he be wroth, and strike you dead;
Sure thy kiss is not such a one.
With unbelievers, Hypocrites shall waile.
Judas, thou know'st mine haunt. I' th' very place
Me to betray
Just there
Ev'n where
With me to pray
Thy feigned lips were wont, hast thou the face?

What means thy search? wretch, thou'rt the fugitive;
Your Lanthorn Light,
Sirs, also shews
Your works are darkness, and you night.
Why force you what I do n't refuse?
Is it my life you seek? 'tis that I give.
Jesus of *Nazareth* you're come to take;
Why I am he.
They all
Down fall!
Can majestie
Upon such Rebels such impression make?

My Lord, thou needst not flee, nor *Peter* draw!
They run, they run:
Backwards they fall;
Yet to be taken, thou comest on,
Yielding thy self unto their thrall,
Who cannot slip thy curb from off their jaw.
Servants are let go free, while th' master's bound.
Bold *Peter* now,
To show his
Prowess,
Is word and blow:
But the meek pris'ner gently cures the wound.[139]

139 For an account of Peter cutting off the servant's ear see John 18:10, and for Jesus healing the wound see Luke 22:50.

Thou chid'st thy Champion while thou friend'st thy foe,
Sweet Prince of peace!
The wounds of foes
Thou'st rather heal with gentleness,
Than thine should steel to flint oppose.
Peter's too hot to hold, I fear me so.
What mean your swords and staves? sirs! who's the thief:
You've stol'n the fruit,
And yet
Are set
To make pursuit.
I've only stol'n the punishment and grief.

Was I not with you in the temple still?
Have you forgot
My Sermons there?
Yet all that while ye took me not.
And must I now these shacles weare?[140]
Th' *Essential*[141] must the *written* word fullfill.
See my Disciples leave me and they fly:
Each shifts for one:
And so
I too
Could well have done:
But, lo! my bondage is their liberty.

Thus bound they drag me to the high Priest first,[142]
Who am the goat[143]
Doom'd thus to die
More by Heav'ns counsell then their plot,

140 'And Jesus answered and said unto them, Are ye come out, as against a thief, with swords and with staves to take me? I was daily with you in the temple teaching, and ye took me not: but the scriptures must be fulfilled.' Mark 14:48–9.

141 Essential = real, actual.

142 For an account of Jesus' testimony before the high priest see Matthew 26:57, Mark 14:53, Luke 22:66.

143 i.e. scapegoat. This relates to a Hebraic ritual performed on the day of atonement. Two goats are presented to God; one is sacrificed and the other, the scapegoat, is released into the wilderness to carry away humanity's sins. See Leviticus 16:7–10. Jesus sacrificed his life in order to bear the sins of the world and thus sees himself as 'both Goats in one'. See Hebrews 9:28.

For sin, in mine Humanity;
Which though it knew no sin, for sin's accurst.
Then they confess over my guiltless head
Their sins not mine:
Yet I
Did cry,
Something divine
You'l find hath *scap'd* your hands when I am dead.

In my two natures I'm both Goats in one;[144]
Can dye, yet scape;
Can scape, yet *dye*:
I can discharge first *Adams* rape,
Then second *Adams* bands unty.
Sinner, I must do both, or thou'rt undone.
False witness they suborne 'mongst faithless Jewes.
Such is their grudge
Their Lord
They 'ccord
To death t'adjudge
Though witnesses agree not, that accuse.

Art thou the Christ? they captiously enquire.[145]
Not for to know
As sometime did
Johns dear Disciples,[146] but to throw
Mine own confessions at mine head.
They watch my words with an enflam'd desire:
This *Mary* sometimes did,[147] but not as they;
Not life but death
They watch
And catch
From my dear breath,
Both to themselves and me this bloody day.

144 See note to line 962.

145 i.e. they enquire in a way designed to catch Jesus out.

146 A reference to John the Baptist's proclamation of Jesus as the Messiah. See Luke 3:15–17.

147 A reference to Mary, the sister of Lazarus. See John 11:28–32.

Peter steales to their fire, to melt, not fight:
Mine[148] seldome warme
Themselves with such
But quickly rue their dear bought harme,
Saying the warmth's not half so much.
Sirs, is't so this morn? 'twas hot ith' night;
I felt it so. Nor find I ought yet cool,
Except it be
The love
Ev'n of
My friends to me,
Whilst enemies my wisdome fain would fool.

The High Priest rends his cloaths, but not his heart:
Then all condemn me
The Hall throughout,
Who must judge all; Abjects contemn me:
Whom Angels do admire, they flout.
They are the *Ishma'ls*, I bear *Isaack's* part.[149]
Then they blindfold mine eyes, to whom the night
Shines as the day:
I can't,
Sure, want,
Who gave away
So many eyes to others wanting sight.

Oh! how these Bats project to blind the Sun!
Moles plot and think
(How wise they are?)
With a poor clout[150] thus to hood-wink
Jacobs true bright and morning star.[151]
Indeed if't could, you've need it should be done.
How they to make me like themselves devise?

148 i.e. followers of Jesus.
149 Ishmael and Isaac were sons of Abraham. God put Abraham's faith to the test by ordering that he sacrifice Isaac, the favoured son, but spared him once Abraham had proved his obedience. See Genesis 17:15–21. In the epistle of Barnabas, written at the end of the first century, the sacrifice of Isaac is identified as a type of the death and resurrection of Christ.
150 clout = a piece of cloth.
151 The Messiah was said to be of the tribe of the sons of Jacob.

I, and they, wink:
They see
Not mee;
And so they think
I can't see them, although I made their eyes.

Others, for spight, spit on my blessed face,
Which *Moses*, and
Elias too,
Did once ith' mount admiring stand
Transfigur'd then, disfigur'd now.[152]
How men bespatter Gods own looking-glass.
These potsheards then their potter smite with rods.[153]
My white and ruddy[154]
These foes
With blows
Make black and bloody:
I'm box'd by slaves, who rule among the Gods.

Then prophesie who smote thee, some do cry.
Alas! who not?
Yet I'll impart;
Me, for my *seed*, my Father smote;
But never did mine own clean heart.
Scorners, go read *Isaiahs* Prophesie.[155]
He did esteem me stricken of my God;
That stripes on me,
My smart
Of heart,
Mans cure might be:
Man did the fault, and I must feel the rod.

152 A reference to the appearance of Moses and Elijah at the transfiguration of Jesus. See Mark 9:4.

153 God is described as a 'potter' in Romans 9:20–4. A 'potsherd' is a broken piece of ceramic. The poet is suggesting that mankind, represented by the high priests and elders, is turning on Christ its creator.

154 See Song of Solomon 5:10.

155 Jesus recounts Isaiah's prophecy (Isaiah 42:1–4) in Matthew 12:17–21 in order to emphasise the meekness of the Messiah. 'He will not contend or cry out, nor anyone will hear his voice in the streets. A bruised reed he will not break, a smouldering wick he will not quench, until he brings justice to victory.'

Peter, I doubt[156] thy courage will soon coole[157]
At that same fire;
Th' Ague'll[158] come on:
Satan to sift thee did desire.[159]
Now *Peter* prove the rock and stone.[160]
My dear Disciple, don't deny my schoole.
Oh! at first charge, I see my Champion's laid![161]
The shield, the shield
Of faith
He hath
Near lost this shield.
Who play'd the man 'mongst men, fals by a maid.[162]

Whom flesh and blood reveal'd not, flesh and blood
Can teach deny,
Ev'n his dear Lord;
Constant to 's own unconstancy.
Ev'n as if this had been his word,
I will deny, not dye, to this he stood.
Oh! my poor fisher's caught the second time.
I said, abide
In me,
Or ye
Will quickly slide:
But now it seems to be of *me's* a crime.[163]

Then others cry, this man's of *Nazareth*.
He by and by
With cursing doth
Me, that have born this curse, deny;
And swears he knows not when he know'th.
Peter, they say they smell thee by thy breath
To be of me, Oh! that I could so say!
Sirs, don't you hear?

156 i.e. I have no doubt …

157 There follows an account of Peter's denial of Jesus. See Mark 15:66–72.

158 Ague = fever.

159 Satan wishes to 'sift' or separate Peter from Christ: 'Satan hath desired to have you, that he may sift you as wheat.' Luke 22:31.

160 The name Peter means 'stone'. See John 1:42.

161 i.e. laid low.

162 Peter was questioned about his association with Jesus by a maid. See Mark 14:66–70.

163 i.e. to be one of my associates.

The man
Can ban,[164]
Can curse and swear.
That he's of me, Sirs, doth such speech bewray?

Surely you know my speech no more than me.
Peter denies
His Christ —— so crew
The Bird that wakes the sleepers eyes:
I lookt on *Peter*,[165] then he knew
The Cock his Masters Monitour to be.
Peter thus finding all crow over him[166]
Runs forth to weep;
His soul
Now foule
To wrinse and steep;
Ev'n in a spring tide of salt teares to swim.

I have deni'd my Lord, my Lord that's dying:
I have deni'd
My Lord, my Lord
Whom I confest, profest; bee'ng tried
I have renounc'd his and my word;
My Lord that bought me I have been denying.
Now his hot fit's come on. My Christ, when ever,
Through thou know'st what,
Thee I
Deny
In word or thought;
Oh! give me *Peters* sweat, in *Peters* feaver.

By this time is my[167] doom daies dawning come.
Their righthfull King
Jewes having bound
Before an alien Judge do bring.

164 ban = curse.

165 i.e. Christ does. 'And the Lord turned and looked upon Peter, And Peter remembered the word of the Lord, how he had said unto him, Before the cock crow, thou shalt deny me thrice.' Luke 2261.

166 crow = to gloat. The crowd 'crow over' Peter's falsehoods. With a pun on cock crow.

167 i.e. Christ's.

That guilt ith' guiltless might be found,
Butchers object, but I the Lamb, lye dumb.
Herod, and *Pontious Pilate*,[168] Gentiles, Jewes
Counsell and plot:
I am
The Lambe
Must go to pot:
Satan is at mine heel, which he will bruise.[169]

Who art? and, what is truth? *Pilate* enquires.[170]
Bee'ng strange to both,
I find it so:[171]
Yet to my bloodshed lag and loath,
Whilest my own people raging go
To burn King *Davids* branch with Gentile fires.
Take him your selves, saith *Pilate*; Jewish men,
Ease your own grudge.
Say they
We may
No man adjudge
To death. Our *Scepter's* [172]gone. Where's *Shiloh* then?[173]

See you your wants? not what ye have, O yee?
Why, *Shiloh's* come:
My white and ruddy,[174]
This wine and milk, though I be dumb
Speaks it; thy innocence thus bloody.
This is your *Shiloh's* garment: can't you see?
'Tis not so long, O thou my city! since
Hosannahs, cried[175]

168 Jesus was first brought before Pontius Pilate, procurator of Judea, and then to Herod, ruler of the province of Galilee, for questioning. See Luke 23:1–11.

169 See Genesis 3:15.

170 See John 18:37–8.

171 i.e. Christ finds Pilate a stranger to truth.

172 The sceptre is a symbol of authority – the Jews no longer have the power to judge Jesus.

173 Shiloh is a name used to describe the Messiah in the Hebrew text of Genesis: 'The sceptre shall not depart from Judah … until Shiloh come.' Genesis 49:10. The tribe of Judah will eventually find its fulfilment in Jesus Christ.

174 'My beloved is white and ruddy, the chiefest among ten thousand.' Song of Solomon 5:10.

175 A reference to Jesus' entry into Jerusalem on an ass when he was greeted with cries of 'Hosanna' meaning 'grant salvation lord'. See Matthew 21:9.

In thee
To mee,
Me testified;
Thy people gath'ring round about their Prince.

'Tis not so long since I bind my fole,
Mine Asses Colt,
Unto my vine,[176]
To thee. *Jerus'lem*, now revolt;[177]
That I might wash my weeds[178] in wine,
Whilst to the death I'm pouring out my soul.
Judas meanwhile, consid'ring all that's done
Through his foul sinne,
Relents,
Repents
And brings agen
That dunghill-dirt for which he sold the Sun.[179]

For's thirty pieces,[180] thirty thousand woes
Oppress his heart.
Then to his Priest,
I've sinned, and th' innocent must smart.
The wretch bee'ng shriven, so confest.
See thou to that, say th' Priests, see thou to those.
Oh! to what lead doth *ill-got* silver turn?
Judas can't bear
The weight
Of it;
Yet 'twas his dear:
Oh! take't agen. My fingers burn, they burn.

176 'Binding his foal unto the vine, and his ass's colt unto the choice vine; he washed his garments in wine, and his clothes in the blood of grapes.' Genesis 49:11. This is Jacob's prophetic declaration of the supremacy of the tribe of Judah tribe which will culminate in David, and eventually, the Messiah, i.e. Jesus Christ.

177 to revolt = to cast off an allegiance / to fall away from a ruler (*OED* v 1 b). Jesus is contrasting his joyous welcome into Jerusalem when he was hailed as the Messiah with the vicious treatment he is now receiving.

178 weeds = mourning clothes. Christ's robes will be 'washed' with wine, i.e. his own sacrificial blood.

179 dunghill dirt = money. Sun = Son of God.

180 Judas betrayed Jesus for thirty pieces of silver. See Matthew 26:15. The following passage is an account of Judas' repentance and suicide. See Matthew 27:3–6.

Into the treas'ry this they dare not cast:
Oh! 'tis not good,
Poor men they dare not;
Oh! 'tis the price, the price of blood!
And yet to spill that blood they spare not:
Thus *Gnats* do stick, whilst *Camels* go down fast.[181]
They take the money first, and then dispute
Whet'r 't should be so.
Meanwhile
The vile
Traitour doth go,
Bee'ng *self-condemn'd* himself to execute.

A bloody peice of Charitie's the end.
The Potters field,[182]
That strangers might
Be buri'd there, to buy they yield,
Not burying there their own strange spite.
Thus kind to strangers, whilst they kill their friend.
Meanwhile me at a *goodly price* men hold;
Hereto it's come,
One field
Can yield
As great a summe,
As doth the Maker of the world when sold.

Now th'Judge of all stands bound at Pilats bar.
Great God is tried
For's life, by man:
Yet by this stranger justified,
Say mine own people what they can.
Hurried to *Herod* next, and's men of war.
Herod forsooth would see a miracle[183]

181 'Ye blind guides, which strain at a gnat, and swallow a camel.' Matthew 23:24. A reference to the hypocrisy of the Pharisees who follow the outward rituals of faith at the expense of inner goodness.

182 The chief priests, to whom Judas returned the silver, used it to buy 'the potter's field as a burial place for foreigners'. See Matthew 27:7.

183 Christ is sent by Pilate to Herod who 'hoped to have seen some miracle done by him' to prove his divinity. When Christ refuses he is sent back to Pilate in 'a gorgeous robe'. Luke 23:8–11.

And doth, whilst I
Sustain
Disdain
So patiently,
Who could scoule[184] these proud scorners quick to Hell.

In white and splendid rayment then, from thence
I'm re-convey'd
To my first judge
('Twixt whom and *Herod* peace is made,
They in my blood can sink their grudge)
Wearing the type[185] of my cleare innocence.
Saith *Pilate*, see, nor I nor *Herod* can
His crime discry,
Why he
Should be
Condemn'd to dye;
Will you, this feast, that I release this man?[186]

Take him, and scourge him, scourge him as you list,[187]
Oh! What I feel!
My God, what lashes!
Think you my back is stone or steel
Like your hard hearts? O gage[188] these gashes?
And spare your rod, or tell me wherefore is't.
Yet doth mine hand still sway that iron-rod,
Wherewith I can
All those
My foes,
Ev'n as one man,
In pieces break; and make them know I'm God.

Who would have thought all government were laid
Upon these shoulders

184 scoule = scold.

185 type = symbol. Christ is wearing a white robe, a symbol of his innocence.

186 It was tradition for the people to select one prisoner to be released at the feast of Passover. See Matthew 27:15.

187 Pilate orders Jesus to be scourged or whipped. See Luke 23:16. It seems that Pilate speaks this line in the first person. The voice of Pilate is then succeeded by the first person voice of Jesus for whose lament there is no scriptural authority. list = wish.

188 i.e. gauge = to take the measure of.

Thus rent and torn
By cruell stripes? yet they're th' upholders
Whereon both globes oth' world are born;[189]
A load that's light to the stripes of them that strai'd.
I am the fruitfull field now plow'd in furrows,
That ev'ry sinne
Might have
It's grave
To wither in.
I am the rock, these holes are sinners burrows.

Princes, whilest under *Paedagogues* they bee,
Can stand and see,
When they've transgrest,
Subjects whipt for't;[190] why, *Pilate* mee
Thou'st innocent and king confest,
Yet for my peoples faults I'm scourged by thee.
Pilate, thou thinkst these bloody stripes may cease
Their bloody cry,
But blood
So good,
They'll drink them dry,[191]
And their Hydropick[192] thirst will more increase.

Alas! thou think'st to seale me a release
From blood in gore,[193]
But 'twill not bee
Till I have emptied all my store.
Then, sinner, there's release for thee.

189 This refers to the terrestrial globe, the geographical configuration of the earth and the celestial globe, the arrangements of the constellations.

190 This refers to the practice of whipping a servant in the place of a young prince who has been disobedient. Christ comments that in his case the situation is reversed.

191 Christ is suggesting that his accusers will drink the blood from the 'stripes' on his back. Teate uses similar rhetoric in his description of the murder of Protestants by Catholics in Ireland during the 1641 rising: 'Yea thus hungry were these *Rebells of Ireland* grown … that they glutted themselves with so many score thousands of poor Protestants, by them and others, butchered in *bleeding Ireland*; unto which bread God will give the surviving murtherers blood to drink.' *The character of cruelty in the workers of iniquity* (London, 1656), p. 54.

192 hydropick = insatiable.

193 Pilate naively thinks that Christ's 'gore' (i.e. the wounds inflicted from the scourging) will be sufficient punishment, and will prevent his 'blood' (i.e. death).

So dearly must I buy my subjects peace.
Pilates own wife becomes mine advocate:[194]
Her sufferings in
Her dream,
To them
Shee doth begin,
So to prevent my Passion, to relate.

But who can harden his soft cowardise
To take my part,
And shield my right?
Or mollifie their hardened heart
To quit their spleen, or scirrhous spite?
Pilate, have nought to do with Christ, shee cries:
Woman, thy husband's like to've nothing sure
With me to do:
Whilst he
For me
No heart can show;
But to condemn, whom he acquits, endure.[195]

Pilates own Lady plaies the nursing mother;
Whilest Jews reject,
Builders refuse
Fair *Sions* precious stone elect
Which for the corner God will use.[196]
'Ware *Pilate* lest this croud thy conscience smother.[197]
Pilate and I have two hard parts to play;
Pilate, to please
All those
My foes,
Yet me release:
I, to make Heav'n and earth good friends this day.

Time after time he questions and approves
Mine innocence;[198]

194 According to Matthew 27:19, Pilate's wife warned him to have nothing to do with Jesus after having a prophetic dream.
195 Pilate can only endure in condemning Christ, even though he would rather acquit him.
196 See Isaiah 28:16.
197 Christ is addressing Pilate although there is no precedent for his words in the Gospels.
198 Pilate questions Jesus about his claim to be the son of God. See Mark 15:1–5.

And tells the Jewes
That clearly that's all mine offence:
And doth the oyl of courtship use,
Which either more enflames, or nothing moves.
Pilate hangs first 'twixt two bee'ng crucified,
Conscience and fear:
The Rout
Without
For blood appear:
By *Pilates* Privy Counsell 'tis denied.

Will you, saith *Pilate*, I release your King,
Or *Barabbas*[199]
The Murderer?
The Man of Men the Monster was[200]
Yet *Barrabas* they all preferre;
Bloud upon bloud thus on themselves they bring.
Now, O ye Heavens, stand astonished!
And thou, bright Sun,
Be gon:
Get on
Thy mourning gown!
That when I *bow* mine, thou may'st *hide* thine head.

Let *Gad'rens*[201] now for kind commended be;
Yet they preferd
Their herd of swine,
But no *Barabbas* in that Herd.
But, Oh! the hoggishness of mine,
Ev'n of mine only people[202] unto me!
Why ev'n these Butchers trade's a mystery.
There is a skill

199 The crowd have the choice to free either Jesus or Barabbas who has been convicted of murder. According to Mark 15:11, the chief priests 'stir up the crowd' to shout for Barabbas.
200 i.e. Barabbas was the worst monster in mankind.
201 Gadr'ns = people from the Gentile town of Gadara where according to Matthew 8:28–34, Jesus drove demons out of two men into a herd of swine. The pigs subsequently threw themselves from a cliff. This stanza seems to be suggesting that even the possessed Gentiles did not behave as wickedly as Barabbas or those who are plotting Jesus' death.
202 i.e. the Jews, God's chosen people.

That they
This day
Have learnt to fill
Their hands with blood: and that before I dye.

The murder and the murd'rer all's their own
Whilst they thus chuse:
And oh! what wonder?
What fitter head, for bloody Jewes,
Than this *Barabbas* to list under;
Whilst from their head they cast off me their crown?
My Christ, there's yet a sweeter mystery:[203]
Innocent breath
I see
In thee
Condemn'd to death;
That th' chief of sinners might escape thereby.

What shall I do then with your King, saith he.[204]
Him Crucifie,
Cries all the rout,
Oh let him, let him, let him dye!
As if they could not live without
His blood, no more can I Lord, give it me.
Why, but saith *Pilate*, tell me what's his crime,
Or take him you.
Away,
Say they,
Let him dye now,
To find his fault would ask too long a time.

Whilst all can tell me how, none can tell why
I should be kill'd.[205]
Sirs, is't because
I gave you good and righteous Laws
Which you have broke, and I fulfill'd?

203 The poem moves from the voice of Christ back into the interpretive voice of the poet.

204 According to the Gospels, Pilate is reluctant to find Jesus guilty but is overruled by the vehemence of the crowd who demand that he be crucified. See Luke 23:20–24.

205 Again the poem moves into the first person voice of Christ. There is no authority in the Gospels for the speech that follows.

Must I because I let you live, now dye?
Or is it for some injuries of old!
In *Egypt*, and
In the
Red Sea,
And desert Land,
Whereof your Fathers Fathers have you told![206]

Or is't because I said I came from God
To bring a new
And great Salvation,
Greater then th' first, to thee, O Jew!
Proving my mission to my Nation,
By an all-conquering wonder-working Rod?
Is it because your dumbe can speak, that I'm
Cry'd out against?
'Gainst me
Are ye,
O Jews! incenst
Because of all my curses? are they my crime?

Is it because your dead are rais'd, that I
Am grudg'd my breath?
Grudg'd what I give?
Am I therefore condemn'd to death?
Doth't therefore greive you that I live?
Why, I shall quicken the more, when ere I dye.
Then *Pilate* puts me in the souldiers hands:
They plat a Crown:
Alas!
It was
A thorny one[207]
Which he must weare, who Heav'n and Earth commands.

Why, I am *Isra'ls* King; and him I found
Ith' Wilderness,[208]
That howling waste

206 i.e. your ancestors.

207 Jesus is made to wear a crown of thorns and a purple robe by the Roman soldiers. See Mark 15:17.

208 Jesus became aware of his Messianic mission in the wilderness. See Mark 1:1–15.

Whose Musick these outcries express;
Whose only fruits are thorns, I tast:
Cloath'd with their sins I'm with their thorns too crown'd,
Thus I with sinners change,[209] 'tis well for them.
Their thorney Crown
So worn,
And born,
I make mine own,
Yielding for it an heavenly diadem.

Isra'l, that so long brought me no sweet Cane,[210]
Now puts me off
With a poor weed;
For sacrifice, they bring a scoff:[211]
And for my scepter, bring a reed;
Yet by me Princes rule and Kings do reign.
Then in a Purple Robe they me invest:
But that same colour
I wore
Before,
Through stripes and dolour,[212]
Both on my scourged back and tortur'd breast.

Then gath'ring round, ev'n as they list, they flout me.
Haile King! they cry;[213]
And bow the knee,
But not their hearts: (Why, truly I
Ever had some that so serve mee)
Breathing disdain yet can't they breath without me.
They rend my flesh, the temples of mine Head
They smite with reeds:
But I
Surely
Shall quit their deeds,
By rending vaile and Temple when I'm dead.[214]

209 i.e. Jesus will be punished for the sins of man.

210 'Thou hast bought me no sweet cane with money, neither hast thou filled me with the fat of thy sacrifices.' Isaiah 44:24.

211 i.e. rather than honour me by performing sacrifices, they scoff and laugh at me.

212 i.e. Jesus is already wearing purple in the form of his bloody, 'scourged' back.

213 Jesus is mocked with cries of 'Haile King of the Jews!'. Matthew 27:29.

214 According to Matthew 27:51, the veil which covered the entrance to the tabernacle in

In strange disguise (for so are Princes wont
When as they pass
Through strangers lands,
And such *Judea* is, alas!
To me, whilst I am in such hands:)
Brought forth I am that Priests might me confront
A ruthfull spectacle! a man of grief!
Laden with woes!
With thorns;
With scorns
Of bitter foes!
Will not the Priest and Levite[215] yield relief?

Whither, oh! whither, would I, could I flie?
Shall I repair
To th' Altars side?[216]
Spight is there hottest. There they are
That first cri'd, be he Crucified.
Away, say they, O let him, let him die.
We have a Law, the Sonne of Death he is,
Gods Sonne to be,
That makes
Or takes,
Himself, here's he.
Sirs do not quote the *Second Psalm* for this.[217]

Pilate, an Heathen, dreads my reverend name,
Which Jewes despise:
Enquires the more

the Temple was torn in two at the moment of Jesus' death. One interpretation of this event is that because of Jesus' sacrifice, all men now have access to the presence of God.

215 Levites were an order of priests responsible for teaching Hebrew law. This line may be alluding to the parable of the Good Samaritan in which a man who had been robbed and beaten, was ignored by both a priest and a Levite. See Luke 10:31–2.

216 In the Gospels Jesus is challenged to release himself from the cross to prove that he is the Messiah. See Matthew 27:40–2. Here the voice of Christ seems to be answering that even if he were to do so, he could not escape to the Temple, as this is where his accusers, i.e. the Pharisees and chief priests, reside.

217 Psalm 2 suggests that God will smite those who abuse his son: 'Kiss the Son, lest he be angry, and ye perish from the way, when his wrath be kindled but a little. Blessed are all they that put their trust in him.' Psalm 2:12. Christ is attacking his accusers, who are not heeding this command.

Whence I am? whence my kingdome is?
Not of this world, I h'd said before;[218]
So, he my dumbness, I his deafness blame.
Of what he asks I did the truth impart,
And told him so:
But hee,
'Gan flee
The truth, as though
It were some Ghost or Mormo.[219] *Truth! what art?*

With's pow'r of life and death he then doth brave me,
Who hold the keyes
Of *David* still,[220]
To shut and open as I please,
To bind and loose all as I will,
For such Command'ment God my Father gave me:
Yet *Pilates* Conscience in his face still flies:
Now he projects
How mee
To free;
But all th' effects
T' enflame their fury, double their out-cries.

Yet in their anger so much wit they have
As to compound
Something to calme
Poor *Pilates* Conscience, why, they've found
Some *Simples* soveraign[221] as balme;
Oh! 'twas good satisfaction that they gave.
Thou art not Cesars friend if this man go.
Now take your Christ,
Fullfill
Your will,
Do what you list
With him, Jewes, so I sentence, and so do.

218 The voice of Jesus is referring back to his questioning by Pilate. See John 18:36.

219 Mormo = an imaginary monster.

220 i.e. the keys to the kingdom of Heaven. Jesus has the power to 'shut and open' the doors to whomsoever he pleases.

221 simple = a plant used medicinally; soveraign = sovereign: excellent as a remedy. The Pharisees try to salve Pilate's conscience – see line 1483.

Thus he and I swim down one stream this day.
Yet the poor man
Found want of water,
Call'd for a Basin, and began
To wash him from this bloody matter:[222]
Which nothing can, but what he gave away.
Truly his washing clears not him, but me:
He doth proclaim,
That I
Now die
A spotless Lamb:
Then, wretch, what Ocean can compurgate[223] thee?

Pilate, upon us and our children fling
Thou this mans blood:
We Jewes, thus wish.[224]
Is this your so much long'd for food,
To you of all th' forbidden dish?
Pilate then cries, ye Jewes behold your King.
We have no King but *Cesar*, they reply.
Sirs, you forget
Whose hour
Of power
This is as yet.
Satan's your *Cesar,* more than he or I.

Satan, not *Cesar*, bad you plot my fall:
That Prince of Hell,
Philistia's King[225]
Plows with mine heifer, *Israel*:

222 Pilate washes his hands in front of the crowd to deny responsibility for Christ's execution. See Matthew 27:24.

223 compurgate = to vindicate.

224 'Then answered all the people and said, His blood be on us, and on our children.' Matthew 27:25. Here the poet has the voice of Jesus paraphrasing scripture to suggest that the Jews' desire for Pilate to sentence Jesus to death has cursed them. This anti-Semitic belief that the Jews were responsible for Christ's death was common among the clergy of Teate's time.

225 Philistia's King = the King of the Philistines. The Philistines were the enemies of the Israelites in the Old Testament and here the poet is declaring that the Jews, formerly God's people, have now become the instrument, the 'heifer', of their old enemy by rejecting Christ.

Thus to mine end, mine own me bring.
Yet *Sampsons* death's *Philistia's* Funerall.[226]
The Purple Robe then strip they from my back;
Which plainly shews
It's worn
And born
For sinners use,
That of my Righteousness they might partake.

Thus is the truth stript naked: And agen
My seamless coat
They make me weare
Unto mine execution plot,
That by my sweet attonement there
I might an Union weave 'twixt God and Men.
Thence to the place of Sculs,[227] Lo! I their Head
The tree accurst,
Before
It bore
Me, bear it first;
Till I, by bearing it, am almost dead.

Thus mine may learn in me, what burthen he
Must daily beare,
Taking his cross,
That in my waies will persevere,
Reck'ning death gain, counting life loss:
Who stumbles at my cross, can't follow me.
Now are my groanes new pickled in friends tears,
They'd steale, I spie,
This tree
From mee,
By Sympathy;
Which by constraint *Simon* of *Cyrene* bears,[228]

226 Samson, an Israelite judge of legendary strength, was captured by the Philistines but killed himself and them by pulling down the pillars to which he had been tied. See Judges 16:4–31. Again, the poet is equating the Jews who condemned Jesus to the Philistines who were brought down by Samson's sacrifice.

227 Jesus was crucified at Golgotha or 'the Place of the Skull'. See Matthew 27:33.

228 Simon of Cyrene helped Jesus carry his cross. See Matthew 27:32.

But weep not, Daughters of Jerusalem![229]
For me at all
But for your City:
Alas! who can prevent thy fall,
Who shew'st thy builder no more pity?
If they do thus to th' green tree, wo to them![230]
Thus under *Pilates* sentence, and command
Oth' *Roman* State,
That all
May fall
On *Romes* proud Pate;
Ith' place of Crucifixion, lo! I stand.

Rome! thou'rt that *Sodom, Egypt, Babylon*,[231]
Though Misticall;[232]
Drunken with blood
Of all my Martyrs, mine withall
Now mingling with thy *Tybers*[233] flood.
Rome's stored with crosses and now lends me one!
Not *Jabbathah*[234] but *Golgotha's* the stage
The Camp without;[235]
Where I
Must dye
'Mongst all the rout,
Tasting at once both *Hells* and *Heavens* Rage.

Why I am the great Sacrifice for sin,
And therefore must
Without the gate
Unto the Earth commend my dust,

229 'And there followed him a great company of women, which also bewailed and lamented him. But Jesus turning unto them said, Daughters of Jerusalem, weep not for me, but weep for yourselves, and for your children …' Luke 23:27–8.
230 'For if they do these things in a green tree, what shall be done in the dry?' Luke 23:31.
231 Old Testament enemies of God and his people, the Israelites.
232 i.e. mystical = hidden or symbolic. Teate is denouncing both the ancient Rome of Christ's time and, more pertinently, contemporary Roman Catholicism as hidden enemies of God.
233 The river Tiber runs through Rome.
234 Jabbathah = Gabbatha: a name given by John to the place in Jerusalem where Pilate had his judicial seat and where he sentenced Christ to be crucified. John 19:13.
235 i.e. outside.

Whilst my deare blood doth expiate
From all transgressions that those are within.
Behold, my dear Disciple, my dear Mother![236]
Her I bequeath
To thee,
To bee
After my death
Provided for as by her Son, my Brother.

Now see your Brazen Serpent lift on high,[237]
Upon the pole!
My bloody cross
Bears fruit to quit what *Adam* stole:[238]
Justice, I find, may n't go by th' loss,
Yet grace shall reign by righteousness, hereby.
Oh! how I'm stretcht and tortur'd on this tree!
Oh! how each vein,
And nerve
Doth serve
A sev'rall pain!
'Twas man grew loose, and I must straitned[239] bee.

Oh! how those hands, I stretcht forth all the day,
To *Israel*,
Are stretcht again?
That as my Patience did excell,
So now I might exceed in pain;
Whilst sinners to mine heart find open way.
Oh! how my feet, that nere took step awry,
Are pierced through!
Made fast
In hast
My cross unto;
Till the transgressours may find time to flie.

236 'Then saith he to the disciple, Behold, your mother! And from that hour that disciple took her unto his own home.' John 19:25–27.

237 See note to line 136. The poet is drawing an analogy between the healing powers of the brazen serpent and the crucified Christ.

238 quit = compensate. Christ's sacrifice will redeem Adam's sin.

239 straiten = to bind stringently (*OED* 5 d) but also to reduce to distress and misery (*OED* 7).

I am the *doore*, they naile me to the tree:[240]
And, as is fit,
Over this gate
A royall *superscription's* writ[241]
That in *all tongues*[242] might preach my state.
Oh! all ye that pass by, turn in by mee.
To th' cross I'm hing'd in mine humanity.
That from the floor
Ev'n each
Might reach
That living door
Whose upper hinge clasps in with th' Deity.

Romans, and *Greeks,* and *Hebrews* come and look;
These open arms
Shew th' open way,
How by mine, you may ease your harms;
And may become one fold this day:
I am the shepheard, and my cross the crook.[243]
I am the shepheard, and my crook, the cross;
Whereby I gather
And keep
My sheep,
And thine, O Father!
I'll suffer death, ere thou shalt suffer loss.

Living, my bread of life among my Jewes
I ever brake,[244]
For 'twas their right;
Who whilst they spread these arms, do make
A feast for Gentiles through their spight;
That, dying, I might none, that come, refuse.
Come unto me all ye that laden be[245]
With sin and wrath;

240 See John 10:9.
241 'And Pilate wrote a title, and put it on the cross. And the writing was, JESUS OF NAZARETH THE KING OF THE JEWS.' John 19:19.
242 The inscription was written in Hebrew, Greek and Latin. See John 19:20.
243 'I am the good shepherd: the good shepherd giveth his life for the sheep.' John 10:11.
244 See Mark 8:19.
245 See Matthew 11:28.

Come ye
To me;
O come in faith.
I'll bear your burdens whilst my Cross bears me.

Mine hands are not so nail'd, but that I can
Ev'n with these nailes
Still pick the lock
Hung on your heel, if your key failes:[246]
But whilst I preach, alas! they mock.
If thou be *th' Christ*, be thine own *Jesus,* man.[247]
Why Jewes remember what your high Priest taught,
How needfull 'twas
That I
Should dye,
That th' cup might pass
My people, whilst I drink their bloody draught.

But, Oh *Jerusalem*! canst laugh at mee?
And at my griefs?
As thou didst know
My pressures to be thy reliefs;
Repent, believe; and be it so.
But laugh not at me who h've wept over thee,
And yet weep blood, for this thy stupid[248] state.
Father, I pray
Reprieve,
Forgive
These foes, for they
Alas! my God, they do they know not what.[249]

They curse, I bless: I pray whilst they revile,
Whilst Priests do scoff
And sore disdain
The Sacrifice that comes not off

246 Cf. Herbert, 'Church-Lock and Key', lines 1–4.

247 i.e. if you are Christ you should have the power to save yourself. See Matthew 27:41–42.

248 i.e. ignorant, unknowing.

249 'Then said Jesus, Father, forgive them; for they know not what they do.' Luke 23:34.

Th' Altar, but suffers to be slain,
My blood makes intercession all the while.
Who'd rase then raise, the Temple[250] (this is he)
In three daies space;
Yet hee,
We see,
Can't quit this place
Where all the nailes that hold him, are but three.

Yet mock not, passenger;[251] wag not thine head
In so much scorne,
When thou thinkst least,
When I this bitter death have borne,
To earnest I'll soon turn thy jest;
And raise this Temple ere't be three daies dead,
Come down say some, and so convince thy foes:
Which if I shou'd
How sore
A store
Of wrath, and blood,
Would come down too? Sirs, I bear off your blowes.

With the transgressours numbered am I:
On either side,
Truth bee'ng between,
Falshood and theft hang crucified;[252]
Yet if Heav'ns Rolls these men had seen
They'd found me in another Trinity.
But, oh my grief! not only mine own Nation
But those, that be
Justly
To dye,
First scoff at me;
Their partner not in crimes, but condemnation.

Yet can I not forget my dear Compassions:
Though both reproach

250 i.e. who would destroy and then build up the temple in three days. See Matthew 27:40.

251 passenger = passer-by.

252 Christ was crucified between two criminals, one of whom desired forgiveness and asked Jesus to 'remember him'. See Luke 23:39–43.

And flout at me,
My blood for sinners since I broach,
I will not suffer both to be
At once partakers of two condemnations
Th' one I call home though in th' eleventh hour:
And thereby shew
How kind
A mind
I bear to you[253]
That turn, though late, to me your Saviour.

But oh his rare Conversion! oh how he
Justifies God!
Rebukes his mate!
Open his sin! kisseth his rod!
Takes me for Lord, beseeching that
In my Salvation he might sharer be.
Thus on my Cross I work a new Creation:
Loosing the bands
Of sin
Within
From th' sinners hands.
My bitter sacrifice brings sweet salvation.

Thus I give life to others, yet I dye;
I heal their wounds,
And break their bands;
Yet anguish mine own soul confounds
More than these nails do pierce mine hands
My God! why dost thou me forsake?[254] Oh! why?
They rend my garments, cast lots for my coate,[255]
Whilst I hang here;
Shame doth
Me cloath,
Else nak'd I were,
Yonder's thy *Josephs* coat,[256] Lord! dost not know't?

253 i.e. anyone.
254 See Matthew 27:46.
255 The soldiers present at the crucifixion were said to cast lots for Jesus' clothes. See Luke 23:34.
256 A reference to Joseph's multi-coloured coat. See Genesis 37.

The seamless vesture of thy sinless child,
How bloody is't?
My God! my God!
Yet not so bloody as thy Christ
Is all within by thy sharp rod.
O be not fierce to me, for I am mild.
See, how I'm nail'd to this most bitter tree!
How I'm accurst!
How gall[257]
Is all
My drink in thirst!
And wilt thou so, my God, my God! leave mee?

See, how men turn my Glory into shame.
Mocking my faith
And confidence;
Some say he for *Elias* pray'th:[258]
But, Lord, thou know'st my mind and sense.
They flout, they fleere,[259] whilst I call on thy name.
Yet save me, for I'm thine: thine handmaids son
Made of this woman:
Thy shade
This maid,
When known by no man,
Impow'rd to bring forth me, thine holy one.

Father! I'm the only Fatherless on earth:
All others have
Fathers, or had:
O pity, pity, Lord! and save
Thy Fatherless, support the sad.
Oh! leave me not in death, who gav'st me birth.
My God! my God! why dost thou me forsake?
Who never thee

257 Gall is a secretion of the liver, proverbial for its intense bitterness and thus used metaphorically to refer to anything distressing or unpleasant. However, it also refers to an excrescence produced on trees, and its use here suggests Christ drinking 'gall' from the tree on which he is being crucified.

258 According to Mark 15:35–7, onlookers at the crucifixion are said to hear Jesus calling out for Elijah when he was actually calling for his father.

259 fleere = to laugh mockingly (*OED* n2 1).

Forsook,
Or took
One sin to mee,
Except the sins that thou didst bid me take.

They fill the spunge with vinegar,[260] but thou
My soul dost fill
With sharper grief.
Oh! sinner, here's a bitter pill,
Yet for thy sickness sweet relief.
My God! my God! O do not leave me now!
How darkness vailes the land! yet clouds do hover
Darker by far:
Thy wrath,
Lord, hath
Eclyps'd thy star,[261]
Whilst from thy darling thou thy face dost cover.

How both Suns suffer while thy *Son* lies under
Thy fierce displeasure!
Th' Sun bears a part
But mine eclypse it cannot measure.
Lord thy sore frowns do teare my heart
More than the Temples vaile, that's rent asunder.
Now come thy breaches[262] and thy darkness on,
O Jewish Land!
For thou
Hast now
Both rid thine hand
Of thy bright light, and of thy Corner-stone.

Father, the earth's all ague,[263] and I more:
Ev'n rocks are rent,
My soul's more torne:

260 The soldiers offered Jesus a sponge dipped in vinegar or 'wine'. See John 19:29.

261 Jesus' crucifixion was said to be accompanied by a solar eclipse. See Luke 24:44–5.

262 breach = a rupture or breaking. The word is used literally and figuratively in the Old Testament to signal God's displeasure e.g. 'He breaketh me with breach upon breach …' Job. 16:14. God's anger with Christ's crucifiers is manifested in the solar eclipse, symbolising spiritual darkness.

263 ague = fever.

Yet flinty[264] Jews do n't once relent.
My God: leave not mine hope forlorne.
I hav' done.[265] Lord, open th' everlasting Doore.
Father, into thine hands I give my Spirit,
And utmost breath;
Whilst I
Thus dye;
And, with me, death:
That my dear seed henceforth may life inherit.

Then Christ, in sweet submission, *bowes his head*
To all Gods pleasure:
I think on't still:[266]
Lord make the bowing heart my treasure
An heart to bow to all thy will;
That dying I may say, *all's finished.*
This done, my Saviour quickly shews his force:
Graves open flie;
They shake
And quake
That see him die:
The rude Centurion's struck with strange remorse.[267]

Thus Christ lets loose his pris'ners, captivates
His scornful foes;
They knock their breast,
Confessing whom they did oppose
To be Gods SON, now not in jest.
Thus Sampsons death brake the Phylistians pates.
Then with a spear his side a Souldier strikes;[268]
Cleaving the Rock
That may
Each day

264 flinty = hard and unyielding.

265 'When Jesus therefore had received the vinegar, he said, It is finished: and he bowed his head, and gave up the ghost.' John 19:30.

266 i.e. Teate does.

267 A centurion who witnessed Christ's death recognised him as the Messiah. See Mark 15:39.

268 Christ's side is pierced with a spear after his death and 'forthwith came there out blood and water'. See John 19:34.

Water that Flock,
Whose Shepheard is now past all push of pikes.[269]

This is the fountain op'ned for thy sin,
Jerusalem!
Thy *filth*, thy *guilt*;
Here is for each a proper stream,
Water and *Blood*: Let none be spilt:
O quench thy guilt, and cleanse thy filth herein.
Isra'l thy Paschall Lamb, thy Christ is dead,
That Lamb from Heav'n:
Have care,
Prepare,
Purge out thy Leaven:[270]
Mingle no more thy malice with thy bread.

Or if the Jewish lump won't leave their leaven[271]
Make me leave mine:
I have in me
(Lord, nail it to this Cross of thine)
An evill heart of enmity.
Lord kill this enmity 'twixt Earth and Heaven.
Be thou my fort, and hiding-place, my soul
Would lodg in thee:
My Lord
Afford
One cleft for mee.
Thy walls are shatt'red, yet thou'rt timber whole.[272]

Satan and sin I h've seen, i'th' Tragick story,
Shoot through and through

269 push = thrust of a weapon; pikes = pointed tip of a spear but also a thorn. Jesus, the shepherd, is dead and cannot feel the soldier's spear.

270 leaven = yeast added to dough. In the Bible 'leaven' is often seen as an agent of corruption. In Mark 8:15, Christ sees leaven as a symbol for the Pharisees' corruption.

271 'Know ye not that a little leaven leaveneth the whole lump? Purge out therefore the old leaven, that ye may be a new lump …' 1 Corinthians 5:6–7. The Jews should repent their corruption.

272 timber = can refer to both the bodily structure, but also the personal qualities of which a person's character is made. The line refers to the essential Christian paradox of life through death, i.e. Christ's walls (his body) is shattered but his 'timber' (his soul) is whole. See Ezra 5:8.

Thy blessed heart;
Yet not one bone was broken, though
Mount *Sinai's* Cannons[273] plaid their part.[274]
In this rock hide me, till I h've seen thy Glory.
Shall not Christ Crucified far dearer be
To me than Pelf,[275]
Than name
Or fame
Or life it self?
'Twas thus with *Joseph*,[276] why not thus with me?

The Souldiers having broke the others leggs,
But not my Lords;
Joseph, a man
Rich in the goods this world affoards
But more in faith, most boldly ran
To *Pilate*, and Christs lifeless body beggs.
Then in clean linnen wraps that skin and bones,
That martir'd treasure:
And why
Can't I
Take as much pleasure
To cloath thy members, Lord, thy naked ones?[277]

Jewes, now, our king's come down: Sirs do you see him?
Your Temple lies
Flat by the ground:
Will you believe when't doth arise?
Catching your Christ at his rebound?
Why if his own won't have him, Lord! give me him.
Christ having now giv'n death his deadly wound,

273 Cannons = canons: laws or rules.

274 Mount Sinai is where the Israelites fled in their exodus from Egypt and where their covenant with God was ratified. In Galatians 4:24–5, Paul makes Mount Sinai a symbol of the old system of Judaism which in this line the poet holds partly responsible for the death of Christ.

275 pelf = money, especially when gained in a dishonest way.

276 A reference to Joseph of Arimathaea, a 'secret disciple of Jesus' who sought permission from Pilate to have Jesus buried in his personal tomb. See John 19:38–9.

277 Here Teate is referring to his role as a preacher to care for God's children or 'members' i.e. why can he not be as happy caring for the living as Joseph was when caring for the dead body of Christ?

Follows him home:
Invades
Deaths shades,
Enters a tombe,
To see what spoils may in a grave be found.

Great Conquerour, who hast kill'd death ith' duel,
After this art
Lodg'd in a stone?[278]
Rather take up[279] in my poor heart
How hard soever, or how none.
Oh! that I were thy Cabinet, dear jewell!
But *Josephs* rock was pure, that grave was new:
First in a womb,
Which none
Had known;
Then in a tombe
Where none had lain, my Lord lodg'd; this doth shew,

I must be *clean* and *new* first. Yet thy passion
And streame of blood,
What did it mean,
That Purple yet a Christall[280] flood?
Was't not the making of me clean?
Doth not not thy rising mean my renovation?
Then make and take for such this heart of mine
And dwell in it;
This breast
Is best
That I can get,
Had I a better, Lord, it should be thine.

Surely the King of terrour I could brave,
If my Lord would
This Sepulcher,
This heart, as his own quarters hold;
I would nor goale nor goaler fear.

278 i.e. tomb.
279 i.e. start to live.
280 i.e. crystal. 'And he showed me a pure river of water of life, clear as crystal, proceeding out of the throne of God and of the Lamb.' Revelation 22:1.

O how my Saviours Corps perfume the grave!
Lord, make this heart of mine a living one
Through thy deaths merit
Convey
I pray
To me thy spirit,
Who thy dead flesh didst Coffin in dead stone.

With th' *Arimathean* Counsellour combin'd
A learned Rabbi[281]
To shew Christ kindness;
An *Israelitish* Doctor: may be
Some wiser man will blame my blindness,
And Antichrist in *Law* and *Learning* find.
But may my soul with blessed *Joseph* dwell
And *Nicodem*:
Yet, down
With th' Gown,[282]
Cry some of them
Who scarce I doubt from these can bear the Bell.[283]

A spicie mixture, 'bout an hundred pounds,
Who came by night
To Jesus brings
T' embalme his Lord, that gave him light,
With Aromatick precious things:
Yet not one half so precious as those wounds.
Now Jesus (*Jonah-like*),[284] Heav'ns sealed one,
Enters the deep:
But shall
The Whale,
The grave, him keep?
See, Souldiers watch, and *Pilate* seales the stone.

281 A reference to Nicodemus, who brought myrrh 'weighing about one hundred pounds' to perfume Christ's tomb and embalm the body. See John 19:39.

282 i.e. those of the clerical or legal profession.

283 to bear the bell = to take first place, to lead. The expression refers to the bell worn by the leading sheep in a herd. Teate is suggesting that those 'sheep' (i.e. Christians) that criticize the clergy could never improve on the example set by learned men such as Joseph of Arimathaea and Nicodemus.

284 The poet is drawing a comparison between Jesus sealed up in the tomb and the Old Testament prophet Jonah who was swallowed by a whale. See Jonah 2.

As *Daniel's* seal'd when cast into the Den,[285]
Malitious Jewes
Require a seale,
And watch, which *Pilate* won't refuse,
Lest some the Coffin'd Corps should steale.
They'l keep the Sun from rising; Crafty men!
Lo! in a Garden stood the sealed Tomb.
Adam the first
Hav'ng bin
For sin
Ith' Garden curst
To th' Grave. My Saviour thus fullfills the doom.[286]

Then dawns that blessed light that ever since
Makes one day shine
More than six other;
For should six week day lights combine,
One Lords-Day brightness would them smother,
With thee, *Thy Day*, Lord, *riseth* and proves Prince.
That Day is now obscur'd wherein Christ slept;
That Day's made bright
In which
That rich
And orient[287] light
Quit that blind prison where he had been kept.

Surely that day's the whole weeks *Jubilee*[288]
(That day's the best
Which my dear Lord

285 The poet is drawing an analogy between the Pharisees demands that Christ be sealed in his tomb to prevent him rising (Matthew 27:62–6) and the Old Testament prophet Daniel who was cast into a lion's den by jealous advisors to King Darius, but was spared by God. See Daniel 6.

286 The word 'doom' signifies both the last day of one's life, and was also used to refer to judgements found in Scripture. It may be that Teate is using the term to refer to Old Testament prophesies that foretold the death and resurrection of the Messiah.

287 i.e. from the East.

288 In Jewish history the 'jubilee' was the celebration of every seventh year and especially every fiftieth year which came after 7 x 7. Jewish slaves were to be released and mortgaged land returned. See Leviticus 25:9–13. Here the poet is suggesting that Sunday, that day of the resurrection, is the day when Christ emancipates sinners.

By ceasing from his labour blest,
Labour that cost more than a word)
Wherein redemption set the ransom'd *free*.
This first day finds more then the seventh day lost
Can superadd
And raise
More praise
Than th' other had:
So th' old Commandment is fullfill'd, not crost;[289]

That bids me celebrate what day of seaven
God hath most blest;
And HIS, doth call:
Such WAS the Jewish, Is our rest.[290]
We sowr'd[291] Gods first works by our fall,
Till Christs last Passover purg'd out of[292] the leaven,
Was not Christs Buriall part of's Humiliation?
His day of rest
From that
Dark state,
Shall't not be blest?
Shall I less prize a new than old Creation?

Redemption is a making old things new.
Rouze, Christians then:
Though dead before,
Let *Lords dayes* find you living men;
That with your Christ can rise and soare.
And for the Christian, quit thy Sabbath, Jew.
The first in sin runs first to th' Sepulcher,
Poor woman kind;[293]
But Christ
Is mist;[294]

289 i.e. the commandment that designates the Sabbath as a day of rest. See Leviticus 19:3.
290 The Christian and Jewish days of rest both fall on Sunday.
291 i.e. soured …
292 'of' is correctly deleted from the second edition of *Ter Tria*.
293 Mary Magdalene was the first to discover the tomb empty. 'The first in sin' is a reference to Eve or womankind. See Matthew 28:1–10, and John 20:1–18 for the story of Christ's resurrection on which the following passage is based.
294 i.e. missed.

Oh! they can't find
Their Lord; though two of his Life guard appear.

The two bright pointers of that blessed Star
His countenance,
Who h'd roll'd the stone,
Strikes keepers hearts, at's first advance,
As dead as what he sate upon.
Thieves were, now Angels Christs attendants are.
Say th' women, who shall roll the stone away?
'Twas done before.
Thus may,
I pray,
I find my score
Quit to mine hand,[295] when I cry who shall pay?

Surely my surety did my debt discharge:
Lord, else why should
Thine Angell be
Sent down t' unlock that prison-hold
Wherein my Saviour lay for me?
My surety's free, why may n't I walk at large?
They would with Oyntments, Odours, precious things
Perfume his Prison;
But th' dead
Was fled;
Their *Sun* was *risen*
With sweeter balme with *healing in his wings*.

Mary the sinner, *Mary Magdalen*
Marcheth ith' van[296]
To th' Sepulcher,
But th' stones remov'd, and so's the man;
Shee, missing her dear Saviour there,
To *John* and *Peter* runs, and comes agen.
These run a race, the wager's precious truth.
But *John* outran:

295 to quit a score = to repay a debt. Christ's resurrection has 'quit' the debt of mankind's sin.

296 i.e. in the van = in the lead.

Alas
He was
The younger man.
Happy the man runs after Christ in youth.

Peter, successour to his Masters Cross,
Whilest *John* keeps out
Enters Christs Tombe;
Looks for his Christ but finds a clout,[297]
And winding sheet in Saviours Room:
But Christ is gone. O blessed, gainfull loss!
Mary th' old weeper[298] stands without and cryes;
But stooping down,
Spies here
And there
The Grave cloaths thrown,
Which linnens scarce can serve to wipe her eyes,

See is still anxious, turns her round, and lo
There the Gard'ner stood,
As shee conceiv'd,
Ev'n he that waters with his blood
Each plant of his. Thus Christ's received
By the true seeker oft when't thinks not so.
Sir, if thou have borne him hence (and 'twas well guest)[299]
Tell me, saith shee;
Mary!
Lo I
Ev'n I am he.
Ah! my dear Lord, that word revives my heart.

Yet touch me not, saith he, I'm not ascended:
But go thou rather
And tell abroad
Unto my Brethren, to my Father
And yours I go, mine and your God.
So richly is the poorest Saint befriended!
How studious is my Lord that they should know,
And so partake

297 clout = a piece of cloth. 298 weeper = mourner. 299 i.e. guessed.

Of this
His Bliss
That did forsake
Him in his captive state and sufferings so.

Surely these men that fled then from their colours,[300]
Might have expected
Another kind
Of message should have been directed
From their now rising Lord: but find
Their sins in the Grave buri'd with his dolours.
No word of th' old uncomfortable story.
But say I'm risen:
Let tears
And fears
Take up my prison.
Run tell my Brethren thou hast seen my Glory.

Also the Angel cries, be not affraid:
Jesus you'd have;
I know it well:
But think you *David* in a cave,
Or *Davids* Son must ever dwell?
Come see the place where your dear Lord was laid.
Woman, your Lord's not here; your Lord is risen.
Have you forgot
Your Lords
Own words?
Or have you not?
Seek you the Prince of life in this dead prison?

Run, tell the rest, and *Peter*, Christ is gone
Tow'rds *Galilee*,
As he did say.
With joy and feare away they flee
All dapled like the time of day.
And as they march, behold! they see the SON.
O may my Lord thus evermore appear,

300 colours = the flags or standards raised in battle which the disciples as 'soldiers' should have followed.

And shine upon
Poor me,
When he
Saith, get thee gone,
And unto others, of me, tidings bear.

O blessed meeting! Courtship, and devotion!
All Haile! saith he;
They bowt' his feet;
Light that forbids us courteous be
Was then so dark Christ could not see't.
That master taught his schollers no such notion.
Men, 'tis observ'd the rising sun adore;
Christ's risen now;
And bright
Day light
Beames from his brow;
Shall not all worship the Son of God much more?

Then watch[301] mean while bring news of all that's done.
To th' Priests within,
Ev'n that Christ's risen;
Who seeing him past reach, begin
To plot how they this truth m' imprison.[302]
Christs second Grave-stone is a silver one.
What potent pranks can mighty Mammon[303] shew!
Powerfull pelf
In'ts facts
Out acts
Ev'n pow'r it self:
Money can make truth falsehood, falsehood true.

Money betrai'd my Lord to all these wrongs;
Now they're devising
To keep on foot
Something to cloud this bright Suns-rising;

301 i.e. the soldiers who had been guarding Christ's tomb.
302 i.e. may imprison.
303 'Mammon' is an Aramaic word meaning 'wealth'. A reference to the money with which the Chief Priests were said to have bribed the guards to say that the disciples had stolen Christ's body from the tomb. See Matthew 28:11–15.

And 'tis large money that must do't.
This silver key must turn the souldiers tongues.
Souldiers are taught a sorry tale to tell;
Which should methinks
Nere flip
Their lip;
But that which chinks
So sweetly, can make all sound pretty well.

Say, *Whilst we keepers slept at th' Sepulcher,*
's Disciples came
And stole him thence;
Which if the governour shall blame
We'll mediate and make your defence.
Now hear O Heavens! and O Earth! give eare.
Can'st thus, O Isr'ell, fool away thy Glory?
Is such a wise
Fable
Able
To blind thine eyes?
Is this th' authentick, yet received story?

Why, souldiers, if you slept at th' Sepulcher
Whilst that vast stone
Was rolling back
(Which may a Jew[304] believe, or none)
And some by stealth the corps did take:
I marvaile you could see what men they were.
Or if you saw the thieves, why did you not
Stop or pursue?
So short
Report
Wants so much glue?
See how the last words have the first forgot.

But oh, fond Priests and Elders, whence is it
That you can stroak
These souldiers pates?[305]
Sure such neglect would you provoke

304 i.e. a non-Christian.

305 pate = brains, intellect.

Of all.[306] Yet you're their advocates.
Alas! how fury doth befoole their wits!
Mean while Disciples were so far from thieving,
That, when this newes
They brought,
They saw't,
Yet, they refuse
To take't for truth, being so far from believing.

As two of them were to *Emaus* going[307]
Their busie tongue
Bee'ng well imploy'd,
My dearest Lord stands them among;
No sooner talk't of, than enjoy'd.
Happy the Servants whom he finds so doing.
What is your talk that makes your walk so sad?
Saith *Cleopas*,
Dost thou
Not know
These things? Alas!
A mighty Man and Prophet we have had;

Mighty in word and deed with God and Men:
Jesus was he
Of *Nazareth*
We'd hop'd might our Redeemer be:
But him our Rulers put to death
This bee'ng the third day since. And yet agen
We know not what to think on't, hurried
'Twixt hope and fear;
For some,
That come
From th' Sepulcher,
Assure us that he's risen from the Dead.

But oh this evill heart of unbelief!
This want of faith

306 i.e. above everything else.

307 The risen Christ appears to two disciples on the road to Emmaus but is initially unrecognizable to them. See Luke 24:13–35.

That can provoke
The gentle Lamb of God to wrath,
Setting in ev'ry wheel a spoke,
Clouding the rising Sun with gloomy grief!
O fooles, and slow of heart, replies my Lord,
Slow to believe me!
But oh
Not so
Not slow to grieve me,
Ought not your Christ fulfill the written word?

But Christ can't alwaies hold his chiding story:
Sugars his cheeks
With sweet instructions;
Moses his vaile in pieces breaks;[308]
Proves by Prophetick fair deductions,
Through Seas of sufferings Christ must land in Glory.
My Lord then makes as he would further go:
But they begin
To pray
Him stay,
And he turns in:
Happy, who love their close reprovers so.

This bread of life thus broken when he had,
He breaks more bread
And makes them eat;
Their Lord's their Shepheard, they're well fed,
Body and Soul, with blessed meat,
My soul, seek Christ first; and those things he'll add.
Just now my Lord makes them see who he is,
Then slips away.
And, oh!
'Twas so
With me[309] last day,
One moment op'ned and seal'd up like bliss.

308 By explaining how his resurrection fulfils the prophecies of Moses, Christ reveals his identity and breaks his 'vaile' or disguise in pieces. The disciples then acknowledge him and beg him to stay. See Luke 24:27–30.

309 i.e. the poet.

When Christ was gone, say they, we might have guest[310]
What light 'twas brought
So bright a day
To darkest Scriptures: might have thought
The *risen Sun* was in our way
Finding our hearts so *burn* within our breast.
Then they return back to *Jerusalem*
Brimfull of joy
To feast
The rest;[311]
But they are coy
Till Christ Himself stands in the midst of them.

And 'tis so still. Whoever's sent about
To tell thy story,
Hardness of hearts
And unbelief blinds all thy glory:
Lord, who believes? Lord, who converts?
Till thy deare presence puts all out of doubt.
Their doores bee'ng shut, and hearts much more, that even
My Lord to put
All out
Of doubt;
(None else can do't)
This newes imparts in person to th' eleven.

Yet oh how hard a thing is this believing?
A sprite appears
As they suppose;
The same that in their storms of fears
Walk't on the Seas when winds arose.
Phant'sies fooles-bolt,[312] how't hinders truths receiving.
Jesus salutes them with a peace be to you
Once and agen:
'Tis I;
Sirs, why

310 guessed (with a pun on 'guest').
311 i.e. to inform the other disciples that they have seen Christ.
312 Phantasie = mental apprehension of an object of perception (*OED* 1a.) Fools are bolted (fettered) by a dependence on sensory perception rather than faith, e.g. 'doubting' Thomas (see note to line 2317).

SON

Distrust you then?
Why do you let such thoughts arise, why do you?

Down doubtings; I'm got up: And ready have
(Sirs, come and see
And feel, I pray)
A Tombe, dead unbelief, for thee
Dig'd in my side but t' other day,[313]
And for your doubtings, in each hand a grave.
If these suffice not, handle, feel my feet,
There are two more.
Doubt not,
I've got
All as before:
Rather than miss their faith their sense he'll meet.

Then for the further feeding of their faith
He calls for food;
They give him fish,
And Honey-Combe: but, oh! his blood
And body is a sweeter dish.
Then, breathing, take the Holy Ghost, he saith.
Now doth the frost-nipt tree of life recover:
Puts forth again:
New springs,
And brings
Fruits that remain
Spirit and Life, so prove's Deaths Winter's over.

Thomas mean while bee'ng absent from the rest[314]
Freezing from th' fire,
(Like them that miss
Th'assemblies Christ is wont t'inspire
With sweet assurance, joy and bliss)[315]
Can't feed his faith with hear-say of a feast
He must first hold a Coroners inquest:
Must see Christs ayles,

313 Christ is urging the disciples to feel the wound or 'tomb' in his side to kill their 'unbelief'.

314 See John 20:24–9, for the story of doubting Thomas.

315 i.e. those who do not go to Church.

And must
First thrust
Ith' print oth' nailes
His fingers; e're this faith enter his breast.

His faith must go on stilts, or not at all:
See with the eye,
Feel with the hand,
His faith must in his fingers lye,
His faith must in his feeling stand,
At th' bound from sorry sense he'll catch the ball.
Th' week after, he and they be'ng all together,
With blessed greeting
(Increase
Of peace)
Christ Crowns their meeting.
Thomas, saith he, come reach thy finger hither.

As men are wont who've Children to be taught,
My Lord was fain
(Though ev'ry letter
In's hands and feet were printed plain)
With's finger teach him spell the better,
The Child to faith by fealing must be brought.
My Lord! and my God! (how this sight relieves me!)
Poor *Thomas* cries.
Christ saith,
Thy faith
May thank thine eyes:
Blessed is he who sees not, yet believes me.

Disciples after this, a fishing go:[316]
But nothing's caught,
Throughout the night;
Till Jesus comes, and brings a draught:
Lord shew me so which side's the right,
When to catch souls thy Gospel net I throw.
Christ look't into their cup-board just before:
Children, have ye

316 See John 21:1–14.

Got meate
To eate?
Else come to me:
I've food and firing[317] for you on the shore.

Hence sinfull cares; infest my soul no longer,
Base diffidence:
Doubtings retreat:
Soul, mind thy Saviours providence:
Do thine own work, and he'll find meat.
Or give thee somethings[318] better if thou hunger.
Dinner bee'ng done, Christ speaks of working then:
And so should we:
Our whet,[319]
Not let
Our food should be.
Shepherds[320] Christ feeds, to feed his sheep agen.

Shepherds who love to eat but not to seed
Are what they're not,
Not what they are;
(A Paradox, and Gordian knot,[321]
Which Christ will cut, and will not spare)
Shepheards in name, but rav'ning wolves indeed.[322]
Peter, dost love me more than these?[323] I'll prove thee.
Then feed and keep
My flock;
My stock
Of Lambs and Sheep.
All knowing Lord, saith he, thou know'st I love thee.

Peter, when thou wast young, then thou wast free
To come and go

317 firing = firewood.

318 The second edition has 'something's'.

319 whet = appetite. These lines seem to mean that our spiritual food should be something which sharpens our appetite rather than an impediment to it.

320 shepherds = clergymen like Teate himself. Christ nourishes ministers so that they may nourish their sheep.

321 Something of great difficulty. Gordius, a peasant chosen to be king, tied his wagon to a beam with a knot so ingenious that no one could untie it.

322 Cf. Milton, *Lycidas*, lines 112–29.

323 See John 21:15–18.

As thou'dst a mind,[324]
Girding thy self: 't shall not be so
When thou art old, others shall bind,
And gird, and carry thee.[325] Man! follow mee.
Peter replies, and what must this man do?[326]
What's that to thee?
Follow
Me thou.
How busie wee
Are to mind others works, our own not so.

In an appointed mount in *Galilee*,
Christ meets th' eleven:
Chargeth them there,
By all his pow'r in Earth and Heav'n,
To Preach the Gospell ev'ry where;
Baptizing in the name of One and Three.
And in so doing, saith, I'm with you still.
He shews Hells loss:
Deaths gate,
Sins state
Spoil'd by his Cross.
Now is our *Sampson* got[327] on *Gaza's* hill.

To prove my new bought right to ev'ry Nation,
New tongues I give
Unto you: Though
You drink what's deadly, you shall live:
Serpents and sicknesses shall know
And Devils too, that I have wrought Salvation.
As many years as *Isr'el* just had been,
Christ, dais doth spend
'Twixt the
Red Sea
Of's bloudy end,
And Heav'nly *Canaan*: forty daies he's seen.

324 Cf. Herbert, 'The Collar', lines 4–6.
325 A reference to the eventual crucifixion of Peter.
326 i.e. what must I do?
327 i.e. captured.

Mean while Christ summons others from the dead
To evidence
His Resurrection:
From types, from texts, from faith, from sense,
Of proofs how full, how fair collection.
Shew'ng Christ is Risen as the Churches head.
Now, O devourer![328] where's thy victory?
Out of the grave
That old
Strong hold
And eating[329] Cave
Comes meat and sweetness; which who tasts can't die:

Ev'n Christ comes thence. And now in *Olivet*
Where he laid down
In part of pay
For th' purchase of his new bought crown,
His bloody sweat: ev'n there this day
To see's Inthronization Saints are met:[330]
Wilt thou restore the kingdome, Lord, they cry,
To *Isr'el* yet?
For you
To know
Times is not fit:
I'll send my spirit! That's my Lord's reply.

O what an eager foolish thing is man!
Busie to know
What least concerns him!
But to take forth,[331] alas! how slow
The lessons that my God would learn[332] him.
A sieve that lets go th' flower[333] but holds the bran.
Melchisedeck[334] mean time, our Priest for ever,
With lift up hands

328 i.e. death.

329 eating = devouring.

330 For the story of Christ's ascension from the Mount of Olivet, see Acts 1:4–12.

331 take forth = to learn.

332 i.e. teach.

333 i.e. flour. These lines seem to mean that man finds it difficult to retain God's teachings.

334 A priest who served Abraham in the Old Testament, Melchizedek was revered as the archetypal priest-king. Teate is identifying him with the ascending Christ.

On his
All bliss
And grace commands;
Whom clouds receiving from their sight do sever.

But not from th' eye of faith, which fixedly
Pursues their king;
Till Angels do
Tidings of's second coming, bring,
In such sort as they'd seen him go.
Chear up, my drooping heart, thine head's on high:
Yet not so high, but that his heart's as low
As still to mind
Poor thee
Till hee
Hath made thee find
What for thy gain he sometime did forego.

Now's the forerunner ent'red in for thee:
Thy Lord's ascended;
Up and away:
When Christ first rose; this flight he 'ntended:
And art thou quickned here[335] to stay?
May all my life but one Ascension bee.
But I'm all fits and starts, and cannot get
Hold of mine own:
But clouds
Prove shrouds:
And all seems gone:
Sometimes I *rise* with Christ, but cannot *sit*.

Yet am I fixt, whilst Saviour sits in Heaven;
There are no hills
And dales on high:
My Swampes my Saviours merit fills,
That all might in a levell lie,
Making my state, though not my comfort even.
Why art thou then, my soul, disquieted?
Christ dwelt in dust

335 i.e. brought to life on earth.

As thou
Dost now;
Shall I not trust
Him, that drank of my brook,[336] to lift mine head?

Is this the Butler that bore *Pharaohs* cup?
Though he forgot
Joseph ith' Prison,[337]
When rais'd himself, thy Lord will not
Reckon that hee's compleatly risen,
Till all his foes are down, and friends got up.
Down then, thou evill heart of unbelief!
Thou art a foe,
To mee
I see,
To him I know;
A goale would fit thee well, for thou'rt a thief.

Thou pick'st my comforts, and thou steal'st his praise,
His and my loss
We lay to thee;
Betwixt two thieves Christ left one Cross
Void, that there hanged thou mightst bee;
Th' arch-thief of all that rob on Gods highwayes.
Now as Mount *Olivet* for *Sion* Mount
Thou didst forgo,
Teach mee
Like thee,
Sweet Saviour, so
Heav'ns joyes before earths fatness to account.

I determined not to know any thing save Jesus Christ, and him crucified, 1 Cor. 2.2

336 See I Kings 17:4.

337 This refers to the Old Testament story of Joseph who was imprisoned in Egypt with Pharaoh's butler. The butler used Joseph's power to interpret dreams to win back Pharaoh's favour and secure his own release after which he forgot about Joseph who was still held captive. See Genesis 40. The poet seems to be suggesting that Christ will not be like the butler and forget about his people on Earth when he has ascended into Heaven.

Spirit

My Verse proceeds to him that by proceeding
Subsisteth in the Deity;[1]
But can't proceed without his speeding:
This Dove doth teach all other birds to fly.[2]

My callow muse hath pinions but no wings,[3]
Pinions indeed of ignorance;
Yet th' Dove that hatcheth other things
Can fledge mine infant muse with utterance.[4]

But th'ther day I saw a Lamb take wing[5]
And flie to Heaven from an hill:
I watcht to see if any thing
Would fall from him in flight, and found a quill,

Of which I made a pen, and fell to write
The story; writing, found a Verse;
Whilst on mine hand a Dove did light,
And bad me with the Lamb the Dove rehearse.[6]

My Master from mine head but th'ther day
The Clouds did take: unkind? or kind?
For whilst my Master went away
His mantle dropt, which whoso seeks may find.

1 The poem 'proceeds' (i.e. moves on) to the third person of the Trinity, the Holy Spirit, who both 'proceeds' (i.e. originates) from God, and exists in God.

2 The Holy Spirit is represented as a dove. See Matthew 3:16.

3 Pinions = feathers. The poet's muse, unlike the Holy Spirit, can not ascend to God.

4 'And they were filled with the Holy Ghost, and began to speak with other tongues, as the Spirit gave them utterance.' Acts 2:4.

5 The poet is referring to the ascension of Christ (the 'Lamb') into Heaven and thus continues from where the previous section 'Son' left off.

6 i.e. And told me to write about the 'lamb' (i.e. Christ) whilst under the inspiration of the 'dove' (i.e. the Holy Spirit).

I seek it: Blessed Spirit! Come and spread
Thy beaming wings and cover me
In thy bright light thy Poet lead
That in thy light would fain discover thee.

'Tis only Sun-shine that can shew the Sun,
Alas! my Lord, my spirits flesh;
Dark-Lanthorn light is next to[7] none:
My Frost-nipt blooms[8] what Sun beams can refresh?

Since then my carnal mind can never shew
O who, or what, dear Dove! thou art:
The spirit of my mind renew
And it shall reimburse what thou'lt impart.

Father and Son are God, and God's a Spirit,
And yet Gods Spirit neither is
Father nor Son; yet doth inherit
With both an equall yet distinguish'd bliss.

Father and Son are God, and God is love,
Yet neither Father nor the Son
But their sweet spirit's the sweet Dove:
Each hath his Spirit, yet they both but one.[9]

By this eternall Spirit Christ the word
Offers himself to God and dies:
Yet by his Spirit doth affoard
Of life unto dead sinners all supplies.

This Spirit's infinite: oh! who can flee
His presence and all-searching sight?
Yet he's a wind, which who can see
From whence it comes, or whither it takes flight?

This Spirit's infinite; dwells every where,
Fathoms all hearts, sounds ev'ry deep:

7 i.e. almost. 8 Cf. Herbert, 'Denial', line 24.

9 A reference to the doctrine of the Trinity wherein the Father, Son and Holy Spirit are separate persons but are all God. Cf. Donne, 'The Good Morrow', line 14, in *Poetical works*, ed. Herbert J. C. Grierson (Oxford, 1979).

Yet how few Temples, Lord! are there
Wherein this holy Ghost doth house or keep?[10]

This active Spirit moves in ev'ry wheel.
Works as he will; doth what he lists.[11]
Mans heart's that only brass and steel
That the sweet Spirits motions resists.

This pow'rfull Spirit did the Heavens garnish
And doth renew earths with'red face:
When winter washeth off the vernish
And makes a verdant spring in ev'ry place.

And why not in my soul? Awake and blow
O North wind, and thou South wind come,
Let all my sweets and spices flow
That he that owns my garden, may have some.

Where the Lords spirit is, there's liberty:
Yet a grim Sergeant one day came,
And neck and heels my soul did tie,
Saying, he did it in the Spirits name.

He did his Office, and wou'd not be brib'd:
But as his warrant shew'd a writing;
Spirit of bondage, there subscrib'd
I spied; and found 'twas of his own inditing.[12]

My heart before had been a bird of prey
But now bee'ng conquer'd by a Dove,
I think on't still how't sprangling[13] lay
Crying for quarter[14] to that bird of love.

I markt his bill but saw no Olive branch:
Peace I implor'd, but he deni'd;
What blood he drew, refus'd to stanch
Till I submitted to be mortified.[15]

10 house or keep = dwell or stay. 11 lists = wants to.

12 indite = to compose. The poet is referring to the belief that man must first be possessed by the Holy Spirit in order to be saved. See Romans 8:23.

13 to sprangle = to stretched out / sprawl (*OED* 1). 14 quarter = mercy.

15 Mortification was the process of subduing the body's needs through self-denial, with the object of receiving divine grace.

Dear Dove, said I, convince me, pierce me, grieve me:
Strike through and through this wretched heart
So that thou'lt but at length relieve me
And with thy gentle wings but stroke my smart.

Dear heart, said he, I struck thee for to stroke thee.
Put thee in bonds to set thee free:
That I might better heal, I broke thee:
I'm sent to comfort by convincing[16] thee.

Though I'm all light and peace, yet I did send thee
To a dark prison, holding over
My black rod, but it was to mend thee;
For friends do Fools and Phranticks thus recover.

Remember, man, thy wild and *Bethlem* tricks:[17]
How oft I strove with thee in vain:
Thine heel could kick against my pricks.[18]
Sure 'twas high time to get thee in a chain.

Thou, and *Manasseh*,[19] stood in much more need
Of iron chains, then chains of Gold.
Distracted folk must purge and bleed,
And in their moneths[20] be caught and kept in hold.

Oh blessed bonds! said I, O happy trouble!
O bitter-sweet sweet-bitter smart!
My pain was great, my profit double
Whilst thus thou undertak'st to tame mine heart.

Void, Chymicks! spill your Spirits! quit your art!
Cease from your oft sought, unfound stone;[21]

16 i.e. overcoming.

17 Bethlem = Bedlam, the lunatic asylum in London.

18 See Acts 9:5.

19 Manasseh was an Old Testament king of Judah who was suspected of treason and imprisoned. See 2 Chronicles 33:11.

20 moneths = particular phases of the moon which denoted the suitability of a patient to be bled. Bleeding was often prescribed for those who appeared to be 'phranticks' or madmen.

21 i.e. the philosopher's stone, a substance sought by alchemists in the belief that it had the power to perfect all that was corrupt in nature, for example, transmute base metals into gold.

There's but one Spirit can convert
An iron chain into a golden one.

Dear Dove, thy pris'ner may I ever bee!
Bondage is like to be my state,
If to my self thou leave me free.
He's only free whom thou dost captivate.

Where the Lords Spirit is, there's liberty;
No man can say, Jesus is Lord
But by the Holy Ghost, or cry
Abba, till that sweet Spirit teach that word.

I was a lisper, and a stamerer
And could not skill o' th' Sibboleth[22]
That might my pray'r to God indear
Till this free Spirit gave new speech and breath.

I was a beggar so extreamly poor
I skill'd not how to make my moanes:
But this Dove met me at Gods door.
Supply'ng my want of words with store of groanes.

I was in suit, and could not well make good
My Title:[23] But said this free Spirit,
Soul, take this seal, the seal of blood;
I am thy witness, and thou shalt inherit.

I found a riddle whilst I sought a Text,
But this free Spirit loos'd the knot:
Which when I h'd read, yet what was next
Had not this Spirit prompted I'd forgot.

My barren grounds were chapt for want of rain
Gasping tow'rds Heaven for a flood;

22 i.e. Shibboleth: an Old Testament password that identified the Ephraimites, enemies of the Israelites, as they could not pronounce the 'sh' sound. The poet is saying that he was unable to make God hear his prayers without the aid of the Holy Spirit.
23 title = a legal right to inherit property. The poet is unable to prove his 'title', i.e. his worthiness to inherit the kingdom of God.

This Spirit flowing in amain,[24]
Told me that he had brought me that's as good.

I searcht mine heart, found so much dross and tin
So little else; I fell a mourning
Both for my gross and splendid sin:
Then he to me the spirit was of burning.

I fell a burning when my God did chide me:
Water, said I, or I'm undone:
This streaming Spirit streight suppli'd me
Till all those scorching flames were quencht & gone.

I fell a chilling till my heart grew stone:
Scarce had I left one warm desire:
My frozen heart was next to none:[25]
Then said this holy Spirit, I am fire.

I fell a melting when I felt his heat;
My soul was broached at mine eyes
The ice was thawn to tears and sweat
Which with fresh gales this Spirit gently dries.

These fontinells[26] thus dri'd pride rais'd a tumour
And then the Spirit's fain to take
His Lancet and let out the humour:
But, oh! mine heart how did it burn, and ake?

Which this dear Dove perceiving straightway goes
T' a precious box,[27] and thence applies
An ointment made of *Sharons* Rose;[28]
Which both the swelling cools, and mollifies.

24 amain = at full force. 25 i.e. almost dead.

26 Fontinell = fontanel. Both a fountain, used here to symbolise weeping eyes, and an outlet for the discharge of humours from the body (*OED* 2). According to Galenic medicine, physical health was determined by the equal balance of four humours natural to the body.

27 i.e. a medicine case.

28 Sharon was a plain in the north of Palestine famous for its wild flowers. The 'rose of Sharon' referred to in Song of Solomon 2:1 was read as a symbolic reference to Christ.

When I was none, this Spirit made me be,
And live, and breath: when I was worse
(For worse than nothing, sin made me)
For my rebuilding freely did imburse.[29]

My stony heart this Spirit hatcht to flesh:
My fleshy heart did circumcise:[30]
My bleeding heart with balme refresh,
Those tears that fell from bleeding Saviours eyes.

In native gore when I polluted lay,
Hav'ng gone to wash, to salt, to swath me;
His counsells were my salt that day;
His laws my swadling bands: his grace did bathe me.

With milk for Babes this comforter did fill
Both Testaments, the old and new;
But how to come by't I'd no skill
Till he those breasts of consolation drew.

He took me by the hand, and taught me go,
For I went all by forms before,[31]
Till's holy unction made me know
A new and living way to Fathers door.

I got upon a hill, would fain decry
Heav'ns *Canaan*[32] from earths wilderness
But being there, could nothing spy
Till with his eyesalve he mine eyes did dress.

Over against Heav'ns haven on the shore,
I stood and waited for a wind;
Then did his Spirit waft me ore
In heart, in hope, in faith, in joy of mind.

Arithmetick and th' art of measuring
I h'd studied, but bungled still;

29 imburse = pay out. 30 circumcise = purify.

31 i.e. I merely observed outward 'forms' or the formalities of faith whilst neglecting my inner state.

32 Canaan was the 'Promised Land' that the Israelites inherited from God after their escape from Egypt and forty years in the wilderness. See Joshua 14.

The measure of a span[33] to bring
Or number of my dayes I could not skill:[34]

Then this free Spirit gave a watch to me
Which ev'ry day wind up I must,
To tell me how my time did flee;
But I forgot, and let it stand and rust.

Then being griev'd that I'd so disrespected
Both guift[35] and giver, did indeavour
To wind it up but t' had collected
Such soil[36] as from the wheels I could not sever.

Then did I mourning to the donour[37] go;
Confess'd my fault, shew'd him the soile
It gather'd whilst I neglected so:
Do not despaire said he, for I am oyle.

This is the Spirit of all life and bliss
Yet when I felt him first, I died:
The fountain of my life he is,
Yet but for him I h'd neer been mortified.

This Spirit in mine heart doth sheed[38] abroad
Gods dear and never dying love:
Yet not a day but his sharp rod
Doth me severely chastise and reprove.

This Spirit rais'd my Christ, yet casts me down
Doth cast me down, and yet uphold:
Mine humblings are my joy, my Crown;
My fear doth make my faith more firm and bold.

Calms are not alwayes profitable for me,
Therefore the winds are sometimes high;
This Spirit blusters and is stormy,
That I might groundfast[39] in humility.

33 i.e. a lifetime.
34 i.e. add up or work out.
35 i.e. gift.
36 soil = a moral tarnish.
37 i.e. donor or giver.
38 sheed = shed; abroad = over a wide area.
39 i.e. be firmly fixed.

This Spirit is my good and only guide:
Yet walk ith' Spirit, Scriptures say.[40]
My conduct, and my path beside
This Spirit is; my Captain, and my way.

Man, walk according to thy native light,
Say some, and thou shalt perfect bee:
Perfect indeed as noon's at night;
Lord, in thy Spirits light, light let me see.

A spirit there's in man but th' inspiration
Of the Almighty only can,
By no less than a new Creation,
Enlighten't; such a dungeon sin made man.

Mans spirit is the Candle of the Lord;
Which who would see by, first should light
At Gods own fire, ev'n Gods own word:
Gods word's his mind sent us in black and white.

For since th' incarnate word his tender love
In blood to write us condescends,
What wonder that his own dear Dove
In ink and paper praies us to be friends?

Nor Son nor Spirit had I understood
Bee'ng sunk so deep in sins dark grot
Had not the Son took bone and blood
Had not the Spirit pen and paper got.[41]

The Son, in humane nature clad, doth raise
My conscience out of guilts dark grave,
The Spirit, cloath'd in humane phrase,
My mind out of blind ignorances cave.

The Son in servile form came down among's
Serving to purchase us command:[42]

40 See Galatians 5:16.

41 Referring to the Calvinist belief that man can be saved by contemplation of Christ the Son's bodily sacrifice and studying Scripture, which according to puritan belief was composed under the direct guidance of the Holy Spirit.

42 i.e. to buy our freedom.

The Spirit fell in cloven tongues,[43]
As who would lisp that we might understand.

Surely this Spirit of all Spirits fram'd
That Book of Books, my Bible dear:
A thing that's all things can be nam'd:
Food, physick, treasures, pleasures, all are here.

A glass that shewes to ev'ry man his face;
A staff that helps the lame to walk:
A spur that makes him mend his pace:
A light that shews what, and what not, to balk.[44]

A Book that makes the simple truly wise:
A Book that proves the wisest fools:
A Book that helps the Readers eyes:
A Book that baffles, and befools the schools.[45]

A Book whose ev'ry leafe, whose ev'ry line
Out shines the milky way as far
As if Heav'ns light should all combine
To darken and obscure one painted star.[46]

A Book that told my story ere I was:[47]
A Book that tells me what shall be
When I'm no more: what doom shall pass
On States, on Churches, Persons, and on me.

This Book's truths standard, nay, 'tis truth it self;
So well's the Spirit here pourtrai'd;
This Book doth sanctifie the shelf,
The heart, I mean where it's sincerely laid.

43 When the Holy Spirit empowered the apostles to preach Christ's teaching they began to speak in 'cloven tongues', i.e. different languages. See Acts 2.

44 balk = shun or avoid.

45 schools = the academies where ancient Greek or Roman philosophers taught.

46 painted = coloured so as to deceive (*OED* 1 b). 'Painted star' may be a reference to the elaborate liturgical rituals of both the Roman Catholic Church and high Anglicanism which were rejected by puritanism in favour of prayer and reading Scripture.

47 A reference to the Calvinist doctrine of predestination, i.e. God knows whether a man will be saved or damned before he is born.

Yet some by reason, some by newfound light
Not only leave to question take
But mend this Book and set it right
By Tables of Errata's[48] they would make.

So much is good, and 'tis Canonicall,
As to mans reason is commensur'd:[49]
Gods light, by mans, must stand or fall:
And so the Sun by th' Sextons Clock is censur'd.[50]

Methinks I love the Author for the Book:
The Book for the' Author much more love;
When op'ning into it I look
My God, I can't forget thy sweet-spread Dove.

The gentle wings I feel, and hear the mourning
Of that dear Turtle waiting still,
Upon my grieving and returning,
To bring an Olive-branch of peace ith' bill.[51]

The lines, I grant, are not all of one colour,
Yet all make up mans doom and duty
Some promise joy, some threaten dolour
Variety makes up the Turtles beauty.[52]

This Dove *Bezaleel* and *Aholiah* taught[53]
All curious works for th' Sanctuary:

48 'Tables of Errata' were lists of errors and corrections affixed to the back of printed books. The poet seems to be censuring those who would challenge and seek to correct the literal truth of the Bible.

49 i.e. commensurate.

50 censure = judge and calculate (*OED* 1). The poet is suggesting that man's reason should be equal to comprehending the divine: just as the 'sexton's clock' can estimate the movements of the Sun, so man is able to understand God's creation. Cf. Henry More, *An antidote against atheisme* (London, 1655), p. 7: 'I define God therefore thus, An Essence or Being fully and absolutely perfect … But to be fully and absolutely prefect is to bee at least as perfect as the apprehension of a Man can conceive, without a Contradiction.'

51 turtle = turtledove. In the Old Testament story of Noah and the flood, a dove brought an olive branch to the ark as a symbol of God's promise of a new world for his people. See Genesis 8:12.

52 Turtles beauty = the beauty of the Holy Spirit. See Psalm 74:19.

53 Bezaleel and Aholiab were Israelites of the Exodus from Egypt whom God filled with 'the spirit of God, in wisdom, in understanding, and in knowledge, and in all manner

But Scriptures are more finely wrought
Shewing most art, where they seem most to vary.

As when this one sweet Spirit is call'd seaven,[54]
Perfection's meant in unity:
A Spirit filling Earth and Heaven
That operates in all, but diversly.

Some reckon seaven Suns to ev'ry week,
So many Moons to ev'ry year,
As shee turns th' whole face or half cheek,
And doth by turns first sit, and then appear.

This Spirit makes in *Sampson* strength excell,
And in a *Moses* Government,
And wisdom in a *Daniel*,[55]
And all much more in Christ, where't dwelt unpent.[56]

This Spirit doth transcribe the Gospell-story
On th' fleshy tables of mine heart.
Christ's Cradle, Cross, his Grave, his Glory
All's acted on that stage by th' Spirits art.

To his Birth answers my Regeneration:
Heart-Circumcision suites to his:
To's Cross and Grave, mortification:
And Grace and Hope to's Rising and his Bliss.

And then as Christ makes intercession for us,
The Spirit in us, intercedes:
With crying blood our Christ doth store[57] us
With sighes and groanes the Spirit in us pleads.

This Spirit is unbounded, yet believers
In earthen vessels this rich treasure

of workmanship.' (Exodus 35:31) so that they were able to make all the items for the 'sanctuary' or church.

54 'Grace be unto you, and peace, from him which is, and which was, and which is to come; and from the seven Spirits which are before his throne.' Revelation 1:4.

55 Samson, Moses and Daniel were archetypal Old Testament leaders.

56 unpent = unconfined.

57 store = furnish.

Only receive as he delivers,
And he dispenseth each one but a measure.

This Spirit is eternal, never dies,
An unextinguishable fire:
Yet in mens hearts oft gasping cryes
Oh! if you quench me thus I shall expire.

This Spirit is a Dove, yet to contest
With Crowes, and Vultures is he fain;[58]
Whilst, in his room,[59] mans wretched breast
Doth lusts unclean, wraths, rapines entertain.

This Spirit is a Dove, yet's vexed often
By foolish man, that peevish wasp
Whose heart nor Sun nor show'r can soften,
Man grieves him without whom he could not gasp.

This tender Spirit who but man would grieve?
If I my Comforter make sad,
Who only can sad hearts relieve,
Alas! my God, who then shall make me glad?

Grieve, foolish heart! be't to thine own perplexing
Be thou as melted wax in me,[60]
That thou shouldst set this Dove avexing[61]
That sweetly seales redemption unto thee.

Give, stubborn heart, relent, since for thy sake
The Lamb of God not only blood,
But ev'n gods turtle tears doth take,
Let thy repentance still help on the flood.

Melt, stony heart! till all becomes one river:
Doves do delight near ponds to dwell:

58 fain = willing. 59 i.e. the body.

60 'my heart is like wax; it is melted in the midst of my bowels.' Psalm 22:14. Cf. Teate, *A scripture-map of the wildernesse of sin* (London, 1655): 'The more the Sun shines upon the wax, the more it softneth it; the more it shines upon the wilderness, the more it scorcheth and hardens it: Now speak soul, Art thou like wax under a judgement, a mercy, a sermon? Hast thou a relenting, giving, mourning, melting heart?', p. 11.

61 i.e. that you should vex this dove …

Groans are best musick to a griever:
Such is Gods dove, whose groanes thy duty tell.[62]

Shew not thy self vexatious to a Dove,
That cannot grieve thee without grieving:
Ev'n Publicans yield love for love.[63]
Quench not truths Spirit by thy unbelieving.

Afflict not this dear guide: go not astray:
Nor look back from an holy life:
While th' Spirit saies this is the way,
Have salt in thee; remember, man, *Lots* wife.[64]

Check[65] not this Spirits checks, but let them bee
Taken for kindness, as they are:
His smitings reckon[66] oyl to thee
Say, smite my rock, my God, and do not spare.[67]

Grieve not this Holy Ghost, by entertaining
Such inmates as he cannot bear;
If bands of lusts thine heart be training
What room for this sweet Spirit can be there?

Seek holyness, seek peace, make after[68] Union:
Let Meditation stir this fire:
Pray'r blow it up; let sweet Communion
Maintain it burning still, and raise it higher.

Quench not the smallest spark in thy weak brother:
What flames are on that hearth of thine,
Boast not, nor yet deny or smother.
Rather desire thou for to burn then shine.

62 i.e. tell thee, heart, what thy duty is.

63 A 'publican' was a tax collector in Biblical times. The poet is saying that even tax collectors, who were perceived as sinners, loved when they were loved.

64 A reference to God's destruction of Sodom. Lot and his family were rescued by divine intervention, but Lot's wife looked back at the mayhem and was turned into a pillar of salt. See Genesis 19:26. The word 'salt' can also mean 'excellence' or 'life': 'Ye are the salt of the earth…' Matthew 5:13. The poet is warning against turning away from a 'holy life'.

65 check = wince at.

66 reckon = are of the same value as …

67 'Behold he smote the rock, that the waters gushed out, and the streams overflowed' Psalm 78:20.

68 i.e. look for or desire.

Some care not for this Dove had they his feather;[69]
A sorry bargain such would make;
Over a while such shall have neither:
Seek thou the Spirits gifts for graces sake.

'Ware sinning, against light and grace, and love;
Know, ev'ry of those sins that are done
Directly against this dear Dove
Comes near to that that never shall have pardon.

If we live in the SPIRIT, *Let us walk in the* SPIRIT,
Gal. 5. 25.

69 feather = attributes.

Faith

From thee, dear Dove,
Yet still in thine embraces,
To Faith, Hope, Love
That Trinity of Graces
Now let me pass, and succour so my Verses
That I may express what my Muse rehearses.

Faith, I'll begin
With thee; for thou wast th' first,
When bloody sin
Had made me all accurst,
That shew'd th' avenger posting[1] after me,
And had me to some refuge-City flee.[2]

Some men would make
Faith and Repentance strive
Who should place take;[3]
But surely Faith's the hive
In which that busie Bee, repentance, makes
Tears drop like honey from mans heart like wax.[4]

For who can grieve
For that which they believe not?
Who can believe
Mans sinfull state, and grieve not?
I did believe the law, and so relented,
I did believe the Gospell, and repented.

I did believe
That God made all things good;

1 to post = to travel quickly.

2 Possibly a reference to Teate fleeing from Cavan to Dublin with his father after the family was attacked in the rising of 1641.

3 i.e. which should take priority, faith or repentance.

4 See Psalm 22:14.

And then did grieve
That I had brought a flood
A flood of sins, and so of miseries
On all: this brought a deluge on mine eyes.

I did believe
That God took flesh, lost blood
So to relieve
Me, and to drown sins flood:
Then girt like *Peter* did begin to swim
In a repentant Sea of tears to him.[5]

Repentance lowers[6]
Yet (like sad rainy daies)
Bring fruits and flow'rs
And floods to wash our waies,
Its Clouds bee'ng fill'd with what bright faith exhales,
But's dry as desperation, when faith failes.

Yet have I heard
That some repented not
That afterward
They might believe. This knot
Is soon untied: First Faith lends tears and grief
Unto repentance, then an handkerchief.

Thus Faith precedes
Repentance, yet comes after;
Followes, yet leads;
As Mother and as Daughter:
As the bright Sun the brackish[7] Sea doth round,
Encompassing Repentance, Faith is found.[8]

Faith, I would tell
Thy story if I could,

5 See Matthew 14:28–9.
6 i.e. lours = to look dark or threatening.
7 brackish = salty.
8 Just as the sun (with a pun on Christ the Son) goes round the earth and hence the sea, faith encircles repentance. The stanza also suggests the alchemical image of the square and the circle, the square symbolizing the mutable, corrupted earth which is perfected or purified by the divine circle or sun.

Where thou dost dwell,
Or what thou art, behold:
But thou art Faith which sense can no more reach
Than death Deity can praise, or preach.

I did ask at
Heav'ns gate for thee, dear grace,
But was told that
There vision held thy place:[9]
Then some infernal fiends said they could shew thee,
But took thee for no grace, for they did rue thee.

I lookt about
On earth to find thee there,
For there no doubt
Thou dwelt if any where;
And yet again th' unerring Scripture saith
When Christ shall come, shall he on Earth find Faith?[10]

Surely not much:
When he shall that day bring
Unto the touch[11]
Each one that wears a ring.[12]
All won't prove Gold that glisters, and is specious,
Nor feigned Faith be then approv'd as precious.

Oh! that I knew
Thee, precious Faith; and could
Thy reall hue,
Thy lustre but unfold,
I should soon draw all eyes from him that hath
Gold rings, to gaze on th' poor when rich in Faith.

Alas! most take
Thee for some pebble, they

9 i.e. in Heaven, faith is sustained by being able to actually see God.

10 See Luke 18:8.

11 i.e. touchstone = a stone rubbed against gold or silver in order to test its quality.

12 'For if there come into your assembly a man with a gold ring, in goodly apparel, and there come in also a poor man in vile raiment; And ye have respect to him that weareth the gay clothing … Are ye not then partial in yourselves, and are become judges of evil thoughts?' James 2:2–4.

Do nothing make
To believe any way;
Only those few that have thee, jealous are
Their Faith is not the right, the right's so rare.

Thou'rt a rich stock,
A Diadem brought forth
Only by th' rock
Of ages, of such worth
That who hath thee, although he hath no more
May well esteem the golden Indies poore.

By thee the just
May live, when wants surround:
And so he must
When other things abound.
Faith makes the conscience good, and that well drest
Is a continual food, a constant feast.

Of the household
Of Faith, I'm sure I've read,
And dare be bold[13]
They want no houshold-bread:
Faith daily sets on the believers board[14]
The Heav'nly bread of th' everliving word.

Others look by
Their trades to be maintain'd:
Why should not I
To be by faith sustain'd?
Thou art the calling: man but misapplies,
To other trades, the name of mysteries.

The mystery
Thou art, yet th' *Oedipus*[15]
That dost untye
All doubts and knots for us.
Nothing is hard to thee: where thou canst not
Unriddle, thou'st a sword to cut the knot.

13 i.e. I am bold enough to say … 14 board = table.

15 Oedipus was the ancient king of Thebes who solved the riddle of the Sphinx. Faith allows man to 'untye all doubts' just as Oedipus untied the riddle.

How blind were man
But for thy piercing eye?
Who nothing can,
No, not himself, descrie.
Thy clue[16] guides through both Labyrinth-like waies
Of mine own heart, and through the Scriptures maze.[17]

I should be set
And pos'd at first and last
Ith' Alphabet,[18]
But that, dear Faith, thou hast
Taught me to know my letters. Who but thou
Could make me th' *Alpha* and *Omega*[19] know!

Or to know him
Aright? alas! my sight
Were dark and dim
But for thine eyes, thy light
Who seest him that is invisible.
What flesh and blood perceives not thou see'st well.

Pray'r 's a blind beggar,
If it do want but thee:
It may be eager,
But right it cannot bee.
Hope were an hopeless thing, but that thou dost
Allow it spend upon thy proper cost.

Faith makes pray'r know
Where t' have its Ammunition,
And teacheth how
To levell each petition
Of clam'rous sin; quick prayer, by Faith, gains cope,[20]
And brings salvations tidings back to hope.

16 clue = a ball of string (such as one used to guide oneself out of a maze).

17 Cf. Francis Quarles, *Emblemes* (London, 1635), IV. II, lines 19–29.

18 to set = to put before a person a specimen of work (such as the alphabet) to be followed or copied; posed = to be puzzled or perplexed. The sense seems to be that Teate would still be copying and puzzling over his alphabet if Faith had not taught him to 'know' his 'letters' (i.e. Scripture).

19 Alpha and Omega are the first and the last letters of the Greek alphabet. God is called 'Alpha and Omega' in Revelation 1:8.

20 Prayer is able to 'gain cope', i.e. overcome sin, with the help of faith.

In pilgrimage,
I went to Calvery,[21]
That bitter stage
Where my dear Lord did dye;
Where missing him, I cri'd out, where is he?
Faith whisper'd to me, go along with me.

Faith brought me to
A door, but it was lockt:
Faith bad me go
And knock, and so I knockt:
Then th' door flew open, and a Lamb did stand
Cry'ng, take both fleece and flesh.[22] But I h'd no hand.

But as my moan
I made with tears and grief,
Faith lent me one,
So I took the relief:
Which having got I found that this believing
Both gives me Christ, and is of Christs own giving.

But as I thought
To h've carri'd home this gift,
A Cross was brought
Which I was bad[23] to lift
Or leave the rest; I try'd but could not bear it:
Said Faith, I'll lend thee shoulders, do not fear it.

With much ado
I got this blessed pack,
Christ and's Cross too
By Faith upon my back:
But could not go nor stand, till Faith did meet
Me just a sinking with a pair of feet.

Faith hav'ng new vampt
My soul, I then could walk.

21 Calvary was the scene of Christ's crucifixion. See Mark 15:22.

22 The Lamb represents Christ who pleads with the poet to accept him, i.e. 'take both fleece and flesh' and be saved.

23 i.e. bade.

Reason's sin-crampt;
And 'tis but idle talk
To speak of marching in its strength and might
Till Faith lends reason legs and sets it right.

We stand by Faith
Saith *Paul*,[24] we stand by reason.
Whoever saith
I doubt me, doth speak treason.
They shew their reason best that daily beg,
Lord give us Faith, reason's a wooden leg.

Faith makes me see
What reason's asking still,
How can it be?
Let him take heed that will
Believe no more than he finds reason for
Lest he find reason to believe no more.

When Faith as Queen
Makes reason wait upon her,
Reason's then seen
Look like a maid of honour:
But let that saucy Courtier 'ware his head
That crowds the Queen into the truckle-bed.[25]

In a few miles
March, betwixt this and Heaven,
I found some stiles,
Not few'r than six or seaven
That reason stumbling at; Faith, help me over,
Said I, till poor Lame reason shall recover.

No sooner said
I so, but Faith did lift,
Ev'n as I pray'd,

24 See 2 Corinthians 1:24.

25 truckle bed = a low bed, usually set on castors, that can be pushed under a high or standing bed. To sleep in a 'truckle bed' is a seventeenth-century idiom meaning to occupy a low position (*OED* truckle v. 2). Faith, the 'queen' should not be made defer to her courtier 'reason'.

Me over with my gift;
Which done, I fell aboard[26] that sacred flesh
That so I might my fainting soul refresh.

Bee'ng cold and thin,
The fleece I had receiv'd
I went to spin
And weave; but as I weav'd
An enemy did cast a fiery dart,
Which but for th' shield of Faith had kild my heart.

Where hadst that fleece[27]
Said Satan, thievish sinner,
Of righteousness
That thou'rt become a spinner?
I answer'd, false accuser, not by thieving,
Had I my Righteousness, but by believing.

Believing? what
Doth thou, poor foolish wretch
Tell me of that?
Said Satan, go and fetch
Gods Law Book, and thy Conscience Book, and say
If thou canst stand as righteous any way.

Malicious foe
Said I, cease troubling me,
Or else lets go
To suit ith' Chancery.[28]
Gods Common-Law admits of mine appeales
To th' Law of Faith that Righteousness reveales.

But equity
Requires thy debts be paid;
Said he; said I,
And satisfaction's made
By one that left his Cross, when he was slain,
That I therewith might thee, foul serpent! brain.

26 i.e. started to eat. 27 i.e. Where did you get that fleece?
28 i.e. let us settle our dispute in the law courts.

Then Satan flew,
Quitting the field. Anon
A numerous crew,
A WORLD it was, came on.
Thronging so thick and threefold in upon me,
That, had not Faith prest in, they had undone me.

Earth shew'd her strength,
Her treasures, pleasures, pride:
Giddy, at length,
Poor I began to slide,
Hold, man! said Faith, thou hast a staff by thee;
Christs Cross can help thee stand, and force these flee.

But in this broil
Ere I the Cross could use,
I had a foil,[29]
And got an inward bruise;
Conscience spat blood, pain pierc'd and wrung my side,
Till Faith some better blood, like balm, applied.

Faith also bad[30]
A vein should op'ned be,
Urging I had
Much putrid blood in me:[31]
Content, said I, for I had heard oth' art
Of saving Faith[32] to purifie the heart.

But lest I should
In bleeding faint, Faith took
Some Cordialls roll'd
In Bible leaves, a Book
Whose ev'ry leafe, said Faith, rich drugs conteins
As I compound them, sov'raign[33] for heart-pains.

29 foil = a wound from a sword. 30 i.e. bade.

31 According to Galenic medicine the body was controlled by four humours: blood, phlegm, black bile and yellow bile. Illness was thought to be caused by an imbalance in the humours, which could be corrected by bleeding the patient.

32 saving faith = faith which delivers from sin and death by God's grace.

33 i.e. efficacious.

Alas! said I,
Many those drugs have got,
But to decry,[34]
Finding they profit not;
But strait remembered what the Scripture saith
Th' word did not profit be'ng unmix'd with Faith.[35]

O pow'rfull Faith!
Whose ev'ry smallest grain,
Is sound, who hath
May say, and not in vain,
Mountains of guilt that here so long have stood
Get hence into the Sea of Saviours blood.

This skilfull grace
Did first Phlebotomize,[36]
Then wash the place,
And after wipe mine eyes.
Dear Faith! said I, I see that thou dost mean
Not only for to make me whole but clean.

As soon as I
Was cur'd of this my pain,
Impetuously
The world comes on again.
I took Faith's Cross, and found what Scripture saith
Our victory over the world's our Faith.[37]

Vain world be gone
Said I, vex me no more,
Vexation
And vanity's thy store.
This *Jacobs* ladder[38] helps me to discrye
A surer sweeter world beyond the skye.

34 decry = to disparage or denounce. Many doubt the healing power of Scripture.
35 See Galatians 3:2.
36 Phlebotomize = the practice of opening up a vein to withdraw or introduce fluid. Faith has drawn out the poet's sin and made him 'clean'.
37 See 1 Corinthians 15:55.
38 A reference to the Old Testament prophet Jacob who dreamt of a ladder reaching up to Heaven with 'God's messengers' going up and down. See Genesis 2:12–16.

By this dear Cross
My dearest Lord did climb;
I'll count thee loss
That I may follow him.
His and my Kingdom's not ith' worlds enjoyment,
If 'twere, who knows where it would be next moment?

World thou must be
Set one day all on fire,
Witchcraft in thee,
And blood deserve this hire.[39]
Then shall my dust[40] see by thy bright fire-light
To rise that morning that shall ne're have night.[41]

We do but jest,
Great *Alexanders* story[42]
Is best exprest
When we say this worlds glory
Vanquish'd that seeming victor; sure I am
Nothing but Faith this world ere overcame.

When I begin
To fight, and want supplies,
Faith summons in
Heavens Auxiliaries;[43]
And stores with precious promises that are
The very sinews of that holy war.

And more than this
Brings in rare commander,
Jesus it is,
Not *Mars*,[44] or *Alexander*.

39 hire = punishment.

40 i.e. my mortal body.

41 i.e the final day of the world.

42 A reference to Alexander the Great (356–323 BCE), king of Macedon, who conquered the Persian Empire leading to the spread of Greek culture and language in the Mediterranean region. He is described thus in 1 Maccabees 1:3: '[He] went through to the ends of the earth, and took spoils of many nations, insomuch that the earth was quiet before him; whereupon he was exalted, and his heart was lifted up.'

43 i.e. Heaven's soldiers, the angels.

44 Mars = the Roman god of war.

But he that taught all fingers fight,[45] can quell
All foes, ev'n Christ ith' heart, by faith, doth dwell.[46]

Jerusalem
Above, that City is
Where *Davids* stem[47]
Raigns and remains in bliss
Yet 'tis his royall pleasure here in us
To dwell by Faith as in his Country-house.

Faith makes mans heart
That dark, low, ruin'd thing,
By its rare art,
A pallace for a King;
High'r then proud *Babels* tow'r[48] by many a story,
By faith Christ dwels in us the hope of Glory.

Thus Faith doth raise
Out of vile dust a Court,
Imputing praise,
Honour, and good report.
Hearts, *Rahab*-like,[49] when once they entertain
Heav'ns spies, by Faith, a good report do gain.

If thou believe,
All things are possible:
Faith can relieve
Ev'n to a miracle:
This Faith can wash an *Æthiopian* clean,
Witness the Eunuch of *Candace* the Queen.[50]

45 See Psalm 144:1. Also, cf. Dr Teate, Preface to *Nathanael, or an Israelite indeed* (London, 1657): 'our Preaching was to animate the soldiers Courageously to prosecute so just a warre against such unparalleled murtherers; and our Prayers were, that the righteous God would teach their fingers to fight …'

46 i.e. Christ can only live in your heart if you have faith.

47 i.e. Christ, a descendent of David. See note to line 402.

48 The Babylonians tried to build a lofty tower, the tower of Babel, and were punished for their arrogance by the imposition of different languages. See Genesis 2:1–9.

49 Rahab was a prostitute who lived in Jericho and who helped Israeli spies escape their pursuers. As a reward she was spared when the city was sacked. See Joshua 2.

50 The evangelist Philip baptized a eunuch who was an official in the court of Candace, queen of Ethiopia. See Acts 8:26–40.

And as Faith makes
Us Courts, so Courtiers too:
God pleasure takes
In us when all we do
Is done in Faith; then reck'ning that he hath
Most glory by us, when most strong in Faith.

And as by this
Our service proves his pleasure,
Ev'n so doth his
Hereby become our treasure:
One day in Gods Court Faith doth far prefer
Before a thousand any other where.[51]

'Tis unbelief
Ith' evill, evill heart,
His and my grief,
That makes us ever part:
That Blessed Man whose feet this Faith hath shod,
With, *Noah* and *Enoch*[52] still can walk with God.

By Faith who strives
To walk with God whilst here
Doth live two lives
At once each day oth' year:
And dying *Joseph* like commands his bones
To *Canaan* there to dwell with living ones.[53]

Dear Faith, said I,
My joy, my crown, my treasure!
Tell me whereby
I may do thee a pleasure.
Thou art that lock[54] in which my strength doth lye,
Thee not to tender[55] were self-cruelty.

51 See Psalm 84:10.

52 Enoch was an Old Testament hero who walked with God and was taken straight to Heaven whilst still alive. See Genesis 5:24. Noah was his descendent.

53 When the Old Testament prophet Joseph died in Egypt he requested that his bones be buried in Canaan, the 'Promised Land'. See Genesis 50:25.

54 i.e. lock of hair. A reference to the story of Samson. See Judges 16.

55 tender = care for.

If thou wouldst please
Me better, work me more;
Said Faith, 'tis ease
Only that makes me poore.
But I do use to bid my workmen eat;
Said I, dear Faith inform me what's thy meat.

Said Faith, I came[56]
Out of the eastern lands,
Old *Abraham*[57]
And I have oft shook hands:
My food's an *Hebrew* root that Gardners dresse
On Lords Dayes mostly, call'd the *root of Jesse*.[58]

By hearing I
Came first; and we are fed
Most kindly by
The things whereof we're bred.
Forget not, if you love me, the Church path:
Line upon Line's the way from Faith to Faith.[59]

The carefull foot,
That walks by Scripture LEAVES,
Shall find this ROOT,
Which happy who receives;
So nutritive, Antidotive and good,
Who feeds on it, needs scarce fear any food.

Make but my bread
Of this root when I Sup,
Let th' Dragons head
Be then broke and serv'd up:[60]

56 The voice of 'Faith' now takes over the poetic narrative in order to tell the poet how faith in God is maintained.

57 Abraham, the first patriarch of Israel, was renowned for his faith in God which he proved by being prepared to sacrifice his son Isaac when asked by God. See Genesis 22:1–12.

58 Jesse, who was the father of David, was known as a successful farmer. The descendents of Jesse, David and by extension Christ are called the 'root of Jesse' in Isaiah 11:10.

59 'But the word of the Lord was unto them … line upon line, line upon line, here a little, and there a little; that they might go, and fall backward, and be broken, and snared, and taken.' Isaiah 28:13.

60 'Thou brakest the heads of leviathan in pieces, and gavest him to be meat to the people inhabiting the wilderness.' Psalm 74:14.

Yet Toad stools,[61] one would think, need be well drest
Ere they will make a good dish for a feast.

Art I did gain
Sometime, and that by book,
The Tempters brain
To wholesomeness to cook.[62]
Only have care as ever thou dost mean
To keep me long in health to lodg me clean.[63]

Good conscience is
An old comrade of mine,
Whom I cant miss,
If thou wouldst make me thine,
And keep me, thou must keep him too; that day
Thou partst with him, look I[64] should pack away.

Self confidence,[65]
My nat'rall enemy,
Must be packt hence.
An hand, a foot, an eye[66]
Who hath of's own, will scorn to be my debtour:
Who parts with these, works, walks and sees the better.

Prove that thou art
A Pilgrim; daily dye:
Of death get th' start[67]
And live eternally.
I that in *Abrah'ms* heart dwelt many a day,
To *Abrah'ms* bosom[68] now shew thee the way.

Fear alwaies, Yet
Faint never: Eye the cloud

61 toadstool = a poisonous mushroom.

62 A reference to alchemy wherein base metals were 'cooked' into 'wholesomeness' i.e. gold. Faith is able to 'cook' the 'Tempters brain' (i.e. Satan) into 'wholesomeness' with the aid of its 'book' (i.e. the Bible).

63 lodg = lay to rest. Faith wishes to be kept 'long in health' so that it, and by extension the poet, will be 'clean' (i.e. free of sin) on death.

64 i.e. it looks as if I …

65 i.e. pride.

66 See Matthew 18:8–9.

67 i.e. defeat death.

68 i.e. Heaven. See Luke 16:22.

That doth beset
Thee, that triumphant Croud;[69]
Look unto Jesus: watch th' word of command,
Which, when thou hast done all these things, is STAND.[70]

By Grace ye are saved, through Faith, Eph. 2. 8.

69 i.e. crowd. 70 See 2 Corinthians 1:24.

Hope

Drive on, my Muse, till thou'rt got through:
Let not Hope find thee in a slough:
Let that that drives the Farmers plough,
Drive thine much more.
To th'Hope of *Isr'el* let me yet
In hope my running rhyme commit,
And humbly say, God prosper it;
Or 'twill be poor.

Hope is a door, the Scripture saith;
And so is Christ, and so is Faith;
Who're out of these doors are in wrath
And Condemnation.
Faith into Christ doth first advent're:
Christ into Hope allows me enter:
Hope makes my very Soul to center
On Gods Salvation.

Hope is Faiths expectation:
Faith is the *Moses*, Hope's the stone[1]
That Faith in Pray'r doth rest upon
Till't overcome.
Faith doth upon Hopes tip toe stand
Stretching its neck to look for land
Beyond deaths gulf; and life beyond
The day of doom.

Hope is next door to Heav'ns gate;
'Tis but a step from this to that:
Nay Hope doth Heaven antedate,
And bring down hither.

1 'And he gave unto Moses … two tables of testimony, tables of stone, written with the finger of God.' Exodus 31:18.

Hope's th'antidote against despair;
Coffin of fear; and Couch of care;
Cradle of patience: Hope hath fair[2]
Even in foul weather.

Hope is the mourners Handkerchief:
Hope is the Balme of ev'ry grief.
Hope doth endorse the beggars brief
Ere it's collected.
In Hope I have, what yet I want:
Hope makes me full, while things are scant:
Hope doth consummate, what I can't
Yet see effected.

Hope hath an harvest in the Spring:
In winter doth of Summer sing:
Feeds on the fruits whilst blossoming,
Yet nips no bloom.
Hope brings me home when I'm abroad,
As soon as th'first step homeward's trod:
In Hope to thee, my God! my God!
I come, I come.

Hope sends the Ship to Sea, and then
E're it returns, brings't home agen:
The port of all Seafaring men
Is this GOOD HOPE.
I am a Sea-man too. My Soul,
Though toss'd with doubts when weather's foul,
Doth like some Sea-sick Vessell roul;[3]
Yet Heav'n's its scope.[4]

Hope doth the Souldiers weapon wield:
By Hope the Souldiers Helmet's steel'd:
Hope gives him, ere he fights, the field:
Hope holds his station.[5]
I am a Souldier too. My Sword,
Is that o'th'Spirit, th'two-edg'd word;[6]

2 i.e. is likely to succeed. 3 i.e. roll. 4 scope = destination.

5 i.e. helps him stay in his position.

6 'For the word of God is quick, and powerful, and sharper than any two-edged sword.' Hebrews 4:12.

Now for an Helmet give me, Lord,
Th' Hope of Salvation.

Hope sets the poor Apprentice free
First day he's bound. And why not me?
Thou hast Indentures[7] Lord by thee
Wherein I'm tied.
Mount *Sinais* Covenants they bee
Yet hope doth, Lord, Enfranchize mee
In *Sion*-hill, where all are free
That do reside.

In Hope the School-Boy doth commence
Master of Art, and fair science:
Yea whilst i'th'lowest form, steps thence
To th'Doctors Chair.
I'm a School-Schollar too, My God!
But yesterday I felt thy rod:
Yet still with Hope am girt and shod.
Away, despair.

'Tis hope that doth the sower feed;
Who seems to cast away his seed,
But doth preserve in very deed
And mend his store.
I am a Seeds-man too, my Lord!
And but for Hope thou would'st affoard
Thy blessing, when I sow thy word,
I had forbore.[8]

I am a Seeds man; every teare
I sow in Hope, 'twill bring an eare
Fit for thy floor in time of yeare
For thee to gather.
Were't not for Hope the heart, some say,
Would break; yet Hope led me one day
Weeping along the Milkie way
To thee, O Father!

7 The contract by which an apprentice is bound to his master.
8 i.e. not have done it.

I am a Seeds man casting bread
On th'waters[9] where it seems lye dead;
Yet Hope assures me't shall be fed,
And then restor'd.
Hope doth the pris'ners bolts unlock:
His fetters doth in sunder knock:
Hope drives the Freeman's trade and stock.
My dearest Lord!

I am a captive too. Sins chain
Doth hold and hamper, but in vain:
By Hope I'm saved, and set again
At liberty.
I am a Tradesman too. Thou art
That God with whom I deal. My heart
Takes Heav'n to be the only mart
Thither trade I;

Exporting groans and broken pray'rs
That scarse can clamber up the stairs.
Importing rich and precious wares,
Ev'n joy and peace.
Joy that exceeds all understanding
Oth' Spirits sealing, Christ's own handing:
Peace that is of Gods own commanding,
And can't surcease.[10]

Hope makes the labourer to run
A race as 'twere with each daies Sun[11]
Paying his wages ere's work be done,
And mine much more.
I daily dig and delve within
Stubbing at th' roots and stumps of sin
And but for Hope one day to win
I should give ore.

O come that long'd for day! come quickly!
This Hope defer'd makes my heart sickly.

9 'Cast thy bread upon the waters: for thou shalt find it after many days.' Ecclesiastes 11:1.
10 i.e. come to an end.
11 Cf. Donne, 'The Sun Rising', line 4.

Grace is a Rose, but sin is prickly
And still adheres.
Amphibion like the Diver tries,
Whet sharp with Hope, t'anatomize
And geld the deeps:[12] his hop'd for prize[13]
Forbids his feares.

I am a diver too. Thy word
Doth richer rarities affoard:
A greater deep, and better stor'd
With Pearls and treasure;[14]
Angels desire to dive into
These deeps; and so I daily do:
Whose Pearls are rich and Cordiall too;
Health, Wealth, and Pleasure.

'Tis Hope that makes the racer fleet,[15]
Bringing the wager to his feet,
Make haste, saith Hope, what? don't you see't?
You've won, you've won.
I am a racer too. My race
From sin to glory is by grace;
Hope sets Heav'ns Bliss before my face,
And then I run.

I heard the witty world once say,
The bird ith' bush may flie away:
Take Heav'n who will, 'tis present pay
For which we trade.
To Faith and Hope I told this story;
Their havings are but transitory,
Said Faith: said Hope, and I have glory
That cannot fade.[16]

Hast it? said I; Hope, shew it me.
What's this, said Hope, thou here dost see?

12 Amphibion seems to be an invented name for a pearl diver. whet = sharpened; anatomize = investigate closely; geld = take the value from.

13 i.e. pearls.

14 See Matthew 13:45–6.

15 fleet = fast.

16 i.e. 'Their havings (possessions) are but transitory,' said Faith; said Hope, 'And I have Glory that cannot fade.'

Said I, an Acorn: No, said he
But 'tis an Oake.
What is't, said Hope, thou see'st fast by?
A grain of Mustard-seed,[17] said I.
A plant, said Hope, reaching the sky;
And thou'dst right spoke.

Then I perceiv'd the meaning was
Hope ripens seeds of Grace to Grace:
Makes Grace, when grounded, Mount and pass
To th' highest story.
Hope shew'd me then a sparkling stone
What's this, said Hope, that I've got on?
I strait reply'd, tis Grace begun.
Said Hope, 'tis Glory.

Then learnt I that Grace inchoate,
By lively Hope doth maturate:
And rip'ning, doth anticipate
Heav'n here on Earth.
I spake to Hope of a reversion[18]
I had in Heaven since conversion:
Said Hope, why cast you an aspersion
On th' second birth?

Reversion sounds, said Hope, to mee
Your state at present dead to bee;
But I have Heav'n in hand, you see,
Whereon I live.
I am Faiths present recompence:
My Grammar knows no Future tense:
The Verbs that make up all my sense
Are Substantive.[19]

Who're these, said Hope, thou see'st before,
Prostrate and begging at a door.
Said I, they are Heav'ns Parish Poor:

17 See Matthew 13:31–2.
18 reversion = a return to an old way of thinking. Here it seems to mean a temporary loss of faith on the poet's part.
19 Substantive = the verb 'to be', i.e. hope lives in the present moment.

Said Hope, they're Kings.
Kings? said I. But where are their Crowns?
Their Scepters, Kingdomes, Countries, Towns?
Their Ermine Robes, and Purple-Gowns,
Those royall things?

I can, said Hope, tell where they bee:
Safely they are reserv'd by mee,
Safely reserv'd from them and thee:
Look here are they.
All's lockt. Hope, lend's the Key, said I.
Hope fetcht a Bible presently,[20]
On which when I h'd but cast mine eye
I found a Key.

The right key 'twas oth' door of Hope;
Enter, said Faith, thou needst not grope:
I turn'd the key, and th' door flew ope,
And I went on.
But O the things that there I saw!
Jewels of joyes, in foiles of awe!
But blab not, Muse. Know'st not the Law?
Peace, and have done.

'Tis not allow'd thee to display
The brightness of Hopes holy day.
Unutterable things to say;
Muse, do not vent're;
Hope shew'd me, but I can't say what.
Only let him that questions that,
But get the key, that then I gat,[21]
And let him enter.

Then let him say, If ever he
The like things unto those, did see:
Or yet can utter what they bee
That there he saw.
This only can I say, that there
Crowns, Scepters, all enameld were

20 i.e. immediately. 21 i.e. got.

With Grace and Peace, with Faith and Fear,
With Love and Awe.

True Hope though pleasant, yet is gracious:
Not light, though lightsome: Not audacious,
Though bold: though joyous, not salacious:
Merry, not vain.[22]
Hope can rejoyce, but never rant:
Alwaies feeds high, but revell can't:
Chast Scripture comforts that provant
Doth Hope sustain.

The word whereon I hope, doth urge
Pureness: the fire wherein I forge
The Anchor of mine Hope, doth purge
My dross, my tin.
That Hope makes not asham'd, but sure
The bottom's rock, and shall endure;
That makes me strive, as God is pure,
To purge my sin.

True Hope's a *Jacobs* staff[23] indeed:
True Hope is no *Egyptian* reed,[24]
That springs from mire, or else can feed
On dirt, or mud.
By Hope just men and sanctified
I'th' Ocean safe at Anchor ride,[25]
Fearless of wrack by wind or tide,
By ebb or flood.

Hope's the top window of that ark
Where all Gods *Noahs* do imbark:
Hope lets in skie-light, else how dark
Were such a season?
But wouldst not be engulf'd, or drown'd

22 See 1 Corinthians 13.

23 Jacob crossed the river Jordan to escape from his brother Esau using his staff (Genesis 32:10) which is evoked here as a symbol of courage and righteousness.

24 According to David, a staff made of 'Egyptian reed' would break and pierce your hand if you tried to lean on it. See 2 Kings 18:21.

25 'Which hope we have as an anchor of the soul, both sure and steadfast …' Hebrews 6:19.

When storms and tempests gather round,
Ere thou canst Anchor, try the ground:
Hope must have reason.

Hopes Anchor-hold cannot be good
Where th' bottom's all or only mud.
Shall th' Sinner in his Native blood
To Hope pretend?
Or th' Hypocrite strengthen his mast,
(Who boldly doth Hopes Anchor cast
On's sandy bottom) when at last
Heav'ns storms descend?

'Ware Cob-web Hopes, when God shall come
With's besome[26] of impartiall doom
To sweep mans heart, that inner room;
Shall they stand sure?
Oft have I seen a branch in spring
Rent[27] from the root, yet blossoming,
As 'twere some Hopefull growing thing.
But can't endure.

He that is at the pains and cost
To plant and water it, next frost
Is like to see his labour lost,
And hope to perish;
Surely 'twill pose all skill and art
But onley his, that can convert
This *lively Hope* in a *dead Heart*
To plant and cherish.

And where there's but a name to live,
Though for a season Hope seems thrive,[28]
When such give up the *Ghost* they give
Their *Hopes* up too.
Good Hopes through Grace. And whosoever
Part Righteousness from Hope endeavour

26 Besom = a broom made of twigs tied round a stick. See Isaiah 14:23.
27 i.e. torn. 28 i.e. to thrive.

The Helmet from the Brestplate sever,[29]
Which who would do?

But let what waters will assaile,
The Hope oth' righteous cannot faile,
Whose Anchor's cast within the vaile
Till th' flood asswages.
His Hope's no Lott'ry, hit or miss;
But an Inheritance it is:
Christ is in him the Hope of Bliss,
That rock of ages.

Mine eyes are unto *Sion*-hill[30]
Longing in Hope, yet waiting still
For he that shall, will come, and will
Not alwayes linger.
Therefore in Hope will I rejoyce,
Yea, when the floods lift up their voice;
When Seas shall roare, to drown their noise,[31]
I'll turn a singer.

I'll turn a singer, and my song
Shall be by book,[32] lest I go wrong:
For I h've not skill'd of musick long,
Or holy mirth.
Weeping into the world I came,
Bringing a world of sin and shame:
Bearing the first Apostates blame
Ev'n at my birth.

The fruit old *Adam* and his *Eve*
Did so long since together thieve,
Wringing my mother[33] made us grieve

29 'But let us, who are of the day, be sober, putting on the breastplate of faith and love; and for an helmet, the hope of salvation.' 1 Thessalonians 5:8.

30 'Yet I have set my king upon the holy hill of Zion.' Psalm 2:6.

31 See Psalm 98:7–8.

32 i.e. the poet shall live in conformity with Scripture.

33 Labour pains were said to have been a punishment for Adam and Eve's original sin. 'Behold, I was shapen in iniquity; and in sin did my mother conceive me.' Psalms 51. 5.

And groan together:
And as I thus did weeping come
Out of one grave, I mean the womb:
My face was tow'rds a deader Tomb
And I bound thither.

My life was but a Bondage through
The fear of death, that fatall slough.
But lively Hope forbids me now
All slavish fears.
Oft I have been contemplating
Of death that melancholick thing;
Weeping, till Hope hath made me sing,
Drying my tears.

Author and rock of all my Hope,
That hast deaths prison doors broke ope,
So fastning to Faiths Cable-rope
Hopes anchor strong.[34]
What though I sail through foaming Seas?
Billows are Pillows,[35] Beds of ease:
Deaths blast rocks me asleep in these:
Waiting ere long

At thy shrill suddain voice to rise,
And rub deaths dust out of my mine eyes
When death shall have disgorg'd its prize
Safe on the shore.
Then hold my rudder in thine hand
Who put to Sea at thy command
Till I may make some new-found land
Oh! help me ore.

I need not want an anchor, Lord,
With wood and iron, bee'ng so stor'd,
With what thy Cross and Nailes affoard[36]

34 'Which hope we have as an anchor of the soul, both sure and steadfast …' Hebrews 6:19.

35 Billows = large waves.

36 The image of Christ nailed to an anchor is found in Donne's 'In Sacram Anchoram Piscatoris'.

Had I but skill.
Anchors, I see, by th' Forgers art,
Have both a strait[37] and bending part:
Hope strengthens, yet it bows the heart
To wait Gods Will.

The Scripture saith, that tribulation
(And 'tis a strange Concatenation)
Works patience;[38] as if vexation
Did make more quiet;
And Patience works Experience:
Experience, Hope: Yet Patience,
I'm sure, doth live on Hopes expense
For daily diet.

Thus have I seen the Grand-Childs purse
For the Grand-Siers support disburse;
Thus Hope doth Patience feed and nurse;
Patience again
Doth tutor Hope, and teach it know
All points of Heavenly Courtship; How
To wait on God, to bend, to bow,
To bear his train:

To follow him in all his wayes,
And so to hold e'en all its dayes,
Seeking that honour, glory, praise
That God shall give.
Patience of Hope makes Heaven smile
To see the troden[39] Camomile,
Whilst underfoot, spring up the while
And the more thrive.

When death comes with his leaden foot,
Hoping to crush mine hope ith' root,
The utmost hurt that death can do't
Is but to make
Mine Hope grow up into fruition;

37 i.e. straight.

38 'Rejoicing in hope; patient in tribulation; continuing instant in prayer …' Romans 12:12.

39 i.e. trodden.

Whilest Faith's translated into vision,
Mending thereby my souls condition,
Doubling my stake.

What though mine Haven, Heaven lye
Beyond the dead Sea? what though I
Decease? mine Hope shall never dye,
Never decay.
What though I walk through th' vale of tears?
Hope is a staff that ever bears:[40]
Hope is a rod chasing my fears
Guiding my way.[41]

What though revengefull Papists burne
Dear *Bucers*[42] bones, still Hope's his urne
Till's ashes to a Phoenix turne
And live afresh.
What though deaths scorching flames presume
To turn my moisture to dry fume?
My soul shall one day reassume
Calcined flesh.[43]

Therefore my dying tongue shall sing:
Yea ev'n my flesh, that fading thing,
Shall rest in Hope for that day-spring
All th' night of death.
And when I lay my weary head
And bones ith' grave as in a bed,
Let not the mourner say he's dead,
But slumbereth.

40 i.e. bears me up.

41 'Yea, though I walk through the valley of the shadow of death, I will fear no evil: for thou art with me; thy rod and thy staff they comfort me.' Psalm 23:4.

42 A reference to Martin Bucer (1491–1551) a German Protestant reformer who refused to negotiate with the Roman Catholic church over his theological beliefs regarding the nature of the Eucharist. He died and was buried in Cambridge where Queen Mary ordered his bones to be dug up and burned in the market place as a symbolic punishment for his heresy. When Elizabeth came to the throne she commanded that the dust from the spot where his bones had been burned be placed in an urn, and buried beneath a monument in Great St Mary's church.

43 Teate is espousing the belief that the soul sleeps until Judgement Day, and then returns to its body in the grave before ascending to Heaven. Cf. Donne, Holy Sonnet 'At the round earth's imagined corners, blow'.

Yet bonie death sometimes looks in
Bringing a list of all my sin,
Pinching mine Hope, till it looks thin
And's like to dye:
Death in my very face doth stare
So gastly, as if't meant to scare
And fright mine Hope into despaire,
While sin stands by.

Ah Conscience! Conscience! when I look
Into thy Register, thy Book,
What corner of my heart, what nook
Stands clear of sin?
And though my skin feels soft and sleek,
Scarce can I touch my chin and cheek,
But I can feel deaths jaw bone prick
Ev'n through my skin.

Yet why art thus cast down, my soul?[44]
Hope still in God, and on him roule.[45]
If Heaven smile, what though death scoule,[46]
And Conscience loure.[47]
A Book of my dear Christs I have
By which I look[48] my God will save
My soul from sin, my flesh from grave,
And from deaths pow'r.

O death, where is thy victory?[49]
That I might live, my Lord did dye;
He fled thee not, but made thee flie,
Hav'ng drawn thy sting.
Thou hadst of teeth a double row,
Till Christ by's Cross took thee a blow
When fastning on him. But thou'rt now
A tooth-less thing.

44 See Psalm 42:5. 45 roule = to meditate upon (*OED* roll v2 6 b).

46 i.e. scowl.

47 lour = to look angry or sullen. If Heaven imparts grace, it does not matter that the poet's conscience is troubled.

48 i.e. hope.

49 'O death, where is thy sting? O grave, where is thy victory?' 1 Corinthians 15:55.

Well maist thou bark, but canst not bite,
Bending thy brow, shewing thy spight:
Death do thy worst: Hope sets me quite
Beyond thy spleen.
What though my death seems written in
The very parchment of my skin
With the black ink of my foul sin;
Yet have I seen

On both hands of a friend once slain,[50]
But since return'd to life again,
A better story Printed plain,
My sights but dim;
Yet in the print oth' nailes I see
Life in a Savours hands for mee,
Whilst as he hung upon the tree,
Hope hangs on him.

And still shall hang on him untill
My bones have learnt to climbe that hill
Where now he sits, and whence he will
Yet come down hither,
That he may gather into one
Each dust of his, and scatt'red bone;
Then shall he, as a living stone
Translate[51] me thither.

And now, my Lord, what wait I for,
Standing, and knocking at thy door?
I stand and knock at th' door of Hope
Till knocking makes the door stand ope.

We are saved by HOPE, *but Hope that is seen, is not Hope*, Rom. 8. 24.

50 i.e. Christ. 51 i.e. transport.

Love

From Faith and Hope I come *sweet Love* to sing,
For ev'ry Anchor hath its ring
Whereby 'tis wedded to its Cable-Rope.
Love makes the match 'twixt Faith and Hope.

'Twixt Grace and Grace no marriage can be made
But where this golden ring's first had.
O golden Love, thou circling, endless thing!
All grace concenters in thy ring.

What though mine heart be flinty rock and stone?
Yet flints have fire: And have I none?
No spark of Love, thou god of Love! for thee
That hast twice over hammerd mee?[1]

There's not one spark kindled upon thine hearth
But at first glance it quits the earth,[2]
As if it knew the element of fire
Were some Diviner thing and high'r.

Lord, I can feel there's such a thing as Love
Warm in my breast, and feel it move;
I find I love my Child, and so doth he:
And shall I not, my God! love thee?

Is Love the only fire that doth descend?
Or is my God, my God, no friend?
Sure all my doubts and fears cannot disprove
The condescention of thy Love.

1 'And Moses lifted up his hand, and with his rod he smote the rock twice: and the water came out abundantly and the congregation drank.' Numbers 20:11.

2 'Yet man is born into trouble, as the sparks fly upward.' Job 5:7.

The Elements, we find, invert their course,
Fearing a *Vacuum* would be worse:[3]
And did not Love stoop low, when God did dye
To fill up mans vacuity?
Reader! stop here,
And drop a tear!

When Love that, ev'ry Ev'ning, makes my bed
Had not whereon to lay his head,
Except you'l call that bloody Cross and bitter
A Love-sick Saviours bed and litter.

When Love it self being as rich as store
To make me rich did become poor:[4]
Unless those tears and bloody drops that fall,
You'll Pearls account and rubies call.

And can the flaming Element of Love
To store my wants drop from above?
Why can't mine Earth as well to Heaven grow,
As Heav'ns Love-fire come down so low?

Why may I not, *Elijah*-like, aspire
To ride to Heaven in that fire,[5]
That fire of Love that came from thence down hither,
On purpose sure to help me thither.

When Love to hatred did himself expose,
And prick's own foot to ease his foes,
Printing full proof in his chapt, parched skin,
What flames of Love there were within.

When Love unthought, unsought for, did come down
Exchanging, for a Cross, his Crown,
Love undesir'd, Love undeserv'd did take
Mans game to play to save mans stake.

3 The poet is suggesting that God's love is the only kind of 'fire' to travel downwards (from Heaven to Earth). God's love will 'stoop low' to grant salvation to man.

4 Cf. Herbert, 'Easter Wings', lines 1–5.

5 Elijah was an Old Testament prophet who fought the Tyrian princess Jezebel against the introduction of pagan worship and was taken up to heaven in a fiery chariot. See 2 Kings 2:11.

Whilest flames of wrath so sorely did contest
With this Love-fire in Saviours breast
Heightning the heat so far till's blood boyl'd ore,
Issuing out at ev'ry pore,
Lord! can the eye,
That reads, be dry?

Ah! if it can; let not the writers bee:
No tears of Love, my God! for thee?
Lord! could Love make thee take my sins as thine?
Sure then thy sorrows shall be mine.

The stripes that rent thy back, shall smite and knock
My breast, till they have cleft my rock.[6]
Their'n[7] that in thine hands left such a print
Shall strike some fire out of my flint.

Shall I not love that friend that lov'd me So,
So Lov'd me when I was his foe!
Lord! let not want of Love encrease my score!
My debts were great enough before.

Make me thy Love so burning hot to feel,
As to dissolve and melt my steel:
And burn my stony heart to fervent lime,
As I h've seen fire turn stone sometime.[8]

My heart is thine; Lord thou hast bought that stone,
And thou hast fewel of thine own:
Wil't not quit cost?[9] great great builder! if it will,
O throw mine heart into thy kill.[10]

Lime is an usefull thing in building sure:
And lime of stone will best endure:

6 'And Moses lifted up his hand, and with his rod he smote the rock twice: and the water came out abundantly' Numbers 20:11.

7 i.e. therein.

8 'And the people shall be as the burnings of lime' Isaiah 33:12. The poet wishes the warmth of God's love to dissolve his 'stony heart' as limestone dissolves into lime when heated.

9 i.e. Will it not repay my debt to you? The poet is hoping that giving his heart over to the fire of God's love will grant him salvation.

10 i.e. kiln.

Knowledge puffs up, but Love is *edifying*,[11]
And growes the stronger by long lying.

Oh that I had that lime of Love that is
(As by *Antiperistasis*)[12]
Hotter for water! I would often then
Weep till I even flam'd agen;
But now I mourn,
That I can't burn.

Can't burn? Alas! my God, I'm burning ever:
But oh my burning is a Fever.
Such *hecktick heat* doth too too plainly prove
That I am but *infirm* in Love.

Lord, dost not see how Giants[13] do invade
Thy right? my God, confound their trade,
Who using lust for lime, by Hellish art,
Would rebuild *Babell* in my heart.

'Tis not so long my God and Saviour since
Thou didst expell th' usurping Prince[14]
Rasing[15] his works and strong-holds built within
With lime of lust and piles[16] of sin.

Can I Love sin, that hatefull cruel thing,
That grinds[17] the Serpents forked sting?
Shew'ng death how twice at once to murther me?
And can I not, my God, Love thee?

Can I love sin, that puts me on the wrack[18]
Till bones do break and sinews crack?
And can I not Love him that climb'd the tree?
Wracking himself to take down me?

11 i.e. morally instructive and sustaining, with a pun on 'edifice'.

12 Antiperistasis = contrast or contrariness of circumstance, a paradox.

13 Most likely a reference to the Philistines, who fought against King David. See 2 Samuel 21:16–18.

14 i.e. Satan from Heaven. 15 i.e. razing, destroying.

16 piles = stakes driven in to the ground to serve as foundations for a building.

17 grinds = sharpens. 18 wrack = rack.

Can I Love sin, since hatred ne're had bin,
Never bin heard of but for sin?
And can I not love LOVE, that came to dye,
To kill hatred and enmity?

Love sin, that founded Hell at's own expence?
And not my God that saves me thence?
Alas! how strangely Love its mark can miss!
Oh that mine head and heart for this
Were both one flood
Of tears of blood!

Or can mine heart like *Josephs* Mistriss, make
Love to the Servant?[19] and mistake
These things below for my dear God above
To whom I owe ev'n all my Love?

And then when these chast Creature-comforts flie
Rather then yield, or gratifie,
Can I complain unto my Lord, and say
That they did tempt, then flie away?

Alas! poor Creatures would not be abused:
And must they yet be thus accused?
And God in them? and that I may be found
Guiltless, must guilt reach God at th' bound?[20]

Thou gav'st me these to prove thy Love to me,
But not to steal my Love from thee:
I cannot Love the giver, for his gift;
Alas! my God, that's a poor shift.[21]

Why? shall I court the Bearer, that doth bring,
Forgetting him that sends the ring?
All Creature-good in this world or the next
Be'ng but a comment on Loves Text:

19 Joseph was thrown into prison for repelling the advances of Pharaoh's wife whilst a courtier in Egypt. See Genesis 39:7–21. The poet hopes that he can follow Joseph's example and forgo sexual for spiritual love.

20 at the bound = at the first opportunity. If you lose 'Creature-comforts', you should not blame God.

21 shift = a plan.

This whole Creation be'ng but one round drop
Hanging down from loves fingers top,
If all the world were Pearl, yet why should I
Desire to wear it in mine eye?

So that for this worlds Love I should not see,
My dearest Lord, how to Love thee?
Can I so love the world? And can't I yet
Love God that made both me and it?
Lord, I must cry,
Here's Witchery!

If the world be th' inchantress, Lord, I pray
Hasten the Gen'rall Judgment day!
For sure my Love, when't sees the witch a burning
To its right wits will be returning.

But rather I suspect 'tis Hells black art
That from my God thus charms my heart.
Remembring 'twas the wilie Serpents plot
That first brake the True Lovers Knot.[22]

When *Balaams*[23] Divinations could not move
From Gods dear *Israel* Gods dear Love,
But God that lov'd them once, would love them still,
Though *Balaam* went from mount to hill.

He next instructs the *Moabites*[24] to lay
Adult'rous Loves in *Isr'els* way,
To quench their Love to God through wanton fire
And thereby to incense Gods ire.

And if this world play the *Moabitess*;
'Tis Satans project, Lord, I guess;

22 A reference to Satan's corruption of Adam and Eve.

23 Balaam was a prophet responsible for causing the Israelites to sin (Numbers 31:16) after which he became a mercenary who cursed others for money. Hence a person who follows religion for financial gain is associated with Balaam.

24 The Moabites were a tribe which, according to Genesis, originated from an incestuous union between Lot and his daughter. There were many conflicts between the Moabites and the Israelites during the reign of Saul and David. See 2 Samuel 8:2. In Teate's time, the term was often applied opprobriously to Roman Catholics.

Who see'ng he can't divert thy Love from mee
Would thus divide my Love from thee.

And, is mine heart divided? ah! my God,
Whose cloven foot[25] thereon hath trod
The print discovers.[26] What though *Balaam's* dead?
Thou God of peace! bruise Satans head.

But I am most affraid the worst's within:
The witch-craft of my native sin.
Sin winds and circles, Lord, so many wayes
Till sin ofttimes the Devil raise;
Lord! thou art fire,
Give sin her hire.[27]

Burn up this witch, her crafts, and Philtre-pots:[28]
Sins books of curious arts, charms, knots,
By thy refining Spirit, that I may
Get warmth of Love to thee that way.

Who hath bewitch'd me that I am so coy
When thou woulst fain my Love enjoy,
Thou, blessed Three, stand'st suing for mine heart
Who only canst fill every part?

Dear God! who hath bewitch'd me that I can't
Deny the courting world a graunt,[29]
That never yet could fill my heart, unless
It were with griping emptiness?

The garment of thy goodness is entire;
Can keep me warm without a fire:
To which this whole creation's but a shred,
Each Creature's but one single thred.

25 whose = the one whose … (i.e. the devil's cloven foot).
26 discovers = reveals. 27 hire = punishment.
28 philtre = a magical potion which was said to excite sexual passion in the drinker.
29 courting world = romantic love; graunt = permission. The poet is frustrated at his inability to forego the 'courting world', which here stands for all the temptations the earthly world has to offer.

To give these things their due, they're good for uses
And lovely too, unless their juice,
By Love inordinate, be dryed up,
Leaving behind an empty cup.

And is gold rich? and can the mine be poor?
Theirs at the best is borrow'd store.
Nay, so long borrow'd that it now grows old:
O that my Love could wax as cold;

As cold to earth, as earth is in decay;
But more intense to God each day!
Who'll soon serve earth for all its glitt'ring grace
As we do serve old Silver-lace,[30]
Lord! fire this pile
Of man mean while.

I h've heard good husbands say, that they that borrow
Their stock today, may break[31] tomorrow:
Sure the worlds credit cannot long hold good.
'Tis much the world thus long hath stood.

Consid'ring when the world's in fullest trade
How poor and sorry payment's made
Him,[32] that owes all, and must his right recover;
Sure th' world must then all trade give over:

Shall I not therefore deal ith' interim
Less with the world, but more with him,
With him whose Love's an unexhausted spring
Of ev'ry good and perfect thing.

Methinks mens trading with the world might stop
At thought of this, who keeps her shop.
Alas! my God, the world is Devill-ridden:
The thing is known, and can't be hidden.

30 Silver-lace = ornamental braiding on clothes. The poet is commenting on the transience and superfluity of the physical world by suggesting that we have as much use for it as old silver-lace.

31 i.e. go bankrupt.

32 i.e. to him …

Hell hath deflour'd the earth, and now I see
'T would put its leavings off to me,
Dawbing false paint on th' face oth' wrinkled Creature,
Hav'ng worn and spoil'd its native feature.

The earth's all *Egypt* now: And *Egypts* curse[33]
Is over all the world, or worse:
For *Beelzebub* with his swarming train
Hath all things flie-blown.[34] To be plain

There is no flesh that's sweet, but Saviours, now,
Which Satan tri'd, but knew not how
To taint. All's dogs meat else. Lord! teach me chuse
And I shall all the rest refuse,
And only wish
For that one dish.

A dish that's wholesome, and 'tis healing too.
Ah my dear God! what shall I do
To Love thy flesh enough, that tasted once
For ever heals my broken bones.

Set thine apart, all other flesh is grass:[35]
And is my soul an oxe or ass?
That it should Love no higher then my beast?
Or can my soul such fare digest?

Come, Trencher Criticks,[36] you that eat by book,
And in your food for physick look,
Your Cook must be some small Apothecarie;
Will you allow a Verser varie

From your received rules? and be content
To try a new experiment?

33 A reference to the seven plagues with which God punished the Egyptians for refusing to free the enslaved Israelites. See Exodus 7–13.

34 flyblown = contaminated through contact with flies and their larvae.

35 'All flesh is grass, and the goodliness thereof is as the flower of the field.' Isaiah 40:6.

36 trencher = a wooden plate for food. The poet is addressing fastidious eaters; i.e. those who may reject Christ's spiritual nourishment.

Flesh in a feaver's good Divinity,
Which who most eats, scapes best, say I.

Provided that the flesh be sound and good
(For I would be right understood)
As never did, nor could, corruption see:
Ah my dear Saviour! I mean thee.

Alas! how low in an high burning Feaver
Of Gods displeasure, never, never
To have been cured otherwise, did sin
Once bring me, till I did begin

To fall aboard[37] that sacred flesh? And then
How soon did I grow well again?
Then welcome, gentle guest, if thou hast not
To prize and Love thine health forgot,
Come sit down here
And Love this Chear.

Or tell me, is it sweetness and delight
That rather doth thy Love invite?
What more delicious, sweeter thing can be
Than that sweet blood was shed for me?[38]

When I Repentance take, that purging pill
I take it in this Syrup still:
What purgeth, pains; and would too much corrode
But for this sweet emulgent[39] blood.

You curious Palates, that can't let one glass
Without a strict Examen pass
Come tast, and tell me if (this blood) this wine
Ben't generous and genuine?

The Vine is Divine, nay 'tis some what more;
And can the blood oth' Grape be poor?

37 i.e. to start to eat.

38 Cf. Herbert, 'The Agony', lines 13–18.

39 emulgent = mollifying or soothing.

'Tis this High-Country-Wine that fills my cup,
When at my Saviours board I sup.

Wine, that's as sweet as wrath of God is bitter,
Which, who hath tasted is the fitter
To rellish this rich liquor. Wrath makes dry,
But here's the cup of Charity.

This is the grace-cup.[40] Nothing's sweet nor good
Till dasht or sprinkled with this blood.
Men are but Swine, wines are but swill before
This blood man to himself restore.

A Wine so good, fal'n Angels might not tast it,
Who therefore did contrive to cast it
Upon the ground; which when they thought to spill
They broach'd for man against their will.[41]
Lord who can love
Thy blood enough?

Or do you Love for Loveliness? Come hither;
My Lord is Lovely alltogether.
Alas how am'rous wits forget their duty
To this supream and perfect beauty!

You fond admirers of a skin-deep hue,
To dusty beauties bid adiew,
To dusty beauties that have marr'd your eyes:
Ah my dear God! that wit were wise!

It cuts my heart to see much silken wit
And snares and halters made of it.[42]
Halters to th' owners, snares to th' passers by.
How fast *loose* wit can wantons tie,

40 grace-cup = a drink taken after prayers or on parting.

41 broach = pierce (a cask) to draw liquor. The 'fal'n angels', i.e. Satan, contrived to spill the 'wine', i.e. 'Christ's blood', without realising that his death would be mankind's salvation.

42 Teate is contrasting religious verse to that of poets who use their 'silken wit' to attract women.

And stake them down! till first the lover burns
In heart, and then in Hell by turns.
But say his Love be chaste, and shee a flow'r;
All's next to nothing the next hour:

'Tis kill'd with kindness, dies when complemented,
And soonest fades when 'tis most sented.
Whose Muse doth dress his Mistress, hangs a Verse
To day upon tomorrows Herse:

Friends must be then call'd in to have away
What wanton wit adores today.
Skin-beauty's but a *Sodom*-apple[43] just:
When crusht, it turns to stench and dust.

The wanton world complains their *Love is blind*,[44]
And I must needs be of their mind;
Whilst for such walking shades they cannot see
My dearest Lord, how to Love thee
Yet thou art faire
Beyond compare.

Had I a wit, and had I grace I'd bring
My Saviour an enamel'd[45] ring,
A ring whose Posie[46] should be this alone,
Stars get ye gone, the Sun hath shone.

Stars? I mean glow-worms; earthen beauties which
Ith' dark do sparkle in a ditch,
And fools mistake for *Stars*; till touch informs
And proves them to be *sillie*[47] *worms.*

But, Lord, my Muse unworthy is to bear
The shoes that thy fair feet do wear.[48]

43 A 'Sodom-apple' was an apple with a fair appearance which dissolved into ashes when touched. The expression is used idiomatically to refer to anything hollow or specious.

44 A proverb deriving from the legend of Cupid and Psyche. Venus was so jealous of Psyche's beauty that she sent Cupid to put a spell on her so she would fall in love with an ass.

45 enamel'd = ornate, beautified.

46 posie = a short motto inscribed within a ring.

47 sillie = lowly, humble.

48 'he that cometh after me is mightier than I, whose shoes I am not worthy to bear.' Matthew 3:11.

Fairer for bee'ng so swift, swift to shed blood;
Their own I mean to do me good.

How fair's thy face then? may I, Lord, one day
Have leave to see, though none can say
How fair it is. My dear, the Sun's a Clod
To thy bright face, fair Son of God!

Wherein still fresh and fresh together growes,
With vallies Lillie, *Sharons* Rose.[49]
A rose that ne'r bare prickles of its own;
Yet sinners thorns did Saviour crown.

And shall I Love my Champion less for scars
He gat in waging of my wars?
Thy bruises are but beauty spots, my dear,
That make thy Love more fair appear.

Who loves for fleshy gloss and silken skin
May find a *Serpent* oft *within*.
But thy deep wounds, Lord, prove thee that thou art
All-Lovely to thy very heart.
Beauty thus deep,
Will hold and keep.

Or is it Knowledge, Learning, Science, art
That takes the more ingenious heart?
Come, bookish man, and sit a while down here;
Till thou hast read my dearest dear.[50]

What's that that's printed in his hands and feet?
The print is plain, man, dost not see't?
A mystery that learned flesh and blood
Never taught yet, nor understood.

I h've sometime stood and wondred at the Owles
How they should prove *Minerva's*[51] Foules:

49 'I am the rose of Sharon, and the lily of the valleys.' Song of Solomon 2:1.

50 i.e. contemplate Christ's broken body.

51 Owls were known for their wisdom due to their association with Minerva, the Roman

But since have learnt that learning's blind as Love
Till both be tutour'd from above.

Oh what a Dungeon is the mind of man,
Let *Pallas*[52] paint it what she can!
Some would not be such fools, but that they're wise:
And might see better but for eyes.

Lord, shall I Love to know, and not know thee,
In whom all Wisdoms treasures bee?
Great Magazine![53] whose wisdom's infinite,
Give me that Panoplie of light.[54]

An *Epictetus* or an *Antonine*[55]
Ith' dark make a shift to shine:
But being by thy Sun-light understood
Alas, my God, prove putrid wood.

Shall ventrous Students ev'ry Toads-head look
For Pearls of knowledge? And thy book,
Thy works lye by unlov'd, unlook'd into?
Thy Pupills, th' Angels don't so do:
But help their sight
By Gospell-light.

Or do I Love for likeness? Ah, my dear,
Whose Image was't I first did bear?
Whilst yet I stood in Primitive perfection,
Lord, what was I, but thy reflexion?

goddess of wisdom and the arts. The poet is suggesting that the pursuit of wisdom for its own sake is folly: 'and hence it came to pass that ambitious men chose Jupiter as their patron … those greedy for knowledge, Apollo and Minerva…' Calvin, *Institutes*, III. 20. 5, p. 855.

52 Pallas is the Greek equivalent to the goddess Minerva.

53 magazine = a storeroom for ammunition. Wisdom is stored in God as weapons in a magazine.

54 See Ephesians 6:11–13.

55 Epictetus was a Greek philosopher and Antonine relates to the Roman emperors Antonious Pius and Marcus Aurelius who were known as philosophers. The poet is saying that Greek and Roman wisdom is nothing to that of God. Students should study the Bible instead of the classics.

So like thee that thy self thou couldst not Love
But Love me too: Nor could I move
Thy Love from me, till I thy likeness lost,
Thine Image bee'ng sin slur'd and crost.

But now I'm hatefull grown and hating too;
Alas, my God, what shall I do
To Love thee and to be belov'd of thee?
My Lord, thy Love preventeth[56] mee.

For since the ground of liking likeness is,[57]
Rather then my poor Love thou'dst miss;
Since cursed sin made man unlike his maker,
God of mans likeness was partaker.

When sin, to mans undoing, had undone
Gods Image; God next sent his Son
In likeness of poor sinful flesh, thereby
Condemning sin ith' flesh to dye:

My God was hungry, thirsty, naked, poor:
In fears, in tears, in sweat, in gore:
Was tempted, was betrai'd, forsaken, sold,
Was captivated, kept in hold.

Was judg'd, condemn'd, was kill'd, was buri'd then
That he and I might rise agen
In one Divine and sweet similitude,
And love in likeness be renew'd.
And can I yet
Thy Love forget?

Or do I Love for consanguinity?
For nearness and relation? why
For me Christ took, and shed that *Blood* of his;
And do I ask how *near* he is?

My Lord is much more mine, than I mine own;
My Lord was mine, when I was none:

56 i.e. goes before.
57 i.e. one of the reasons that we like things is because they are similar to us.

My Lord, when I was lost and gone astray,
Was both my Shepheard and my Way.

Surely my Lord and I am near akin,
Ere since my Saviour was made SIN
For me, and I made RIGHTEOUSNESS in him.
He is my head and I a limb:[58]

He is the Vine, and I the branch: the root,
Whereof I am a slip or shoot:
Of my salvation he the captain is,
And I am a reprize[59] of his.

He is my Father, I his feed: nay he,
In travaile of his soul, bare me:
My brother too, born for adversity;
The *Joseph*[60] of the family.

He is my Maker, yet mine husband too;[61]
This Potter me his clay did wooe:[62]
And rather than he'd miss the match did make
Him a *clay-body* for my sake.[63]

Ev'n all men Love *their own*, and shall I not?
Help Lord, and I will knit the knot
In full acceptance of thy free donation,
Clasp hearts and hands in sweet relation;
Lord, thou art mine,
Make me more thine!

Or do I Love for suitable supplies
To all my wants? sure I want eyes
Or I could not want Love, my Lord, to thee,
In whom all blessings treasur'd bee.

58 i.e. the poet and Christ are of one flesh, yet the poet is merely Christ's 'limb' or servant.

59 reprize = repeat. Christ's resurrection grants salvation to all men.

60 Joseph was the prophet Jacob's favourite son. See Genesis 37–47.

61 'For thy Maker is thine husband; the LORD of hosts is his name …' Isaiah 54:5. Jesus is both God, the 'Maker' and man, the 'husband'.

62 'But now, O LORD, thou art our father; we are the clay, and thou our potter; and we all are the work of thy hand.' Isaiah 64:8.

63 God made Christ out of human flesh so he might save mankind.

O that my drop into a Sea could swell
Of Love to him, in whom doth dwell
All fullness, as in bank or house of store,
Ev'n Grace and Bliss for evermore.

Thine[64] bee'ng once asked if they would away,
O whither shall we go? said they
The words of life eternall, Lord, thou hast,
And that's a stock can never wast.

Goodness is all contracted in thy face,
As Sun beams in a burning-glass:
Oh that I lay in some directer line
That I might burn whilst thou dost shine.

Am I sinner? thou'rt a propitiation:
I h've wrought confusion, thou salvation.
I h've purchas'd death both for my self and thee;
But thou to life hast ransom'd mee.

As God, thou *seest*; as man, thou *feel'st* my grief;
As *both*, thou'rt suitable relief:
My Creditour, and yet my Surety too:
Paying and *pard'ning* what I owe.

Creatures are Cisterns,[65] leaking vessels, they
Cannot supply themselves one day
And me much less. My springs are all above
My light, my life: Why not my Love?
Oh 'tis thy right:
Accept my mite.[66]

Or is it Love that sharpens Love again?
My Saviour, every grinding pain

64 i.e. thy apostles.

65 i.e. men are imperfect, 'leaking vessels' and cannot provide adequate spiritual nourishment for themselves let alone others: 'For my people have committed two evils; they have forsaken me the fountain of living waters, and hewed them out cisterns, broken cisterns, that can hold no water.' Jeremiah 2:13.

66 mite = a small, insignificant contribution. See the story of the 'Widow's Mite', Mark 12:42.

Of thine on Earth, and present Intercession
Pleads for a Love beyond expression.

'Tis Love I live upon. And do I yet
Suspect thy Love! or question it?
Lord, if my Living be n't full proof, thy dying
Gives evidence beyond denying.

Herein is Love without dissimulation,
Thy Love thou provest by thy *Passion*,
Whose every wound with open mouth cries out
We are Loves Vouchers,[67] if you doubt.

When Heav'nly Hoasts first saw thee breathe if then
They run and preach good will tow'rds men
If thus they comment on thine Infant-breath,
My God! what thought they of thy death!

Oh! how he[68] Lov'd him? if who saw thee shed
Tears for thy friend *Laz'rus* bee'ng dead,
Cryed out; What might they've said that saw thee dye
Bleeding for me, thine enemy.

And dare I? can I yet renew that grief?
Doubting thy Love, through unbelief.
If I but say I Love, how doth it grieve me
If yet my Friend will not believe me.

And dare I yet suspect the God of Love
Who saies, who swears, who dies to prove
He Loves me? Shall I fail in proof of mine
And then, to make amends, doubt thine!
Doubling thereby
Each injury?

I find, I feel, I see, and can't I say,
He Loves me? doubts out of my way!
Doubtings by Demonstrations overcome
Sure then, if ever, may be dumb.

67 i.e. we are evidence of Christ's love.
68 Most likely a reference to Jesus and his love for Lazarus mentioned in John 11:5.

Or if I needs must doubt and jealous bee,
Lord Ile suspect my self, not thee.
My soul! lov'st thou thy Lord? say yea or nay,
My God I'm gravell'd[69] what to say.

Yet will I hold mine heart to th' Scrutiny
Till it affirm or else deny.
Deny? my God! I dare not, nay I cannot,
And yet, methinks, affirm I may not.

O that I could. This only can I say,
Dear Lord, that I cannot say nay.
Thoughts in again![70] (Loves no such neutrall thing)
You must a certain Verdict bring.

Only be sure, for 'tis your own behoof,[71]
Your Verdict stands on certain proof.
Alas my thoughts can never solve this doubt
Unless thy Love, Lord, help me out.

My God what crouds of witnesses seem strive
To be depos'd oth' Negative?[72]
My seldome thoughts of thee, my cold devotions,
Heartless profession, lifeless motions;

My wanton Daliance with the world and sin:
My want of kindness to thy kin;
My little longing when thou'rt out of sight
Or lab'ring to regain the light,
I sigh to say
How these plead NAY.

These? ah my God! and many more than these;[73]
My little little care, to please;
Or fear, of grieving thee, my want of leisure,
For thee; and in thee, want of pleasure.

My numbe Lethargick zeal when men defame
Thy Saints, thy worship, waies, or name,

69 gravell'd = perplexed.
70 i.e. doubt comes again.
71 i.e. it is for your own benefit.
72 i.e. to testify to my faults.
73 Cf. Donne, 'A Hymn to God the Father'.

How say I that I Love thee, when mine heart
So poorly plaies the Lovers part?

My Love commands mine eye, mine hand, my purse;
Can I Love thee, yet serve thee worse?
Or must my friend of all friends be deni'd
What I yield all I Love beside?

Alas! my Lord! such proof had almost got
A Verdict past, I Love thee not;
But that one witness came and crost the rest
Stifling that Verdict in my breast.

Yet t'was not much that witnesse had to say,
But sorely weeping cri'd, I pray
If't be as you pretend that there's no fire,
Whence is this *smoaking flax*[74] desire?

My Jesus! thou'rt my Judge, the Judge of all,
To whom my Love must stand or fall
Thou that knowst all things knowst that I abhor
My self for Loving thee no more.

My Dear! I h've sometime long'd, and do I not
Long yet that thou wouldst loose one knot
To tye another? what's this life to me,
If I must still be strange[75] to thee?
To Love is life,
Else life's but strife.

Oh that I were a Graduat in that Colledge
Where Love is known that passeth knowledg:
Where smiling Saints do comprehend and dwell
In Love incomprehensible.

Where perfect Love casts out tormenting fear:
Nor *theirs*, nor *thine*,[76] is doubted there:

74 smoaking flax = a burning candle. Although the poet does not love God sufficiently enough to warrant a fire, he has the 'smoaking flax', i.e. the *desire* to do so.

75 i.e. unfamiliar, unknown.

76 i.e. neither the love of the saints nor God is doubted …

Where full-eyed[77] Love may see to interline
Thy text with some short Notes of mine.

But whilst I'm low as earth, short as a span,
Fleet as a shade,[78] narrow as man,
The height, length, depth, and breadth, of Love to measure
I have nor skill, my God, nor leisure.

Love that's as High as Heav'n, for thence it came
And thither with it bound I am;
Love that's as long as length; eternity
Must say how long, for so can't I.[79]

Love that's as deep as Hell, for thence it took
Me; And the day's down in my book.[80]
Love that's as broad as sin that spreads all over,
Yet, Lord! thy Love my sin doth cover.

Th' Astronomer what Houses stars do keep
Can tell, the diver gage the deep;
But I, poor Christs-Cross[81] Scholler, cannot spell
LOVE, though a monosyllable.

Lord I could be content mine earth might turn
To ashes, so my soul might burn,
And all my powers become one Holocaust[82]
Reaching thy Love and life at last;
Lord, stir this fire
And raise it higher.

Here's a poor broken heart, a Sacrifice
Which yet thou'st said thou'lt not despise,

77 full-eyed = perfectly visible.

78 i.e. as shifting and impermanent as a shadow.

79 i.e. for I cannot.

80 A reference to the 'book of life', which contained details of the works of every man's life so that they may be judged accordingly. See Revelation 20:12. The poet is aware that his sins have been recorded in his 'book'.

81 Christs-Cross = the alphabet, so called because a cross was printed at the start of the alphabet in students' school books.

82 Holocaust = something which has been totally consumed by fire or, more generally, a sacrifice of any kind.

I bind it on thine Altar in desire[83]
Heav'ns favour set it all on fire!

Lord shall I ever be a Questionist?[84]
Help me commence[85] in Love to Christ:
Or still incept'ring? pass a grace[86] mine heart
May once be master of this art.

But as I said, methought, I heard one say,
Away bold Freshman you must stay
Your time: there's many 'n act ere this degree,
And here there must no hudlings[87] bee.

Lord if it must be so, my now Condition
I tender to thine own Tuition
Till I have better arguments to prove
I'm more proficient in thy Love.

Charge thy self with me.[88] Me and all that's mine
Subject I to thy discipline,
Lord, I will have no mind distinct from thee
Who givest all that's thine to mee.

If others ask me, can you walk abroad?[89]
Ile answer, Go and ask my God.
Where thou saist go, though flesh and blood stay,
I'le creep[90] if I can't run that way.

Or if I, as I fear I shall, transgress
This law of Love I now express,
I'le humbly strip my self next serious thought
Till thou hast whipt me for my fau't:

83 'he hath sent me to bind up the brokenhearted, to proclaim liberty to the captives.' Isaiah 61:1.

84 Questionist = Someone who habitually questions the validity of religion, but also a university undergraduate in the last term before graduating.

85 commence = to be awarded a full master's or doctoral degree: Teate is developing his 'graduat' conceit.

86 pass a grace = to grant a dispensation to a student who has not, officially, fulfilled the criteria to take a degree. Teate wishes that Christ will recognize the sincerity of his love and grant him salvation through grace.

87 hudlings = hushing up or keeping out of sight.

88 i.e. take charge of me. 89 i.e. outside. 90 creep = crawl.

Then kiss thy rod;
And cry, my God!

Then if thou smile, thy favour, Lord, shall be
Like rain upon mown grass to me.
Or like warm Sun-beams that succeed some shower
Till joyes poor Bud's a full-blown flower;

But I will watch lest some *Old Adam* seed,
With joyes fair flower, put forth some weed.
Which when't first peeps, thy weeding knife Ile borrow
Lest the ground harden by to morrow.

Ile mark thine eye; a better brighter Star,
Than that that guides the Mariner.
My dull remisness, Lord, thine eye, shall whet
To more observance, when sharp set.

Thy quick and hasty look shall quicken mee:
Ile away to my Book, or Knee.[91]
Ile chide my busie play-fellows; Away,
My master frowns; I dare not play.

Lord, I'le see by thine eyes; thine ev'ry beck
Shall be my Bridle curb, and check.
The *Watch*[92] thou giv'st me, Ile keep for thy sake:
And wind it up when ere I wake.

The *Book*[93] thou gav'st me, that blood-guilded Book,
Ile ever, ever in it look
Till I find thee there, and my self, thy beauty,
And learn to know and do my duty.

Then shewing to others, See the token Love
I'le say hath sent me from above:
Keeping the cleaner hands that I may not
Discolour it with any spot;

91 knee = kneeling in prayer.

92 'Watch' is used in the Bible to mean a period in the night when people 'kept watch' for danger: 'Set a watch, O Lord, before my mouth' Psalm 141:3. A 'watch', as in a timekeeping device, becomes a metaphor for the poet's conscience.

93 i.e. the Bible.

Unless a tear
Drop here or there.

The task thou setst me Lord I'le not complain:
Thy work shall be my wage and gain:
Clean as I can I'le do't, if sullied then
My tears shall wash it ore agen.

Thy strict commands and Love-lin'd yoak shall be
A neck-chain of pure gold to me.
Thine hardest sayings when my stomacks queazie
Love shall digest, and make them easie.

Thine is no Labans-service,[94] if it were,
Let Love two Prentiships might bear;
But to be bound, or held in durance by
Thy *Royall Law*, is liberty.

Mine heart shall be less *loose*, and yet more *large*
Be'ng stretcht out unto all thy charge:
And where my life falls short of either table
Love shall *fullfill*; for Love is able.

If thou wilt come, and take an Inventory
Of all thats mine; I'le not be sorry:
If thou wilt search and ransack all I have
I'le help thee, or thine help Ile crave.

If ought I have displease, or if I doubt,
I will, for sureness throw it out.
If I can pleasure thee with ought that's mine:
Ile quit my Title, Lord 'tis thine.

If mine heart fit thy walking, thou shalt have it;
If not, yet Love shall mend and pave it
With such clear solid stone ev'n all within
As yet can weep for ev'ry sin,

94 Laban was the father of Rachel who required Jacob to do fourteen years of labour in return for his daughter's hand in marriage. See Genesis 29:1–30.

Washing thy feet
When men don't see't.

Mine heart be'ng thus possest, when strangers come
I'le say thou'st taken up my room:
Then if thou ask whose purse or parts are these,
I'le answer, thine Lord, if thou please.

If on mine Houre-Glass thou then lay thine hand,
And ask whose is this running sand,
Ile answer, Lord, the little's left is thine:
But what's run out is no more mine.

Or if thou ask me, who are those at th' door?
Smiling on them; Ile say, my poor,
Ile *draw my soul out* when thy *Lazar*[95] knocks
My *Cupboard* shall be th' poor mans box.[96]

If others come, like those poor *Greeks*,[97] to mee
With a, Sir, we would Jesus see,
Ile gladly tell them where my Lord doth Sup
Do'ng all I can to help them up.

If others curse thee *Shimei*[98] like; if they
Cast dust, Ile blow the dust away
With sighs and groans; if they thine honour stain
I'le weep and wash it clean again.

Or else I'le chide or fight if thou shalt bid
(But first of all with Traytours hid
At home) I'le fear no colours whilest above
Thy Banner over me is Love.

Who sues to be a favourite of mine
Ile ask him first if he be thine,

95 lazar = beggar.

96 The 'poor man's box' was a collection box for the destitute. The poet will feed the poor from his own cupboard.

97 In the New Testament 'Greeks' meant all gentiles. This line refers to a deputation of Greeks who came to see Jesus. See John 12:20.

98 Shimei, a descendent of Saul, cursed and threw stones at King David. See 2 Samuel 16:5–10.

If not, Ile pray him to be reconcil'd
To thee, that so my Love to th' Child
May all be found
Thine at the bound.[99]

Or when thy tender Lillie bleeds, my God
Torne with those cruel horns abroad
Or rent with Schismes at home and heart-division,
Ile what I can play the Physician.

Ile plead with thee with them; if things grow worse
Ile bleed my self to turn the course
When I thy Peoples Hearts divided see
Surely mine Heart shall broken bee.

Thy Love hath lent me all the balm thats thine,
Why should not then thy sores be mine.
My God they shall: but chiefly when my Passion
Or lust provokes thine indignation.

Ile be reveng'd on one, my self I mean,
And grieve till thou art pleas'd agen.
Passions shall live like *Gibeonites*,[100] their Law
To hew thy wood and water draw.[101]

So all I have shall serve thee till I know
My Love hath life, and find it grow.
Lord, Ile account of all as it conduces
To help Loves growth and serve its uses.

If in the Sunshine of a prosp'rous state
My fire can't burn so clear for that,
Ile rather choose some curteous clouds return
Than see Loves holy fire not burn.

Or if I fail of ought I here profess
And thy rod can't my fault redress

99 at the bound = immediately.

100 Inhabitants of Gibeon who tricked the invading Israelites into signing a treaty and were punished for their duplicity by being forced into servitude. See Joshua 9.

101 See Joshua 9:21.

Rather than live thy grief, Ile yield to dye;
So Love inflict the penalty
That paid my score
By death before.

If Love yet let me live a growing debtor,
Ile study hard but Ile live better:
Live I mean Love; that's the Commandments end,[102]
And that's the life that I intend.

Though Love wax cold abroad, and sin abound,
Hard Frost ore spreading all the ground,
Shall th' heat of Kitchin fire be more increast
And not thy flames within my breast?

Lord, what's a Silver Tongue if't cannot talk,
A Golden Leg if't cannot walk
Faith that can Mountains move[103] when 'tis desired
Or *Martyrdome*, if Love be n't fired?

What if I give my goods and all my store,
But not in Love to feed thy poore?[104]
But if in Love a cup of water cold
Though the drink's mean, the *cup* is Gold.

Love tunes my Pray'rs, makes Praises Musicall:
Which else at best but howl or ball.[105]
Love makes two *Mites*[106] to God as acceptable
As if to bring two worlds 'twere able.

True Love's true beauty, beauties else but paint
No more am I if Love I want.[107]
Lord help me *put on Love* to keep me warm:
To *dwell in Love* secure from harm.

To *walk in Love*, till Love ith' stream do lead
To Love that is the Fountain head,

102 See John 13:34.
103 See 1 Corinthians 13:2.
104 See 1 Corinthians 13:3.
105 i.e. bawl.
106 mite = a small coin of low value. See the story of the 'Widow's Mite', Mark 12:42.
107 i.e. lack.

Or th' Ocean which if I can't comprehend
I'll plung into: that in the end
Lost I may bee,
If *lost*, in thee.

Yet when I think what pent and narrow room,
Ith' Virgins Womb,
The God of Love lodg'd in, methinks mine heart
May hold its part.
Into mine heart O shed thy Love abroad,
My God! my God.
Both be'ng Spirit, what can better suit,
Than th' *Spirits* fruit?
Drink thirsty vessell, till thou fill or break!
but never leak.
The broken Heart, and truly contrite Breast
Holds Love the best:
And the best Love, a Love more worth then wine,
Lord, I mean thine:
Then as the purpose of thy Grace and Love
None can remove
Let me so love thee as to part and sever,
Lord, never, never.
Ungirt, Unblest, we say; my God *Love is*
The bond of Bliss
And *perfectness*; A Grace, whose Bondmen[108] be
The only free.
Works without *Faith* can never, Lord, please thee
Nor profit mee.[109]
Faith without *Love*, can't operate or move
But *works by Love*.
Love is a Grace that stands her ground in Glory,
That upper story.
Love, when Tongues, prophesies, and knowledg fail,

108 Bondmen = slaves. Only those who are slaves to God's love are truly free.

109 A reference to the Calvinist belief that good works do not come from the individual but are rather brought about by God's will and are thus, alone, insufficient grounds for salvation. 'What perversity is it for us, when we lack righteousness, in order not to seem deprived of all glory – that is, utterly to have yielded to God – to boast of some little bits of the few works and try through other satisfactions to pay for what is lacking.' Calvin, *Institutes*, III. 13.

Ent'ring the Vaile,
Proffesseth as Supream and *highest* Grace
The *Holiest place.*
When Faith and Hope do thither wait upon her,
As Maids of Honour,
Sole Love is left as *Queen* of all the Graces
In Gods Embraces.
Meanwhile, Lord, to be *sick of Love* to thee
Is *health* to mee.
They that have not this *sickness* have a worse,
Thy *plague* and curse.

If any man Love *not the Lord Jesus Christ, let him be* Anathema Maran-atha,
I Cor. 16. 22[110]

110 Anathema = accursed. Maran-atha is an Aramaic expression meaning 'O Lord! Come!'

Prayer

Next th' Trinity of *Persons* and of *Graces*
Mans three main *Duties* Muse and Method places.

Who views my God and Grace in all their Beauty
Can't (I should think) but take delight in Duty.

But who believes, Hopes, Loves (I'm sure of that)
Will Love to Pray, to Hear, to Meditate.

Pray'r's the first *breath* put forth in *crying* then
When, through sad *pangs*, poor souls are *born agen*.

Heav'n well commends Faiths *midwifery*, and sayes,
The Child's no *still-born*, for behold he prayes.

Pray'r is the *rapper* at Heav'ns door, *Faith* knocks,
Who's there? saith *Love* within doors, and *unlocks*.

*Pray'*r is the *key;* what e're ith' lock retards;
Pray'r, *oyld* with *mourning*, gently flips the *wards*,[1]

And moves the *Spring*, Gods heart; doth *Ephraim*[2] mourn?
The *bolt* gives back, Jehovah's bowels *turn*.[3]

Pray'r is an *Arrow* from a *well-bent* heart:
Watch the *Returns*, and see what 'twill impart

Of Heav'ns *Intelligence*; i'th' *flouds* decrease
This *mournfull Dove* brings th' *Olive branch* of peace.[4]

1 wards = the ridging within a lock.

2 Ephraim was the patriarch of one of the twelve tribes of Israel. When two of his sons were murdered, he 'mourned' but was comforted when his wife conceived. The incident is related as an example of God's kindness. See 1 Chronicles 7:22.

3 In scripture the term 'bowels' is often used to mean the seat of pity or kindness.

4 A reference to Noah's Ark. See Genesis 8:11.

Pray'r is the sacred *Bellows*; when these blow,
How musically doth faiths *Organ* goe;[5]

Thus Pray'r proves Faith an *Instrument*: and Love
Answers to this *wind-musick* from Above,

In sweet consort, with ravishing consent,
Upon that *Lute* (that dear-string'd Instument)

Whose strings are *Bowels* of that *Lamb once slain*,[6]
Who makes the Musick, bee'ng *Alive again*.

Pray'r is the sacred *Bellows*, when these blow,
How doth that *Live-cole*[7] from Gods *Altar* glow!

By Prayer *Love* burns to *zeal*; and hot desire
Baptizeth the souls fewel all with *fire*.

Pray'r breath's the *gale*, whilest Faith doth *navigate*
Ith' brittle *bark*[8] of mans frail mortall state:

Good Hope's the *Cape*: fair *Heaven*, and *fair wind*!
Whilest Faith, in pray'r, steers the *low ballast* mind.[9]

Pray'r is Faiths *Limbeck*,[10] there the Promise lies
And thence *distills*: mock not Pray'rs *watry eyes*.

On th' *knees* of Pray'r Faith brings forth *Promises*,
As *Bilha* sometimes bare on *Rachels* knees.[11]

5 The use of musical instruments in puritan services was common. Calvin, though distrustful of other forms of art, believed music and singing edified worship. See *Institutes*, III. 20. 32, p. 895.

6 Lute strings were made of lambs' intestines. The image also refers to Christ the 'lamb' whose death brought life to believers.

7 i.e. lighted coals.

8 bark = a ship or boat.

9 'ballast' weighs down and thus stabilises a ship, preventing it from capsizing. Prayer helps to guide a 'low ballast', i.e. an unstable mind.

10 limbeck = an apparatus used for distillation, principally in alchemy. Prayer turns faith into gold, i.e. salvation. Cf. Teate, *A scripture-map of the wildernesse of sin* (London, 1655): 'A Chymicks Limbeck … will extract moisture out of seared sticks and hardest stones: Gods limbeck will melt thee, O thou seared sinner …', p. 11.

11 Rachel was the wife of Jacob who, being infertile, begged her husband to have children with her maid Bilha: '… let her give birth on my knees, so that I too may have offspring, at least through her.' Genesis 30:3. Prayer brings forth promises from God as Bilha, and later Rachel brought forth children.

Pray'r is Faiths *Bucket*, (Pray'r doth upward move,
Drawing its *waters* from those *wells above*)

Chain'd to that *Bucket* of the *Blessing*, so
That that *comes down*, as this doth *upward go*.

Pray'r is Faiths *Pum*p, where't works till th' water come
If't come not free at first, Faith *puts in some*;

Some truly penitentiall *tears*: and then
Pumping the *Promise*, paies it self agen.

Pray'r is the Christians *Pulse*: Pray'r instantly
The *Temper* or *Distemper* will descry.[12]

Some *read*; some *sing* and some their *pray'rs* can *say*,
He's an *Elias*[13] that his pray'rs can pray.

Pray'r lifting up its *holy hands* can dart
To He'ven that hand-granade of the Heart,

Of the *whole Heart*, which kindled with *desire*
In *fervent* motion *breaks*, sets Love *on fire*:

Compassions *burn*; He'ven suff'ring violence,
Grows to *surrender* unto man, propense.[14]

Pray'r's a chief piece of Faiths *Artillery*
Take a *right ground*, mount Pray'r, aym *right*, let flie:

Doth Heav'n hold out? let Heaven hear from Faith
What force Pray'r *home-charg'd* with a Promise hath.

Doth Hell assault? let *fervour* fire this Gun,
And the *report* shall make bold *Legion*[15] run.

12 In the seventeenth century, 'Temper' referred to the proportionate mixture of the four bodily humours, blood, phlegm, black bile and choler, which guaranteed good health. When the humours became unbalanced this led to 'Distemper' or bad health. Prayer can 'descry' or diagnose the health of the soul.

13 Elias = Elijah, an Old Testament prophet.

14 Here, the poet is developing the analogy of prayer being like artillery in terms of the impact it has on God. These lines seem to mean that if Heaven is subjected to the force of man's prayers, it will surrender to them willingly.

15 i.e. Satan, with a pun on a 'legion' of soldiers.

Pray'rs Rhetorick *commands*, when't *begs*, and so
Makes most *victorious* whom it brings most *low*.

Pray'r *lifteth up the Eyes, Hands, Heart* we see,
When Pray'r must humbly doth *bow down* the *knee*.

Pray'r makes Man *Prince with God*; doth *Jacob kneel*?
Saith King of Glory, Rise up Israel!

Pray'r, in the *silent Hannah*,[16] loudly *speaks*;
Pray'r both *Manasse's*[17] *heart* and *prison* breaks.

Elijahs Pray'r doth *pierce* the *brassie* skies:[18]
And makes the *Tears* to stand in *Heavens eyes*.

'Tis not an *armed Amalek* [19]can stand
When Pray'r lifts up a *Moses's naked Hand*.[20]

As *Thunder-struck* Philistines once did fall,[21]
Down tumbles *Rain*, and th' *Enemy* withall,

At th' Lightning Legions Pray'r. Oh who can war,
Where *private Souldiers* such *Commanders* are?

Pray'r bee'ng aboard, the great Leviathan,[22]
In whose close Cook-room *Jonah's* shipt, poor man![23]

16 Hannah was childless for a long time but became pregnant with Samuel after praying to God. 1 Samuel 1–2.

17 Manasse = Manasseh; Joseph's son and the elder brother of Ephraim. Manasseh angered God by constructing false idols and using witchcraft, and was imprisoned by the king of Assyria as punishment. However he prayed for forgiveness, and was returned to his kingdom. See 2 Chronicles 33:12–13.

18 Elijah prayed for the life of a sick boy and was heard. See 1 Kings 18:21–2.

19 The Amaleks were a nomadic people descended from Esau. They occupied part of the Promised Land but were dispossessed by the Hebrews. See Exodus 17:8–16.

20 See Exodus 17:11.

21 A reference to the capture of Samson by the Philistines. Tied between two pillars, Samson prayed for deliverance and was granted the strength to pull the building down, thus killing his enemies, but also himself. Judges 17:28–30.

22 Leviathan was a mythological sea monster destroyed by God in an act symbolizing his power over sin. See Isaiah 27:1. Here the poet seems to be using 'Leviathan' synonymously with the 'great fish' that swallowed Jonah. See below.

23 A reference to Jonah who was shipwrecked and swallowed by a 'great fish'. He was saved after praying for deliverance. See Jonah 1–2.

Makes *Land*, runs th' *Hull* on shore, and open breaks
The Pris'ners way, by *blowing-up* the Decks.

Pray'r undertakes to discipline the SUN:
To teach that *Giant* Postures when to Run,

When to *Retreat*, to make a Halt, to stand:
At praying *Joshua's word of Command*,[24]

This Rowling Eye,[25] in Heavens brow stands still,
Wondring to see Faiths Pray'r thus work its will.

Fifteen Degrees, when *Hezekiah* pray'd,
His *Life*,[26] and ten the *Sun* ran retrograde,

Thus *Pray'r* prevails in *Heaven, Earth*, and *Seas*:
Add but its conquest over *Hell* to these.

Thus th' *Ayre* of Pray'r *choaks* the serpentine brood
Of that old crooked *Dragon* in the *flood*,[27]

Sin, Satans *spawn*, and how the intestine *Thorne*,
Is by true Prayr's *compunction* out-worne!

How th' *Messenger* of Satan's buffeted,[28]
Who came to *buffet*; how the Serpents *Head*,

Under the *knees* of Pray'r is *sqeez'd* at last;
And *Beel-zebub* is himself *out-cast,*

By the rare force of Pray'r, that grows more strong
By Fasting,[29] and more *fresh* by watching long.

24 Joshua was a warrior leader of the Israelites who prayed that the sun and the moon might stay still in order to punish the invading Amorites. See Joshua 10:12.

25 i.e. the Sun.

26 Hezekiah was the king of Judah who prayed to God to spare his life so that he could defend his kingdom from attack from the Assyrians. In response God added another fifteen years to his life and as a sign that he would keep his promise, made the shadow of the sun move backwards by ten degrees. See 2 Kings 20:1–11.

27 See Revelation 12:15–16.

28 buffet = strike or hit.

29 Puritans believed that the power of prayer was strengthened if accompanied by fasting.

The summe of all is Pray'rs stupendious Art,
To bind *Gods hands*, and keep in hold his *Heart*.

Pray'r importuning this *Sampson* hath found,
Himself revealing how he may be bound;

Ev'n God be *bound*, who's infinitely *free*,[30]
Yet faith to Faith and Pray'r Command ye mee.

The Prayer-hearing God the *Father* is;
The Pray'r-perfuming God that *Son* of His,

(With flagrant, fragrant Incense of His Merit)
The Pray'r-inditing God is God the *Spirit*.

Pray'rs Tears are washt in Gods Blood,[31] & its moans
Are *ayr'd*[32] with Gods unutterable groans:

Thus Pray'r prevails with God: yet Praises shall
Not *Pray'r,* but th' God of Pray'r, victorious call,
Who's *All in All*.

Pray alwaies with all PRAYER, *and watch there unto with all Perseverance*, Eph. 6. 18.

30 A reference to the capture and binding of Christ – even God submitted to be 'bound' to save mankind from sin. See Matthew 27:2.

31 A reference to the Calvinist belief that the contemplation of Christ's sacrifice acts as a mediating force between man and God in prayer. 'our prayers are cleansed by sprinkled blood – prayers that … are otherwise never free of uncleanness'. Calvin, *Institutes*, III. 20. 18, p. 875.

32 i.e. the air is filled with …

Hearing

From Pray'r to Hearing I proceed,
For that prepares for this indeed;
But who from Hearing[1] turns his ear away
The Lord *abominates to hear him pray.*

Heark? 'tis Gods *voice*: can man forbear
To hear Him *speak* that made the *Ear*?
Why should the *Head of hearing Ears* make show
Since such *Deaf Ears* upon Mans *Heart* do grow?

Heav'n did to poor Mans misery
Give *ear* before he gave the *Cry.*[2]
Methinks a Saviours words should all sound loud,
Acuted with the *Accents* of his Blood.

What vile *Dishonesty* appears
By Mans disgraceful *loss of Ears*?
And yet let *Syrens sing*, and Satan *knock*;
Mans Heart can *hear* too light, too soon *unlock*;

No *Cords* can *hold*, or *Lusts* be *bound*,
Till *All* is *over-board* and *drown'd.*
When th' Serpent *charms* this *Adder* hears, but when
Heav'n *charms* more wisely, th' Ears are *charm'd* agen.[3]

Most what I see a monstrous sight
Most have *two Ears*, yet neither's *Right,*

1 'Hearing' is used in the Bible in the sense of listening to and obeying God's commands.

2 A reference to the salvation of mankind through Christ's crucifixion.

3 'The wicked are estranged from the womb: they go astray as soon as they be born, speaking lies. Their poison is like the poison of a serpent: they are like the deaf adder that stoppeth her ear; which will not hearken to the voice of charmers, charming never so wisely.' Psalm 58:3–5.

God gave them *two*, yet they'l by no means lend
So much as *one* to such a bounteous Friend.[4]

Sure such a Friend would soon *repay*,
By *giving ear*[5] to what they pray.
God ever takes up Ears on *Interest*,
And doth his greatest *Creditors* pay best.

They teach their very *Ears* to pray
Who *listen* well what God shall say.
The *uncircumcis'd in Ear*[6] bid God deny,
Refusing Him that speaketh, when they *cry*.

The *Deaf Ear'd–Idoll* is abhord
And *Men* like Idols, of the Lord:
Who *deafness* plagues with *deafness*, and doth turn
His *Ear* from *Dives*[7] whilest his *Tongue* doth burn.

Lord therefore to *Deaf Hearers* give
To *live to hear*, to *hear and live*.
Yea into th' *Harvest* send forth *Labourers*
To still thy *floor* by gathering in of *Ears*.[8]

Thou sow'st thy *Word* as *Seed*,[9] and then,
'Tis fit thou reap the *Ears* of *Men*,
As Mary *weeping*[10] heard till *showrs* of tears,
Full *ripe* for thine own *reaping* made her Ears.

What *Heapes* shall in thy *Garners*[11] bee
When *Ears* are *Circumcis'd* by Thee?
Fair *Sion* shall be like an *heap of Wheat*
That *round about with Lillies is beset*.[12]

4 Cf. Shakespeare, *Julius Caesar*, III. 2. 1.
5 give ear = to listen attentively, but also to make a sacrifice.
6 The uncircumcised in ear are those that are deaf to the word of God.
7 'Dives' comes from the Latin for 'rich man' and is a reference to the parable of the Rich Man and Lazarus. Lazarus refused to help the poor when alive, so God did not listen to his cries for mercy from Hell. See Luke 16:19–31.
8 with a pun on 'ears' of corn.
9 See the 'Parable of the Sower'. Matthew 13:3–30.
10 Mary Magdalene wept on seeing the risen Christ. See John 20:11–18.
11 Heapes = wheat; Garner = storehouse for corn.
12 'thy belly is like an heap of wheat set about with lilies.' Song of Solomon 7:2.

When *Malchus*[13] lost an Ear thy *touch*
(A Saviours skill and virtue's such)
Repair'd that Loss: Lord, 'tis but *Ask* and *Have*;
Thou canst find *Ears* in *Lazarus* his *Grave*.

Thou *Davids Heir* of *Davids Keys*[14]
Canst *shut* and *open* as thou please,
Thy still voice loud *winds*, and proud *waves* obey;[15]
Unto thy Word, let not *Mens Eares* say *Nay*.

Thou didst a *Pris'ner*[16] once impow'r
(*Judge Felix* bee'ng *Auditour*)
To give the *Charge* that took the Judge by th' *Ear,*
More *Bonds* did then on th' *Bench* than *Barr* appear.

When Heav'ns great Guns from *tire* to *tire,*[17]
According to thy Word *give fire*
Kadesh doth tremble: *Hindes* do *Calve* for fear;[18]
The *howling* Desarts, and *deaf* rocks give ear.

And is Mans *Heart* more *wild?* more *hard?*
More *full of noises?* stronger *barr'd?*
Yet is the Ear the *key-hole:* Lord put in
Thy *finger*, then the gentlest word will win.

All *turns* and moves; One *Eph-phata*[19]
Removes obstructions out of th' way;
Then th' Ear shall welcome every *second word*
With a *Come in thou blessed of the Lord!*

13 Malchus was the high priest's slave who, while attempting to arrest Jesus in Gethsemane, had his ear cut off by Peter. (John 18:10.) Jesus then healed the severed ear. See Luke 22:51.

14 'And the key of the house of David will I lay upon his shoulder; so he shall open, and none shall shut, and none shall open.' Isaiah 22:22.

15 A reference to Jesus' calming of the storm. See Luke 8:23–5.

16 A reference to the Apostle Paul who was tried by Felix, the governor of Judea. Felix kept Paul bound in prison in order to placate the Jews who wanted him executed. See Acts 24.

17 tire = a volley of gun shots.

18 See Psalm 29:8–9.

19 A reference to Christ's healing of the deaf man: 'And looking up to Heaven, he sighed, and saith unto him, Ephphata, that is, Be opened. And straightaway his ears were opened' Mark 7:34–5.

The Scriptures speak of th' *Learned* Ear;[20]
Sure then thy *tongue* must *teach* to hear,
Morning by morning let thy *Musick* make
The *heavy Ears* of Mans dull mind to *wake*.

If *Sons of God*, fair *Angels*, stand
Waiting the *Son of Gods* command,
(Which when it comes, who sees these Holy things,
Might see their *Ears* converted into *wings*);

If the *Deaf Divill* lends an *Ear*,
Not led by Love but forc'd by Fear,
And if the *sword, plague, famine* only know
By hearkning to his Word they *Come* and *Go*:

In vain doth poor Man stop his Ear
And say in's Heart Hee'l never hear:
Harvests bring *Ears*: and such is the *Worlds end*:[21]
Graves must find *Hearers* then; The *Dead attend*.

Then Happy He that sooner heard,
Hearing before *for afterward*;
God had his *Eares* on Earth, and doubtless He
Shall with *full sheaves* repaid in Heaven be.

If *Sol'mons servants*[22] were so blest
That *conn'd*[23] their *Lesson* from his *breast*,
How Happy 're those *Disciples* then whose *Ears*
Are tun'd to the *true Musick* of the *Sphears?*[24]

Where the *First Mover*[25] is *Free Grace*,
Free *Purpose* moves ith' second place:

20 'The Lord God hath given me the tongue of the learned … he wakeneth morning by morning, he wakeneth mine ear to hear as the learned.' Isaiah 50:4.

21 Judgement day is referred to as the 'harvest' in both the Old and New Testaments. See, for example, Matthew 14:37–9.

22 For the story of Solomon's servants, see 1 Kings 5:1–18.

23 conned = learned.

24 A reference to Ptolemaic cosmology which stated that the heavenly bodies, e.g. the moon and stars, were carried on cocentric, hollow globes or spheres which revolved around the Earth and, on doing so, produced harmonious sounds.

25 The 'first mover' was the outermost of these cocentric spheres which was said to trans-

Third *Orbe's* the *Word of Grace,*[26] in which do shine
As many *Stars* as *Promises* Divine.

These Lessons so Divine, so good
(The *Orbes* bee'ng *Oyl'd* in Saviours *blood*)
Do so divinely correspond, that so
Needs must the *Hearer* the *Diviner* grow;

Then comes that holy *Turtle Dove,*[27]
Gently descending from above;
And stealing through the *Earth hole*[28] into th' heart,
Doth Heav'ns *Intelligence* on Earth impart.

This is a *joyfull sound* indeed,
What *Halcyon* dayes shall hence succeed,
Whilest *Thunders* terror makes Deaf Rebels quail,
Christs voice to his Disciples is *All hail!*

If God that rules all otherwhere
Love so to move the *Orb of th' Ear,*
Sure then the *Blessed* of the Lord are they
That *Hearing* hearken, *Hearkening* that Obey.

The Humble Hearer may invite
God Guest-wise[29] to a Disht Delight
A fervent *whole broke-heart* serv'd up in *Tears*
The *Bread* bee'ng made o' th' *Contrite hearers Ears.*

Nay God invites Himself to *sup*
Where such delights are so serv'd up
By a *clean hand*, where th' *ear* and the *heart's* kept hot
God is Mans *Guest*, and Heav'n will pay the *shot.*[30]

A letter H is not say we,
Let HEARING then mine EARING be:[31]

mit its motion to those spheres below it. The poet is saying that God's grace has an analogous influence over the lives of men.

26 i.e. Scripture.

27 i.e. the Holy Spirit.

28 earth hole = both the physical surface of the ground and human skin.

29 i.e. in the manner or a guest.

30 i.e. pay the bill.

31 'As an earring of gold … so is a wise reprover upon an obedient ear.' Proverbs 25:12.

Thou God of *Israel bore* thy *Servants Ear*,
That I in it this *Jewel* still may *wear.*

Let every one be swift to HEARE. *But be ye doers of the Word, and not hearers only, deceiving your own Souls*, Jam. I. 21, 22.

Meditation

I come to sing the last but not the least,
Be'ng that that *Clencheth* in mans mind and breast
Those *Nails* th' Assemblies masters drive
Not t' eat but to *Digest*, makes thrive.[1]

Sweet, sacred thing! Caelestial *Contemplation*!
Old *Enochs*[2] *Trade*, young *Isaac's*[3] *Recreation*,
That furnishest mans thoughtfull breast
With Greatest *Work*, and Sweetest *Rest*.

Israel's *sweet Singer*[4] us'd when first awake,
His *Lark-like* Rise, upon thy *wings*, to take;
With which, he made his *morning flight*:
Of which, his *Feather-bed* at night.

The nimble *Life-guard* of that Royal mind,
Were *Thoughts*, by thee divinely *Disciplin'd*:
Marshall'd in each dayes *front* and *rear*,
Greatness thus guarded know's no fear.

When anxious musings would invade that soul:
When *Cares* would *clog*, or make it stomack-foul,
Thou didst *exonerate*, Thy *skill*,
Did still prepare the *Stomack pill*.

Thy *Physick*[5] having wrought; and *hungry health*
Thine *hopefull Patient* re-surpriz'd by stealth,

1 'The words of the wise are as goads, and as nails fastened by the masters of assemblies, which are given from one shepherd.' Ecclesiastes 12:11. The good Christian should not just 'eat', i.e. hear, but also 'digest', i.e. meditate on the word of God.

2 Enoch was a legendary Old Testament hero who by-passed death and was taken straight to Heaven. See Genesis 5:23.

3 Isaac was the son of the patriarch Abraham. He is shown meditating in Genesis 24:66.

4 A reference to the composer of the Psalms, commonly thought to be David. See Psalm 63:6–7.

5 i.e. medicine.

Then thou that *honey-comb* didst drain,[6]
And break the *Bone*, that did contein

The *fat*, the *sweet*, which from the *Promise* flow's[7]
(Whereof the sensuall wordling[8] nothing knows)
Thus Meditation first *sets right*
Then *saviest's* the souls Appetite.

Man's fed with *Manna*, void of surfets fear:
Where Meditation's *Cook*, *Digestions* clear:
Mortals thus fed with Angels *fare*,
Converted into *Angels* are.

By *Contemplation* was that *Darling* drest,
When Guest wise Heaven bad him to a *feast*:
John's cloath'd in spirit ; when they call
To keep the *Lords daies* festivall.

In *Contemplations Mount* who dwell, can stretch
Their hand to Heav'n that *Starry Crown* to reach:
And dress themselves in that bright *Sun*
Whilest *under-foot* they tread the *Moon*.

In *Contemplations* Pisgah[9] they, that have
At once a view of *Canaan*, and their grave.
(In this worlds *Desart* wearied)
Do willingly undress to Bed.

Sweet sacred *Meditation*! may I bee
Wrought, recreated, garded thus by thee:

6 Palestine is referred to as a land flowing with milk and honey (Exodus 3:8). Thus, in the Bible, honey is symbolic of God's love and providence to his people: 'My son, eat thou honey, because it is good; and the honeycomb, which is sweet to thy taste' Proverbs 24:13.

7 The fat was the richest and best part of the animal and hence is used figuratively throughout the Bible to represent God's love. God's 'promise' to the Old Testament patriarchs to send the Messiah comes from his love for his people: 'Then he said unto them, Go your way, eat the fat, and drink the sweet, and send portions unto them for whom nothing is prepared …' Nehemiah 8:10.

8 i.e. a poet devoted to describing earthly pleasures.

9 Pisgah is the mountain from which Moses was allowed to view the Promised Land before he died. See Deuteronomy 3:27.

Physick'd and *fed* by the *Dispensatory*:
By thee be *drest* with Grace, prepar'd for glory.

I.

Then learn O man to part betwixt
Dead earth and th' earth wherewith thou'rt mixt:[10]

Sure *walls of Clay* may higher rise,[11]
Then what in earths *dead dungeon* lies.[12]

The Soul with Earth's already clad,
Earth upon earth would make more sad.[13]

Shall *wings* make massie *Mountains* fly?
Shall *hands* stitch *Earth* unto the sky?

Then *dung-hill drones* scale Heaven may,[14]
And *Muck-worms* creep i'th' *Milkie Way*.

To carry Earth to Heav'n some think:
But must Earth *rise*? or Heaven *sink*?

Nor Earth nor Heaven must be their prize;
But a *fools* (Mah'mets)[15] *Paradise*.

10 i.e. man must learn to distinguish between the physical world and the Kingdom of Heaven.

11 In the Bible, human flesh is often described as 'clay' moulded by God the 'potter'. Here, the sense seems to be that the human body may leave behind the 'dead dungeon' of its flesh and rise up to Heaven.

12 Cf. Teate, *A scripture-map of the wildernesse of sin* (London, 1655): 'Yea, how doe the very houses of clay, that sinners dwell in, spew them up, and cast them forth in a few yeares, as if weary of being so long possessed by them.' p. 29.

13 i.e. the soul is already encased in 'earth' or flesh and it would be a double curse if it remained in the physical world without ascending to Heaven.

14 Cf. Spenser, 'An Hymne in Honour of Love', lines 183–4, *The Yale edition of the shorter poems of Edmund Spenser*, ed. William A. Oram et al. (New Haven, 1989).

15 Mah'met = Mahomet or Maumet: a rendering of the Arabic for Muhammad . In Teate's time, the word was often used to describe a false idol, and specifically by protestants as a derogatory term for catholic imagery and iconography. The word is also used in a punning sense as 'mahomet' was another word for 'pigeon', which in turn was a seventeenth century appellation for 'fool'.

If yet thine Earth to Earth adhere,
Then let the *Dead* the *Dead* interre;

If thou can't *lift* the inferior part;
Yet, as *Gods Offring*, heave thine *heart*.

Thy *Body's* but thy *Beast*, and sure
All else is but its *furniture*:

Leave then thy *heavy jade*[16] below,
Up to the place that God shall show.

Earth's ever moving to Earths *Center*,
Man's for a more sublime Advent'r:

'Tis pitty Dust in th' *Ayre* or *Eye*
Should hinder a *celestiall spie*.

With lumbering Body leave behinde
The low, th' ignoble, *servile mind*:[17]

Such men I mean as can't out-pass
Old *Abrah'ms servents*,[18] or his *Ass*.

The *secret seeker* only knows
What *secrets* Heaven can disclose.

Gods *Holy of Holies* still shuts out
The *vulgar* and unholy rout.

In *secret places* of the stairs
And *clefts of Rocks* lye mine Affaires.[19]

16 jade = a worn out horse, here symbolising the human body. Those that love only earthly things will never ascend to Heaven in the manner of a dove, but remain below like a lowly pigeon.

17 Cf. Henry More, *Philosophical poems* (London, 1647): ' 'Tis true, a never fading durancie / Belongs to all hid principles of life / But that full grasp of vast *Eternitie* / Longs not to beings simply vegetive / Nor yet to creatures merely sensitive / Reason alone can not arrive to it', p. 91.

18 See Genesis 24:35.

19 'O my dove, that art in the clefts of the rock, in the secret places of the stairs, let me see thy countenance' Song of Solomon 2:14.

Angels will scarce in crouds appear.
We say, The *few'r* the *better chear.*

If *busie Ants* of mole-hill[20] birth
Promiscuously converse on Earth,

Let th' High-born *Bird of Paradise*
Scorning the *Earth*, still scale the *skies.*

An *Ant-hill* and Exchange agree,
Save, Men the *greater Triflers* bee;

Thus mortals *toyl* to live *below*,
Whilest Man by toyl to *Heav'n* might go.

What though thou've been *short-winded?*[21] Sure
Heav'ns hill can *Earths green-sickness*[22] cure.

Or what needst dread[23] the *journeys length*,
Whilest all along thy *way's thy strength*?

II

Bee'ng thus Ascended, *Binde* and *slaughter*
Thy sin, thine *Only Child of laughter*,[24]

In this *Mount God will* soon be *seen*
If some Dear sin dont intervene;

Dear sin indeed? whilest Angels *sell*
Their *first Estates*[25] for it and Hell.

20 i.e. lowly.

21 i.e. Although you are out of breath … (from the 'toyl' to reach Heaven).

22 green-sickness = an anaemic disease which gives rise to a morbid appetite. The poet is saying that the sinful effects of earthly life can be counteracted by striving to climb 'Heav'ns Hill', i.e. by leading a godly life. Cf. Teate, *A Scripture-map of the wildernesse of sin*: 'Yea, how doth the very Gluttons, and Drunkards Stomack tell him to his face, that it is weary of bearing his surfeiting, and drunkennesse, and therefore disburtheneth it selfe upon the ground', p. 29.

23 i.e. you need not dread …

24 See the story of Abraham and Isaac. Genesis 22:1–12.

25 i.e. their birthright.

Dear sin! whilest for its *husks* men do
Fair Heavens *houshold-bread* forgo.

A *present flash* and *future flame*
Is the best Income sin can name.

'Twas sin eclips'd the Angels Crown
And what *brought* them, will *keep* thee, *down*.

Man dost not see how *Cherubs* stand
With flaming swords on every hand,[26]

From *rape* of such to guard *Lifes Tree*
As of *dead works* the workers bee?

Ah! *guilty* soul, dar'st *look abroad*,
Or *unagreed* dar'st *walk with God*?

To reconcile dar'st thou aspire
Thy *dress*[27] with that *consuming fire*?

Sure such *Attonement* shall begin,
When *sin* proves[28] *grace*, or *grace* proves *sin*.

Since *Earth's* too dead, too dark, too low;
Sure *Hell* to Heav'n shall never go.

III

BEe'ng thus far onward in this *steep*,
Wouldst further *climbe*? then learn to *creep*.

Who try can tell th' *Ascents* like these
Are the best seal'd on th' *hands* and *knees*.

Angels first *rose*, then *fell*; and so
By growing *too high*, became *so low*.

But *Christ* did raise his *Royall Crest*
By building such a *lowly nest*,

26 Cf. Milton, *Paradise Lost*, I, lines 323–7.

27 dress = conduct.

28 proves = tests.

The *Pharisee* that nothing knows
Of the *true Temple*, boldly goes

Into its shadow there to boast
Reck'ning proud fool *without his Host*.

The *Publican*[29] doth smite upon
His *Heart*, as if 'twere made of *stone*:

Which *stone* despised, though't lay below,
Did to a *Temple* sooner grow.

Unto Gods Altar *nakedness*[30]
God suffers to have no access:[31]

Th' indowments of mens minds we call
Their parts, importing therewithall,[32]

No man of parts can *decent* be
Unless *cloath'd* with *humilitie*,

The *Highest* to the *low* gives grace:
Who *veil* their own shall see his face.

In dust and ashes *self abhor'd*
Are the *accepted of the Lord*.

Most *staring* fair-faced *Dinas*[33] are
Sooner *undone* for being *fair*.

The veil'd *Rebekah Isaac* takes,[34]
And his dear bosom-consort makes.

29 'Publicans' were tax collectors, hated by the Jews because they were paid employees of the Roman occupiers. The poet is suggesting that repentant publicans will get to Heaven faster than 'proud' Pharisees. See Luke 18:10–14.
30 nakedness =poverty or simplicity.
31 access = fever (*OED* IV 10.) Those who come to God's alter 'naked' shall not catch fever.
32 i.e. by this.
33 A colloquial term for a desirable woman i.e. a 'sweetheart'.
34 See Genesis 24:64–7.

How can a *near acquaintance* grow?
Whilest God proud hearts *far off* doth know.

Proud Hearts *know not themselves* and then
Sure Heav'n must needs be out of *ken*.[35]

Whilest the *void Aire* and worthless wind
Brooks no way[36] to be *down confin'd*,

Earthquakes must all things overthrow
Rather then empty Aire keep low;

Gems, Jewels, India's *Treasures* dwell
In meanest Caverns *low roof'd* Cell.

Thus from the *pots*[37] the Lord doth take
And into Crowns his *Treasures* make.

Would'st then be profited by me
From *earth, sin*, and *proud self* get free.

Yet 'tis a *Trinity* indeed
After the which with winged speed

I would pursue, and ever may
Both *body, soul*, and *spirit* pray.

He whom I seek, and ever shall
Is *THREE*, and *ONE*: And *ONE* and *ALL*.

MEDITATE *upon these things, give thy self wholly to them, that thy proffiting may appear to all*, I Tim. 4. 15.

35 i.e. out of sight or beyond reach.
36 i.e. will not allow itself to be …
37 pots = mines.

Appendix One

'EPITHALAMIUM, OR, A Love-song of the Leaning Soul'

The 'Epithalamium' or wedding song is affixed to the end of a sermon by Teate published in 1655 entitled *A Scripture-map of the wildernesse of sin*. The sermon takes its inspiration from a quotation from the Song of Solomon: 'Who is this that cometh up from the Wildernesse leaning upon her Beloved' (Song of Solomon 8:5). In the preface to the sermon, Teate stressed that the Song of Solomon, a book full of erotically charged language, was 'not carnal but spiritual'. This kind of Christian appropriation of the Song of Solomon was common practice among preachers of the time. According to Teate, the Biblical book referred to the defeat of the earthly wilderness, what he calls the 'lost estate of sinners', through 'leaning' (having faith) on the 'beloved' (Jesus Christ). Starting from this premise, Teate wrote a verse allegory of individual redemption set in a quasi-Biblical landscape to complement the more formal discourse of the sermon. As Teate stated in the preface to the Epithalamium: 'the matter … is experience, though the form be Verse. My Text being one of the highest and sweetest straines, Of the Song of Songs, best SONG that ever was Penned; my Discourse being but an Explanation of that Text, and my Verse but a Contraction of that Discourse.'

EPITHALAMIUM,
OR,
A Love-Song of the Leaning-Soul.

An *Orphan*, in a *Bulrush-Ark* bound fast,
(*Vain Childhoods Emblem*) when I h'd suck'd a while,
Like cruell *stepdame Nature*, did me cast,
By *Miry Banks* afloat the sides of *Nile*.[1]

1 Here Teate draws on the story of the infant Moses being cast adrift in the Nile in a 'Bullrush-Ark' (Exodus 2:3) to allegorise the cruelness of human experience at the hands of 'stepdame Nature' or earthly existence.

Here crawl's a Tearfull *Crocodile:*[2]
There comes a *woman* with a *smile.*[3]
The *Crocodile* creeps after me apace,
And *weeps* as't *creeps*, and cries, *thy friend, thy friend,*
I look'd and list'ned, but soon turn'd my face;
Jealous[4] at first: but whilst I did attend,
Did *Educations Eccho send*
A Counter-Cry, *thy end, thy end.*
And now my fear hav'ng put me on my flight,
Poor wretch! what hast[5] I might I made away.
No sooner was I gotten out of sight
Of that *Pursuer*, and into'ther Bay,
But th' *woman* comes, in *bright array*,
Unto that Creek, and makes her stay.
In *curious curles* her *Locks* division'd are
To *Captivate beholders, Golden wire*
Made into *snares*: Her *breasts* are all made *bare.*
(*Naked Temptation's more*, shee counts, *than tire*)[6]
The *hills* where *wantons* make their *fire*
In *sacrifice* to *Lusts* desire.
(I since have heard that she belong'd to th' *Court*:
A *darling Minion* of th' *Egyptian King's*,
That *Syre of Negroes*, to whose *Coasts* resort
Such as will *truck* for *Trade* with *darksome things*,
Whose *soule's at sale*; whole *Egypt* rings
Oth' *Custom* that such *Traffique* brings)[7]
This was her *Haunt*, here *Natures high-tide spring*
The *Children of Gods Israel* (secured
From the *birth-perill*) all *afloat* doth bring:

2 The crocodile was said to weep in order to draw people closer so it could devour them: Teate means the crocodile to represent Satan. Cf. Spenser, 'Visions of the Worlds Vanitie', lines 29–33.

3 The 'woman' described in the poem draws on many Biblical representations of the female as sinful, a symbol of the way in which material temptation corrupts the spiritual life. She has echoes of the Egyptian princess who rescues Moses from the Nile (Exodus 2:5) and who, for Teate, represents the corruption of Pharaoh's court which the righteous Moses must reject to liberate the people of Israel. In a broader sense she is a version of the 'Whore of Babylon' described in Revelation, a figure often taken by Protestant clergy to symbolise the Roman Catholic Church.

4 i.e. eager. 5 i.e. haste. 6 tire = attire or clothing.

7 Teate again identifies the diabolical woman with Egypt, a country synonymous with sin and slavery in the Old Testament.

Whom she by *lying Vanities* allur'd,
And of *full fleshpots*[8] first Ensur'd,
To *Brick-kiln-bake'-meats* oft inured.[9]
My son, said she, how cam'st thou thus afloat
In a *Cold Ark*, and *Colder Element*?
Behold my *Bosom* warmer than thy *Boat*:
What more *restorative* for *Nutriment*?
Here *Bed* and *Board*: My *Breasts* are pent,
I'le *give* thee *all* to *give* them *vent*.
Look, look you, here's *whole Worlds divided Treasure!*
This Breast's the one *half-globe*, and *that* the *other*:
What one can suck them *both*, and want for pleasure?[10]
Honor distills from th' one, and *Wealth* from to'ther
If *busie Conscience* make a *poother*,[11]
Suck hard and that shall quickly *smother*.
With that my foolish heart began to dream
(When I saw milk run down her Breasts so fast)
Of housing in her *Bosom*; and the Theme
How sweet to thought, to sense how gratefull was't?
Affections clos'd and Mind embrac't:
And all towards her made too much hast.[12]
But just as I was stretching forth mine *Hand*,
Having in *heart* quite sold my self that day,
Me thought I spi'd some *Negroes* on the strand,
That fast by, in *close posture*, lurking lay;
And streight bethought what I h'd heard say
Of *spirits stealing youth away*.
Mine *Heart* draws in, suspitious of some Craft,[13]
Mine *hand* it recollects,[14] evades the while:
Meantime, Afflictions *Hurricanos* Waft
Me crosse that Channell; sounding all the while,

8 fleshpots = pots for boiling meat. The phrase is used here with reference to Exodus 16:3: 'Would to God we had died by the hand of the Lord in the land of Egypt, when we sat by the flesh pots …' 'Fleshpots' became an idiom for an unnecessary luxury.

9 inured = burnt. The sense seems to be that by tempting souls with 'fleshpots', she is able to ensure that they burn like meat in the 'Brick-kiln', i.e. Hell. A passage found in 2 Samuel 12:31, describes how David tortured his captives by making them walk through a 'brick-kiln'.

10 Cf. Francis Quarles, *Emblemes* (London, 1635), I. XII.

11 poother = perturbation or fuss. The poet should not let his conscience 'make a fuss'.

12 i.e. haste.

13 i.e. witchcraft.

14 recollects = withdraws or pulls back.

Trust thou no more this *Womans smile*
Than the *tears* of the *Crocodile.*
Transported thus, and landed safe ashore,
I find my soul transported[15] in my Breast;
This Land being so remote from that before,
I thought those Foes in *earnest*, Friends in *jest*
Could never more my soul infest,
This is, said I, the *Land of Rest.*
Shod with *self-confidence, and girt*[16] in mind
I trac't about, not doubting but to light
Soon on such lodging as I long'd to find:
But *stumbled* on the *left* and on the *right*,
Yea this and that did cast me *quite*,
So that more *Waies*, more *Woe's* in sight.
Seeking, alas! my self was quickly *Lost*,
Yet found full many a path where *Beasts* had bin
Thwarting each other, Each by th'other crost:
And I 'midst all perplex't: intangled in
Thickets: it seems 'twas *Desert-SIN*,[17]
And this, or none, must be mine *Inne.*
Thus housed in this dark and shady Bowre,
Yet having *here* and *there* an *hole* for *light*,
The *Sunsets in a cloud*, and half an hour
Draws round the sable Curtains of the night:
This dark *damps hope*, and *fills* with *fright*,
Thus to *see nothing*, O *sad sight*!
My passion now breaks out in flings and throwes,
No *bread*, No *bed*, whereon to *feed*, to *lie!*
I rush't amidst the Bowre and streight arose
A Circling sound, a *wind* [18]went whistling by,
And as it came it seem'd to cry
No food, no food, no food but I.
Thus having giv'n a rush[19] in discontent
Whilst passion did weak Reason overbear,
I heard, and felt as well as heard, a Rent;
(Oh! the sad *Bed*, the *bed of Thornes* was there.)

15 transported = transformed.

16 girt = secure.

17 i.e. the wilderness referred to in Song of Solomon 8:5, and described by Teate as 'The Lost Estate of Sinners'.

18 i.e. the Holy Spirit.

19 i.e. to give chase or to forcibly drive something away.

Sounding as *Cloaths and flesh did teare,*
No bed but here, but here, but here.
I heard the *Lions* roar, the *Dragons* howl,
Fierce *Wolves* and *Leopards* ranging to and fro;
Next lit upon my Lodge[20] a *flaming scroul;*[21]
By th' *light* it cast I read th' *Inscription, Wo.*
I *sate* on *thorns*, yet thence nor go,
Nor durst I cry, my fears were so.
These *howling hunt*, and *hunting howl* the more;
And yet as though the saddest sound did misse
In this *confused Consort, Heavens* roar
With *thunder-claps*: A *fiery Worm*[22] there is
Just in my bed makes such an *Hisse,*
Out-fears[23] are small compar'd to *this,*
Which when I heard, and look'd but saw no aid,
What *self-tormentings* worry, tear, and bait?
I am a *Prey* by a *Prolepsis* made:
Mine heart doth *Death* and *Doomes-day* antedate;
Fear first doth kill, then *re-create;*
Thus *Horrour Hell* doth imitate.
At length through *Crannies* of my black *bed-tester*[24]
Breaks in the *lightsom star* of *long'd for day*:
You never saw a Rising Sun at *Easter*
So drest on its (suppos'd) best *Holy-day.*
Said I, if such be th' *Day-star's Ray,*
What Glory, Lord! shall *Noon* display?
My God, said I, let me but see that *SUN*:[25]
Break day; break heart; Rise Sun of Righteousnesse!
Lo yonder's *He*! *wo's me, I am undone!*
Unclean in heart and lips! yet must confesse
I (*then the least of Mercies lesse*)
Have seen that Sun, 'midst dark Distresse.
Let the remembrance never quit my Breast
How *seav'n daies light* the first appearance brings;

20 i.e. the place where I was lodging …

21 i.e. scroll. An apocalyptic image taken from Revelation 6:14: 'And the Heaven departed as a scroll when it is rolled together'. The poet is anticipating Judgement Day with fear.

22 i.e. Satan, who has entered the poet's 'bowre' i.e. his soul.

23 i.e. fears which threaten from outside.

24 bed-tester = the canopy over a bed: an image for the night sky.

25 i.e. the son, Jesus Christ.

And as a mighty *Eagle* on her *Nest*,
This *mighty Sun* doth *spread* his *beaming wings*:
Mine *heart* was full of *thorns* and *stings*,
But O these *raies* were *healing things!*
Whilst such delights exiled all my fears,
Clos'd up my Rents,[26] compos'd my troubled breast,
Fed busie *sight*, like glory *fil'd* mine *Eares*,
A voice that *cannot* yet *must* be *exprest*:
That joyful sound *for ever blest*
May't with mine heart *for ever rest*.
Bewildred long, but not *Deserted* one
Come with me from the *Lions Den away*,
From *Leopards Mountains*, and from *Lebanon*;[27]
Chosen of old, in *Desert found today*;
While *grace* makes *Wildernesse* its *Way*,
For thee doth *Love-pav'd Charriot stay*.
    Then answer'd I (and *answ'ring brake mine heart*):
SATAN'S a Crocodile; the WORLD'S a whore;
SIN is a Wildernesse: Cut off my part
In this *Black Trinity* that Fooles adore.
My *GOD*, Chief *GOOD*, sole *GUIDE*, thou art:
Here let me *lean*,[28] hence never start.
If my *Desert* kept not thy *Love* from me,
Sure'ts thy *Desert*[29] that I should *Lean* on thee.
My Christ, this is my Groan, my cry.
Let me *Lean* on thee, *Live or die*.
Live, oh! how can I *live* so Love-sickly?
Hold HEAD or *heart breaks*: Let me *Lean* or *Dye*:
Who *dies* and *Leans not*, doth in *Dying Dye*:[30]
Who *Leans* and *dies not*, *leans* too sparingly.
Who *leans* and *dies* doth in the *Bosom* lie,
Oh! my heart breaks Lord, let me *lean* and *die!*

26 rents = the places where I had been torn asunder …
27 'Come with me from Lebanon, my spouse, with me from Lebanon … from the lions' dens, from the mountains of the leopards.' Song of Solomon 4:8.
28 i.e. let me have faith in you …
29 A play on words: Desert = reward.
30 i.e. whoever dies without faith will not be granted salvation.

Appendix Two

'To the WITS of this AGE, Pretended or Real'

This dedicatory poem was included in the 1669 and 1699 editions of *Ter Tria*. It is by John Chishull, Minister of the Gospel at Tiverton in Devon and author of *Two treatises* (London, 1675), *The danger of being almost a Christian* (London, 1657) and *A word to Israel in the wilderness* (London, 1668). Chishull's predilection for versifying and his belief that it could be helpful in spiritual instruction are demonstrated in *A brief explication of the ten commandments intended for a help to the understanding and memories of children* (1665), a page of privately-printed verse, perhaps intended for his own children, or those of his parish. 'To the WITS of this AGE, Pretended or Real' reflects the playful, 'witty' tone of sections of *Ter Tria*.

'To the WITS of this AGE, Pretended or Real'[1]

You Candidates for Fame, who ne're could gain
The Name of WITS, till you darst be profane,
Nor get the knack on't, till the Witty Devil
Gave you a smartness of a Theme was evil,
Who by elated strains, taught you to raise
Some piece of clay, 'bove him who's above praise,
And having lost the God head in it's place,
By flattering lines to set some painted face:
Or with ingenious tartness to deride
The Scripture stile, and all that's good beside,
Let fall your wanton pens, and blush to see
Your selv's out-done by Sacred Poetry.
Let all wise-hearted savo'ring things Divine,
Come suck this TEAT that yields both Milk and Wine;
Loe depths where Elephants may swim, yet here

1 This poem is included in Andrew Carpenter, *Verse in English from Tudor and Stuart Ireland* (Cork, 2003) pp. 321–2.

The weakest Lamb of Christ wades without fear.
And you, great Souls, who bathe in Contemplation,
Come, here's a prize, Wits worthy Recreation;
Myst'ries as sweet as deep, Pray read and try,
You'l be immerst in pleasure by and by.
If words or things will please, here they accord,
Each other their benign aspects afford;
Words fit for Matter, matter fit for Men,
Baxter or *Boyle*[2] may read and read again;
Who weighs the things, will say, TEAT did inherit
The subject of his lines, the Holy Spirit;
He that the Dress, (I mean) his Verses peruses,
Will say, that *Teat's Thrice Three* surely were Muses,
So full of Wit and Grace, 'tis hard to say,
Whether the Head of Heart hath got the day;
A Heart so headed and a Head so hearted,
(Blest Concord) pitty they should e're be parted.
I'le wish that TEAT'S and HERBERT'S may inspire
Randals and *Davenants*[3] with Poetick fire;
May th' *Wits* be *Wise*, and *Faithful*, *Teat*, like thee,
To Consecrate their Pens to thy *Thrice Three*.

2 Richard Baxter (1615–91), one of the best-known Presbyterian (and later Anglican) divines of the seventeenth century, and Michael Boyle (1609?–1702) chaplain-general to the English army in Munster at the time of this poem and later archbishop of Armagh, were two of the most famous clerical writers and wits of the day.

3 i.e. modern poets and dramatists. 'Randall' was Thomas Randolph (1605–35), one of the most promising writers and wits of his day; the other reference is to Sir William D'Avenant (1606–68), a successful poet and dramatist who had been appointed poet laureate in 1638.

Appendix Three

FIDELIS TATUS

This anagram was included in the preface to both the 1669 and 1699 editions of *Ter Tria*. It is unclear whether it was written by Teate or someone else. Anagrams, often in or incorporating Latin, were very popular with seventeenth-century readers. As with emblem literature, they required the reader to decipher the hidden, 'witty' connections between words. In this case, the anagram is based on the literal meaning of the poet's Latin name.

FIDELIS TATUS.

[ANAGRAM]

TELIS FIDATUS,

STATU FIDELIS.

JEHOVAH'S Golden Shaft and
Blazing Sword,
FIDELIS had in Trust
(I mean his Word)

GODS Armour-bearer was
FIDELIS TATUS,
Who was FIDELIS always
in that STATUS.